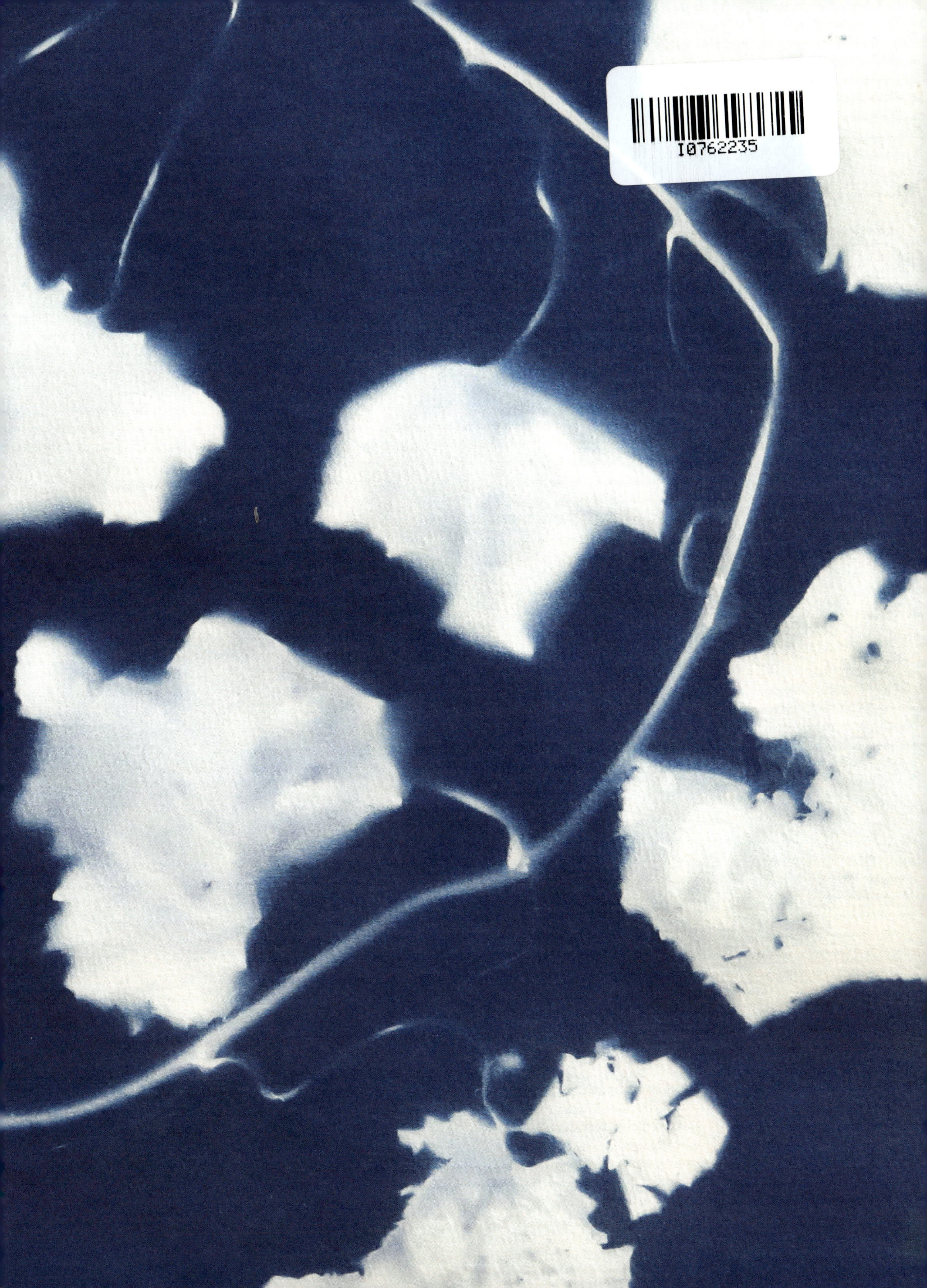

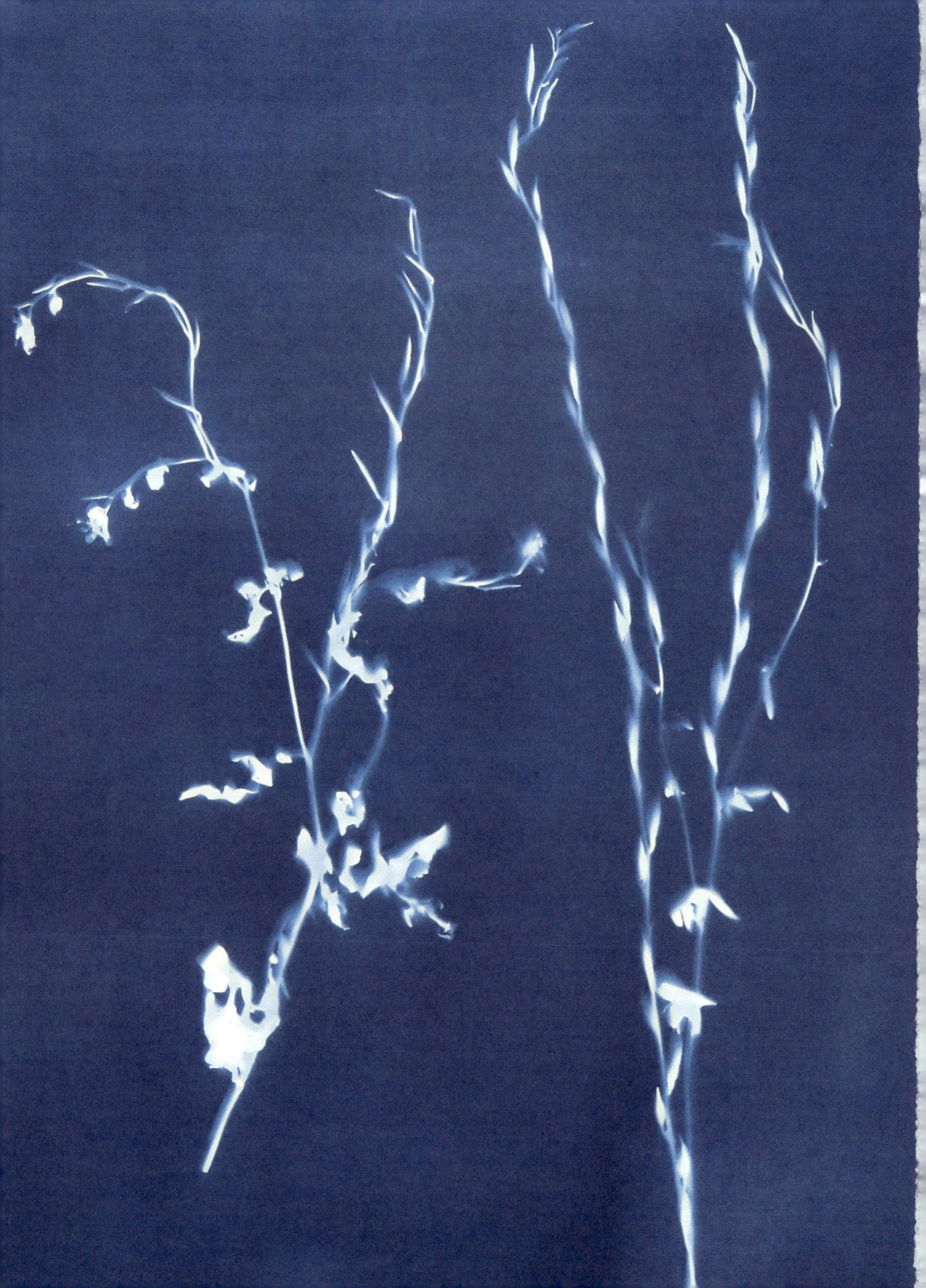

Joy Gregory

Catching F*lies* *with* H*oney*

Whitechapel Gallery

PRESTEL
Munich · London · New York

Work Series

Foreword

Joy Gregory is one of the most significant artists working with photography and film in the UK today. Over the past four decades, Gregory has developed a distinctive and quietly radical practice that combines conceptual rigour with technical innovation, and poetic sensibility with political insight. *Catching Flies with Honey* is the first major exhibition in London to survey her work. It brings together a broad selection of works from the 1980s to the present, alongside a new commission, presented across Whitechapel Gallery's main galleries. Published to coincide with the exhibition, this monograph offers a richly layered reflection on Gregory's artistic journey, her contribution to contemporary photography, and the broader cultural, historical and political contexts that inform her work.

Gregory's practice has always been expansive in scope and sensitive in approach. From early black-and-white self-portraits to film installations and embroidered textiles, Gregory's work moves fluidly across materials and genres. Her enduring engagement with nineteenth-century photographic processes – including salt prints, cyanotypes and kallitypes – reveals a commitment to the material history of the photographic medium and to its conceptual and poetic possibilities. For Gregory, photography is a means to trace hidden histories, to amplify overlooked voices and to create space for different conceptions of beauty.

At the heart of Gregory's work are questions of history, identity and language. She approaches these themes with subtlety, often through fragmentary or elliptical visual strategies. Gregory's self-portraits, for instance, resist conventional modes of visibility and instead offer partial, intimate glimpses of the artist's presence. In other series, found objects – handbags, domestic accessories – are transformed into relics that speak to inherited ideals of femininity, gendered labour and colonial legacies. Elsewhere, landscape and botanical imagery map the entanglement of geography, migration and power.

The title of the exhibition, *Catching Flies with Honey*, is drawn from the artist's own reflection on how beauty can be used as a subversive force. Throughout her practice, Gregory has used formal elegance and visual seduction to draw audiences into deeper conversations about race, gender and representation. Her work challenges reductive expectations about what Black or feminist art should look like, asserting instead a nuanced and multifaceted approach to visual storytelling.

This publication brings together a group of distinguished writers and thinkers: Brook Garru Andrew, Catherine Hall, Rohini Malik Okon, Cheryl Finley, Kate Bush and Penny Siopis, whose essays respond to different aspects of Gregory's work. Their contributions extend the conversations initiated by the exhibition, offering critical, historical and personal perspectives on an artist whose practice has consistently opened new ground.

Joy Gregory: Catching Flies with Honey has been made possible through the generous support of the 2023 Freelands Award. Joy Gregory and Whitechapel Gallery are honoured to have received this important annual award, which champions mid-career women artists in the UK and enables major institutions to realise ambitious exhibitions and accompanying publications. We are also grateful to Cockayne – Grants for the Arts and to the Paul Mellon Centre for Studies in British Art, which supported the research underpinning this project.

We extend our sincere thanks to Arnolfini, Bristol, for partnering with us to tour the exhibition following its presentation at Whitechapel Gallery, helping to bring Joy Gregory's work to new audiences across the UK.

Arnolfini's Director Suzanne Rolt shares: 'That as a gallery devoted to the contemporary visual arts, it's a privilege to welcome Joy Gregory to Arnolfini as part of our forthcoming season. This accompanying monograph provides a fascinating account of some four decades of artistic work, offering insights into a poetic and deeply layered way of capturing the world that so often makes visible the invisible, and gives voice to the unspoken.'

This exhibition and publication affirm Joy Gregory's legacy as a vital voice in contemporary art. Across diverse media, geographies and histories, Gregory's work returns again and again to questions of visibility, voice and the politics of representation. She shows us that the photographic image, far from being fixed, is a site of ongoing negotiation – a place where histories collide, identities shift and new meanings emerge.

Autoportrait (detail)

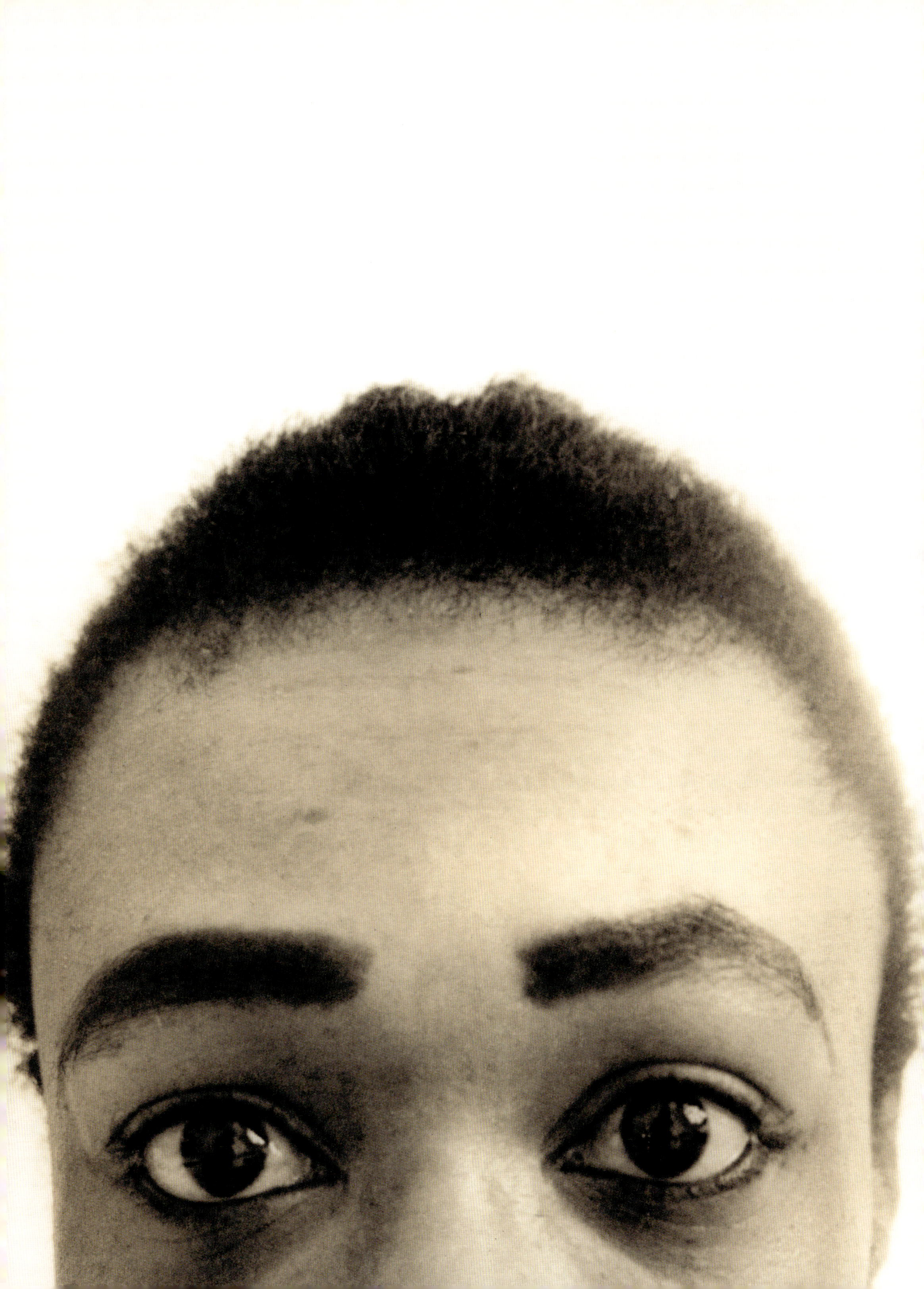

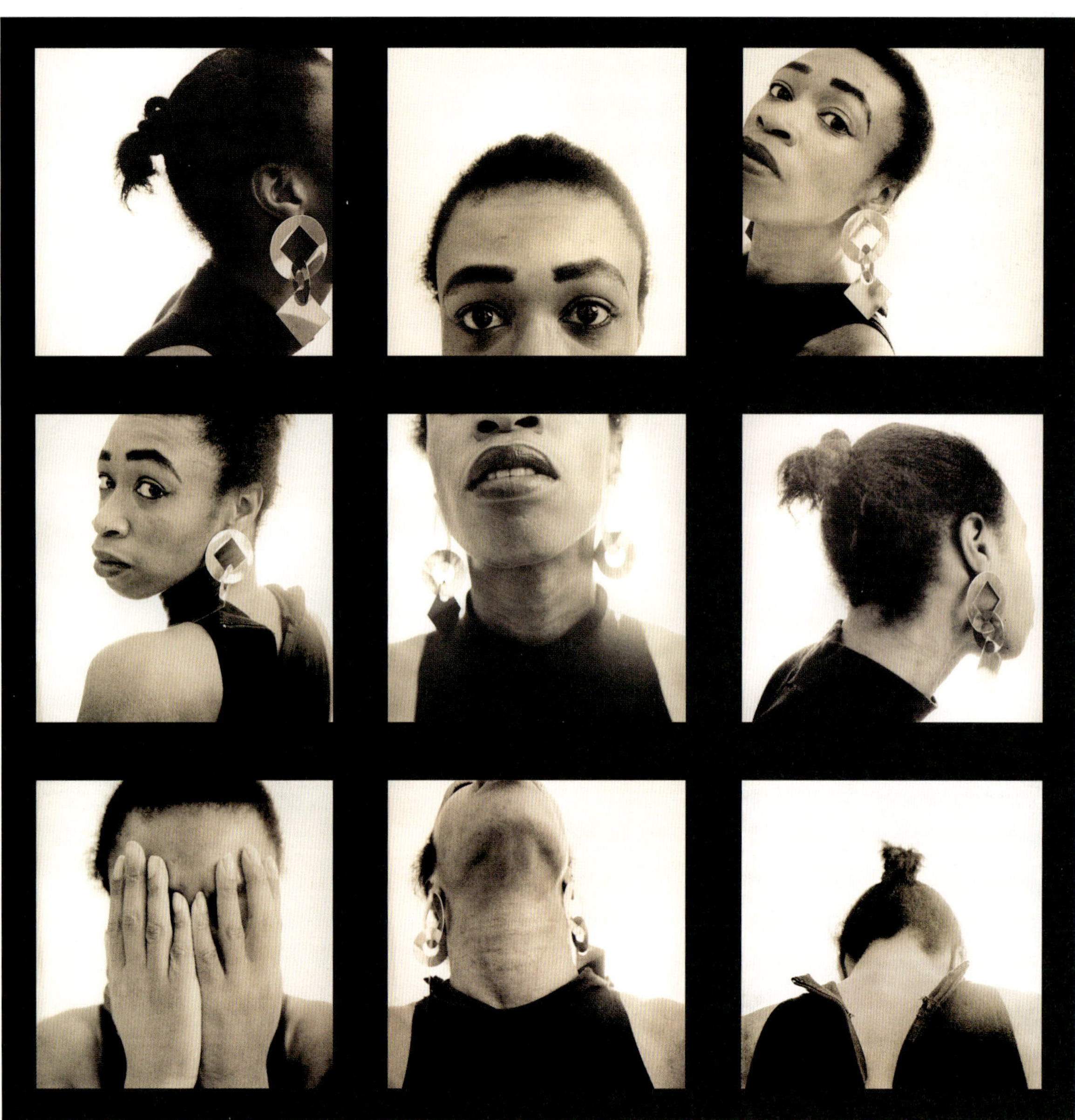

Autoportrait 1989–90

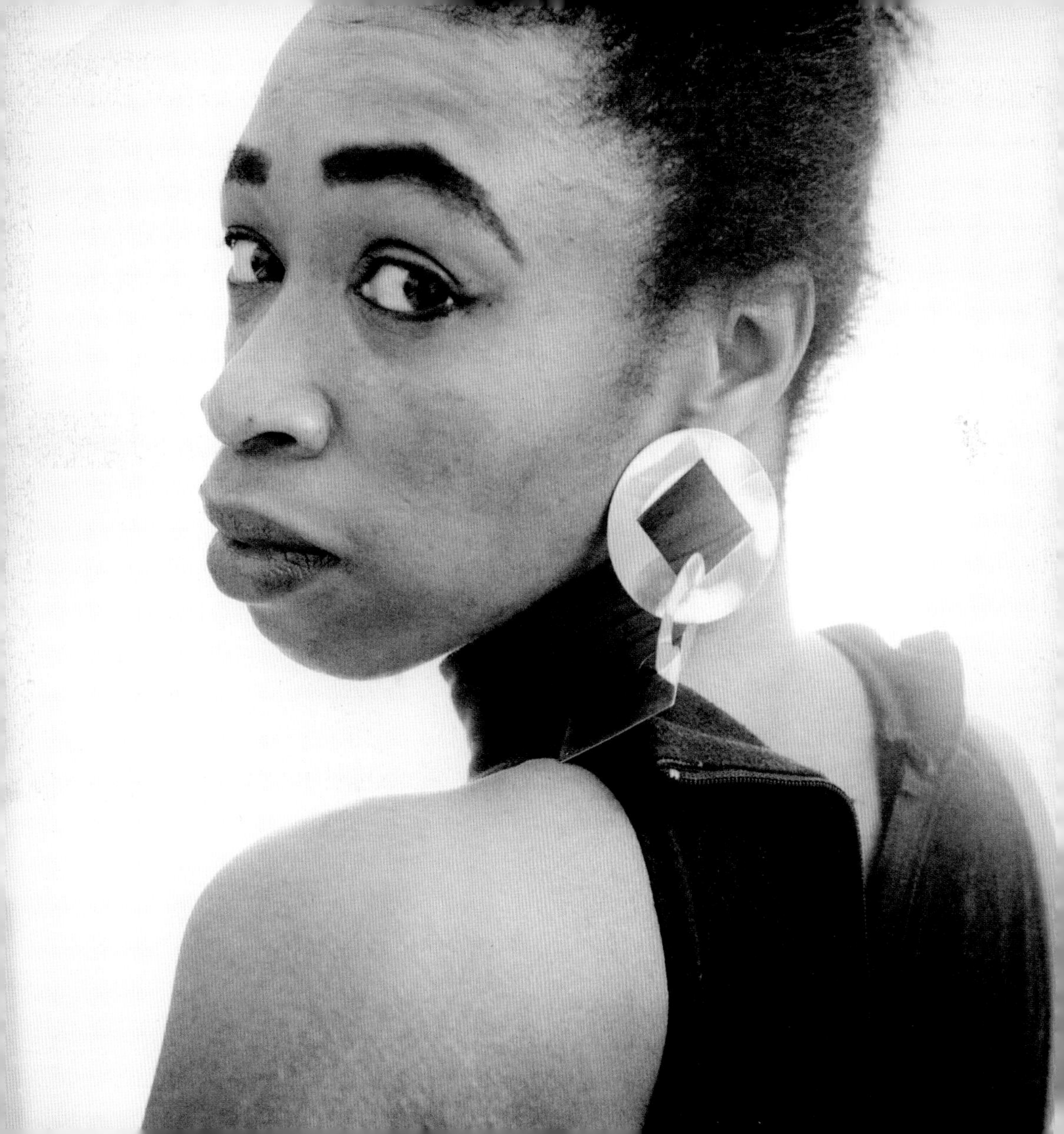

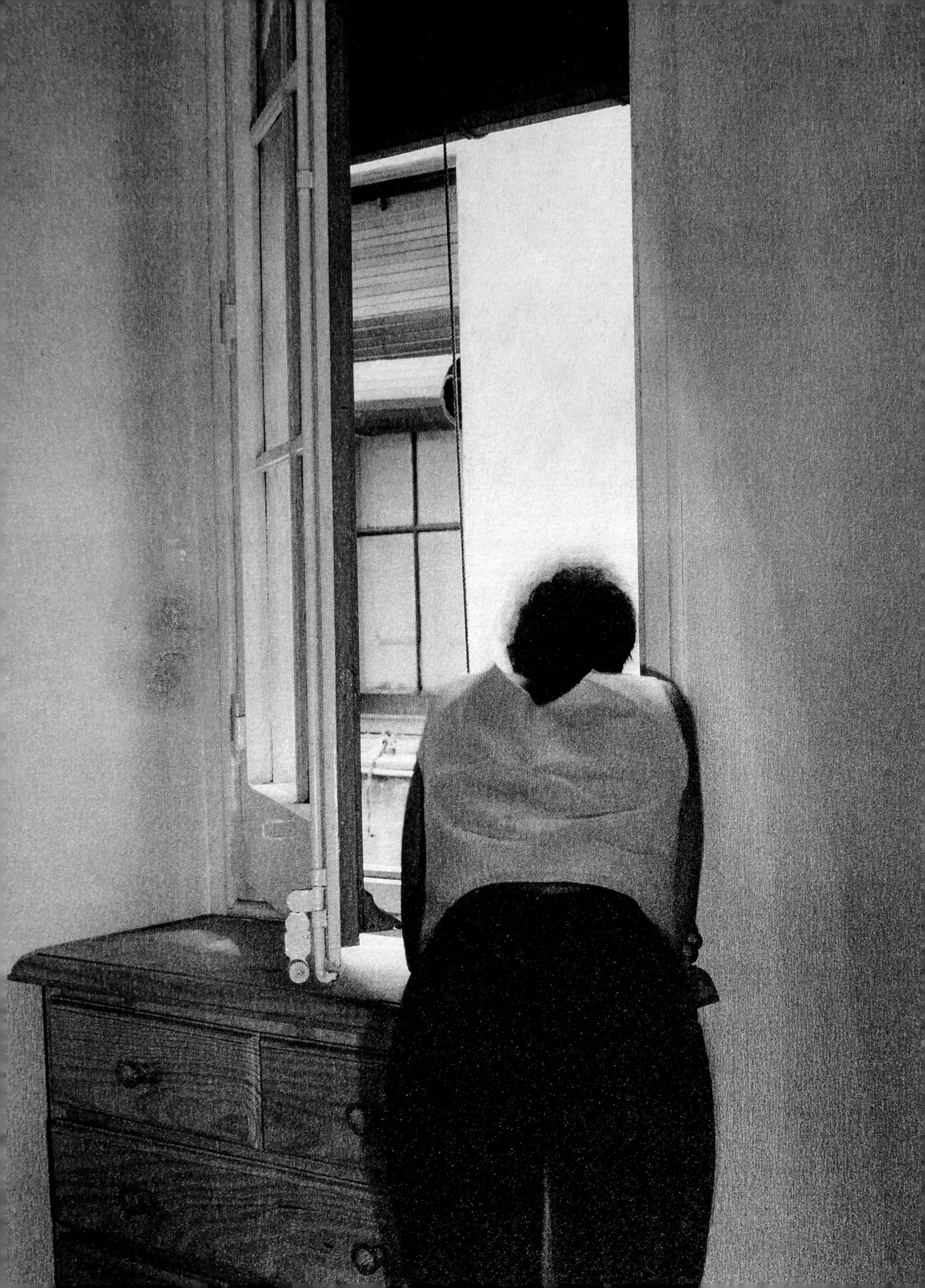

Gilane Tawadros

Catching *Flies* *with* Honey

A woman, with her back to the camera, leans across a wooden chest of drawers, gazing out of the window. There is no view to speak of; only the window of the facing building which is shuttered from the inside. The open window casts shadows over the bare interior walls. There are no harsh and sharp contrasts but soft grey and brown hues. The artist's camera delicately records the creases in the woman's sleeveless blouse, the frizz of her hair silhouetted in the reflected sunlight; the brownish grains of the wooden furniture. The only clue to this enigmatic image is its title and date: *Barcelona* (1988).[1] One of a series of early works by Joy Gregory made between 1987 and 1999 and entitled *Women and Space*, the images were made whilst Gregory was travelling on holiday, mainly in Spain, the only opportunity she had to make photographs at a time when she was juggling three different jobs: working at North Paddington Community Darkroom in London, teaching at Staffordshire University in Stoke-on-Trent and working nights as a waitress in Ronnie Scott's jazz club.

The series reflects poetically on women's relationship to space: the fact that women own very little space or are encouraged to occupy a very small amount of space. Gregory intentionally placed herself in hotel rooms, environments she didn't own, and takes possession of these liminal spaces: stretching out along the length of a bed; scattering her possessions across a room; sitting cross-legged at the table; studying an unfolded map. Reminiscent of Johannes Vermeer's paintings of women in intimate domestic spaces, caught up in everyday pursuits such as playing music, making lace or reading a letter, Gregory's self-portraits

1 See page 21.

Barcelona, 1988 (detail)

resist our gaze and offer us partial and hazy glimpses of the artist taking up space, absorbed in her own world.

From early on in her career, Gregory has experimented with the photographic medium, pushing it beyond its everyday applications to test and stretch its material possibilities. In this and later series, the artist makes works which are more akin to paintings than photographs, using liquid light to create elegant and elusive images. Employing a process which dates back to 1853,[2] the series *Women and Space* was made using a silver-gelatin liquid emulsion which at room temperature is a solid gel but becomes liquid when heated up. It can then be used to coat a variety of surfaces – paper, stone or glass – and exposed and developed in the same way as ordinary photographic paper. Gregory's use of liquid light invests the photographs with an ethereal and timeless quality, suspending the images beyond the specifics of space and time, in spite of their titles.

During the years when Gregory was making these photographs, she recalls that her work 'wasn't considered "Black enough" [and] remembers sending her work, images of fauna and flowers, for consideration in a Black photography exhibition only for it to be rejected. "The whole point of me being able to do my practice was having the choice to do what I wanted, not what someone else dictated I'd be allowed to do. People like me have been told what they're supposed to be doing for generations; I wasn't going to carry on with that."'[3] Instead, inspired by her mother's advice, Gregory concentrated on making exquisitely beautiful and compelling images that would enable her to raise critical questions about race and gender and 'catch flies with honey'.

Gregory's earliest experiments with the photographic medium date back to the mid-1980s when she made medium- and large-format positive prints that dissolve the line between photography and painting. Taking the archetypal subject matter of still-life painting, Gregory conjures a spectrum of different hues, light and shadows to compose dramatic images of tulips and bottles. At the same time, the artist began to create constructed interiors, placing female silhouettes in undefined settings which render them like abstract paintings.

A number of other series of self-portraits followed *Women and Space* including *The Honeymoon Project* (1991–95), *In Search of Self* (1993), *Creating the Subject* (1998) and Gregory's celebrated *Autoportrait* (1989–90) which

2 The first experiments involving silver halide emulsions with gelatinous mediums date back to 1853 and were spearheaded by French chemist Marc Antoine Auguste Gaudin.
3 Lanre Bakare, '"I was told my work wasn't Black enough": Joy Gregory on becoming hot property at last', *The Guardian* (8 January 2024).

was the first time Gregory was 'thinking consciously about being political within [her] work, and [talking] about race'.[4] Made up of nine individual self-portraits, Gregory situated herself at the centre of the frame for the first time, photographing her head and shoulders from different angles and perspectives. As Stuart Hall writes:

> *[T]here is nothing else in the frame, nothing for the eye to see, nowhere else to look, except at the black woman 'in the field of vision'. Or rather parts of her – eyes, eyebrows, mouth, neck, ears, half-profile, hands-covering face – that Gregory allows us to see: for the deliberately distorted staging of these self-images, disrupting the 'normal' distances of viewing, their isolation in space and fragmented shapes, also breaks the frame in a wider sense, refusing the wholeness of the tradition of Western portraiture and, in a counter-move, obliging us to see and look otherwise.*[5]

Wanting to avoid the austere contrasts of traditional black-and-white photography and capture the soft, graduated tones of Black skin, Gregory once again used liquid light to create a set of silver gelatin prints and one-off images that cannot be duplicated. *Autoportrait* (1990) gently underscores the uniqueness of these photographic objects and of the subject of these images, both of which refuse to be bound by the strictures of traditional photographic framing and processes. Over a period of five years, Gregory subsequently worked on *The Honeymoon Project* (1991–95), a series of poignant, intimate images which mirror the voyeuristic experience of peering through a series of small windows or peepholes. Fragmented, indistinct and verging on abstraction, many of the images are hard to decipher: a lone figure walking in a landscape; a street observed from the window of a tall building; the outline of a woman's figure distorted by a window frame. These delicate and emotionally charged photographs were made using the Victorian Kallitype process,[6] 'which enabled Gregory to work with an extended palette of tones and gradations, in order "to depict fleeting moments of hope, desire, isolation and disappointment ... made during a period of extreme vulnerability where the membrane separating life and work was at its thinnest.'[7]

4 Interview with the artist.

5 Stuart Hall, 'Legacies of Anglo-Caribbean Culture: A Diasporic Perspective', reprinted in *Stuart Hall: Selected Writings on Visual Arts and Culture*, ed. Gilane Tawadros (Durham and London: Duke University Press, 2024) 158.

6 The Kallitype printing process is an iron-based photographic process developed and patented in 1889. The process starts when a high quality 100 per cent cotton paper is coated with a mixture of ferric oxalate and silver nitrate. Once the coating is dried, a negative is placed on top of it and exposed to sunlight or UV lamp.

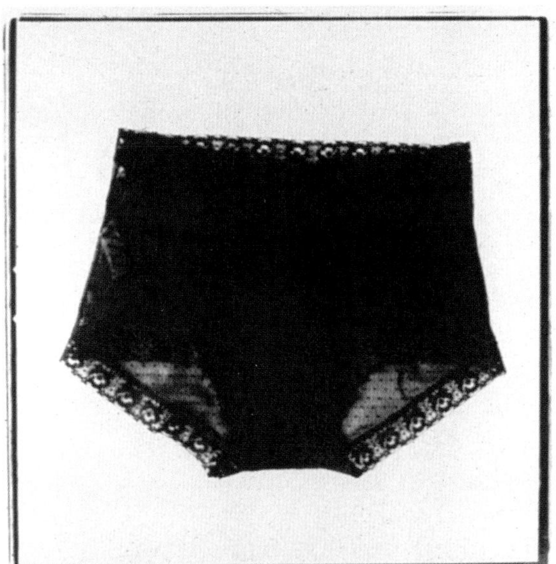

Knickers

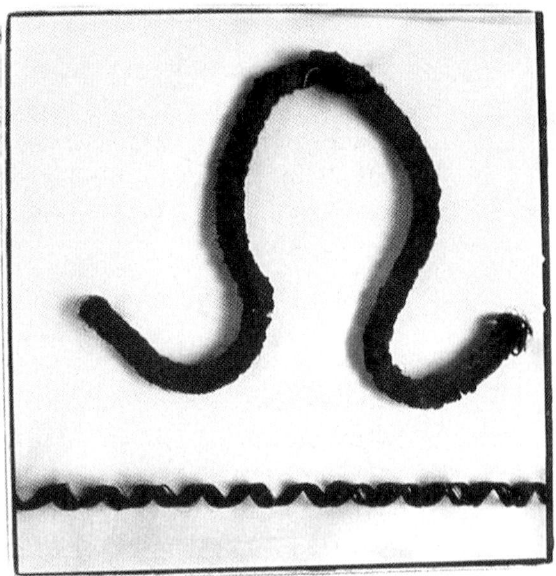

Hairpiece

Gregory's fellow artist Sonia Boyce once described her work as sculpture rather than photography. Working against the assumed reproducibility of the photographic medium, Gregory's works are often unique, irreproducible prints. Her mastery of nineteenth-century printing techniques enables her to transform photography into painting and also into sculpture, rendering everyday female accessories and clothing – hairnet, comb, brush, corset, eyelash curlers, knickers, earrings – into precious things as in her series *Objects of Beauty* (1992–95) and *Girl Thing* (2002–04) which interrogate preconceptions of beauty and the construction of femininity through achingly beautiful images, desirable objects in themselves.

With *The Handbag Project* (1998–present), Gregory's compelling 'photo-sculptures' engaged with broader questions of gender, race and colonialism. Whilst on a residency in Johannesburg, South Africa (SANG / Bag Factory), Gregory became fascinated with luxury objects that had been bought, used and then discarded by white South African women during the Apartheid era and which the artist began to search out and collect: '... satin and pearl gloves that served as a barrier against physical contact, and exquisite handbags, the ultimate symbols of femininity, privacy and power. These objects were for sale in charity shops, often wrapped in their original cellophane, the apparently innocuous remnants of house clearances. They describe a time in history where idleness, power and powerlessness, as well as the objectification of women, were ingrained in society, and contrasted with the lives of other women who shared the same physical space'.[8] Gregory likens these objects to religious relics

7 Joy Gregory, *Joy Gregory: Objects of Beauty* (Autograph) (London: Chris Boot, 2004), 18.

which she uses to make a series of large salt-printed photograms that resemble archaeological remains, by turns alluring and disturbing; the traces of an opulent lifestyle afforded by the exploitation of cheap, female, Black domestic labour.

In 2021, the figure of the solitary woman in an interior returns in Gregory's haunting installation work 'A Little or No Breeze' in which the artist draws on two texts from *A Voyage to Jamaica* (1688), the writings of seventeenth-century botanist and collector Hans Sloane: one in which he charts the weather in Jamaica on a daily basis; and the other in which he records his brutal and nonconsensual medical treatment of Rose, an enslaved woman at the house he is staying, who is suffering from depression. Inhabiting the role of Rose in the film of the same name (one of two films which make up the installation), Gregory is pictured at a distance from the camera, her hands holding the handle of a broom and her eyes averted. Interwoven with extracts from Sloane's weather diary, the Vermeer-like image of Rose standing or seated, slumped on the staircase, her head resting in her hands or gazing into the long distance, moves in and out of focus, between still images and flickering Super 8 film, with the film sprockets materialising and disappearing at the edge of the frame. The image on screen changes like Sloane's descriptions of the fluctuating weather, shifting from colour to black-and-white to almost black and back to colour again. By contrast, Rose remains still, barely moving and her ghostly, melancholic presence is underscored by the soundscape created by composer Philip Miller and based on a reimagined Angolan slave song, originally noted down by freed slave and Jamaican musician Mr Baptiste.

The installation *Seeds of Empire* (2021) comprises two films *Observations: A Little Breeze* and *Observations: Rose* that together make up a single work that tells a single story of two protagonists Sloane and Rose. In *Observations: Rose*, the words of Hans Sloane (the absent but authoritative voice from the seventeenth-century) are interwoven with oral histories of people who have moved to England from Jamaica, talking about the weather and their experience of being in England. Like so much of Gregory's work, this beautiful and complex piece threads together the past and present, bringing into the frame, those stories and experiences that leave little or no trace, seamlessly interweaving different narratives in the same way that she effortlessly intertwines processes of making with aesthetics and subject matter: always, catching flies with honey.

8 Ibid., 88.

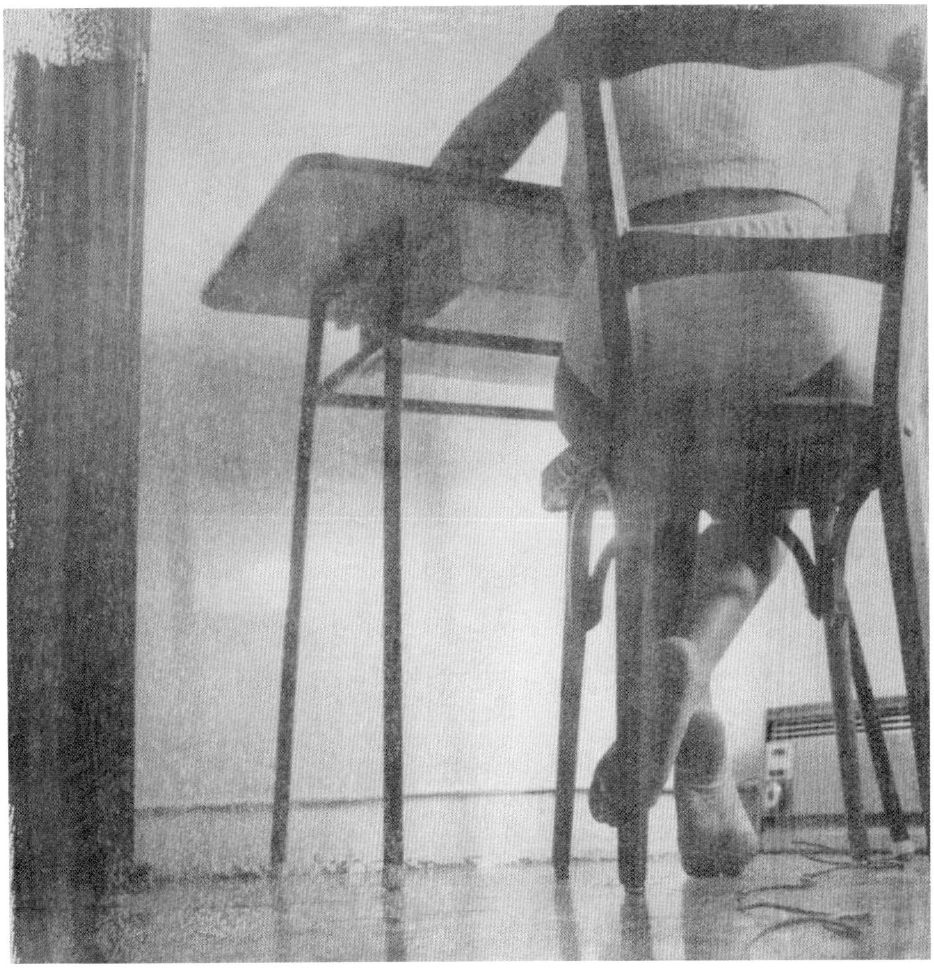

Hotel Normandia #2, Andorra La Vella, 1988

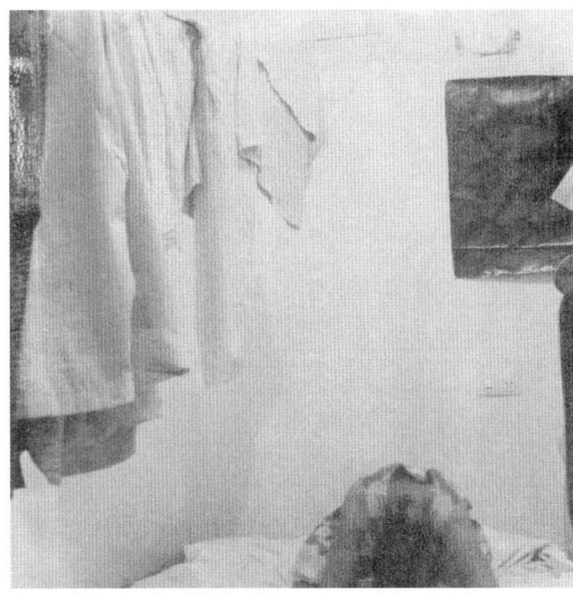

Plaza Sagrada Familia #1, Barcelona, 1988

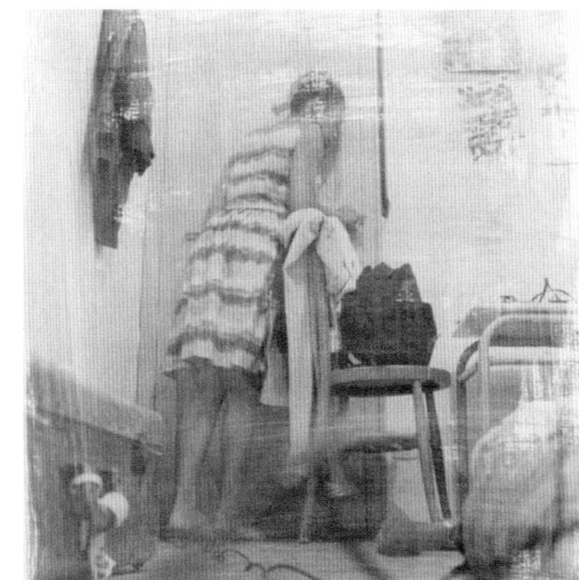

Plaza Sagrada Familia #2, Barcelona, 1988

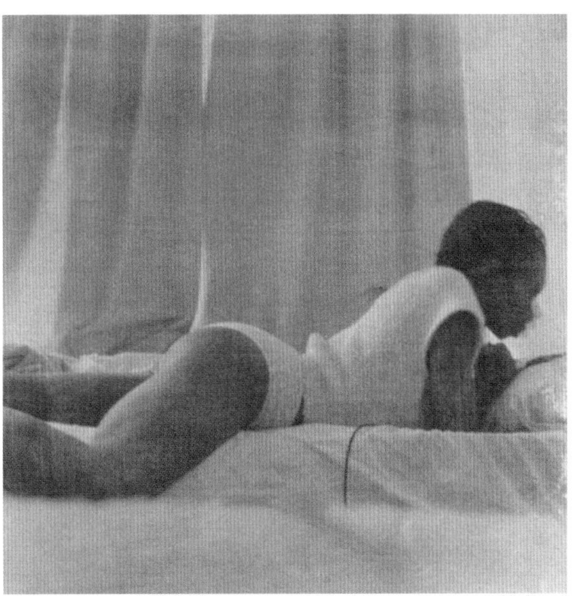

Hotel Normandia #1, Andorra La Vella, 1988

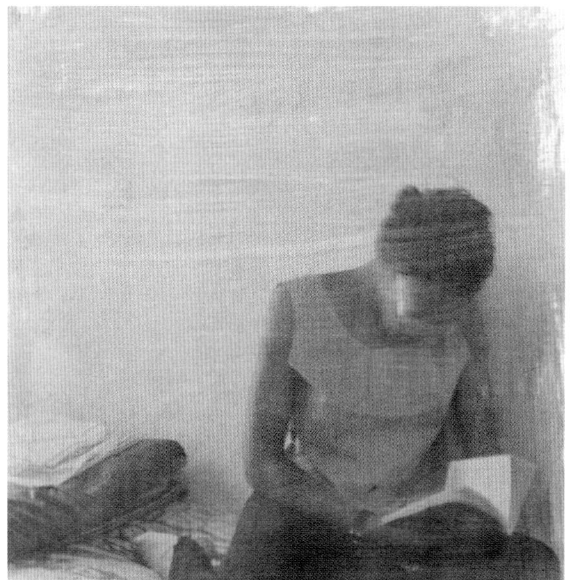

Villaroel, Barcelona, 1988

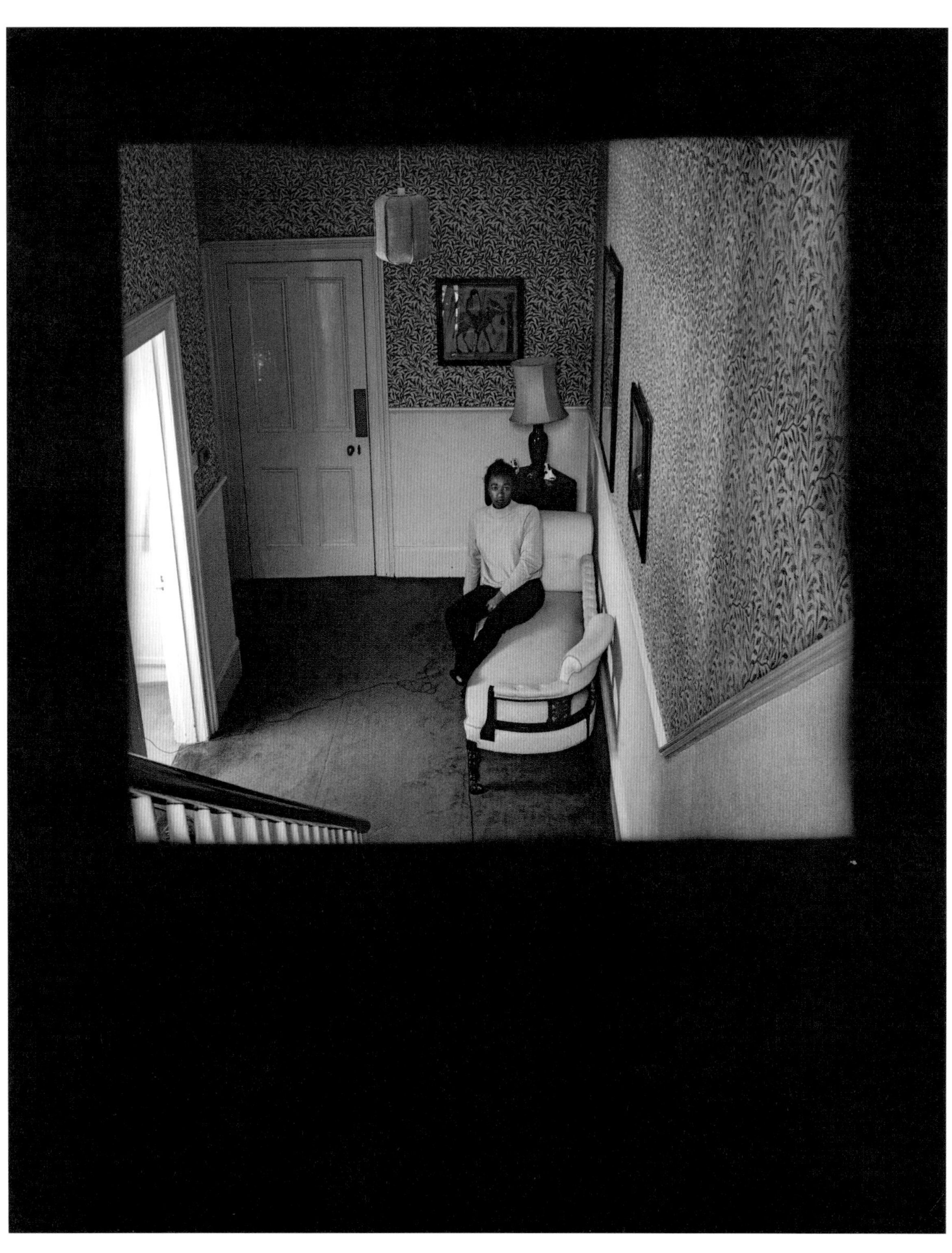

Holland Park, 1989

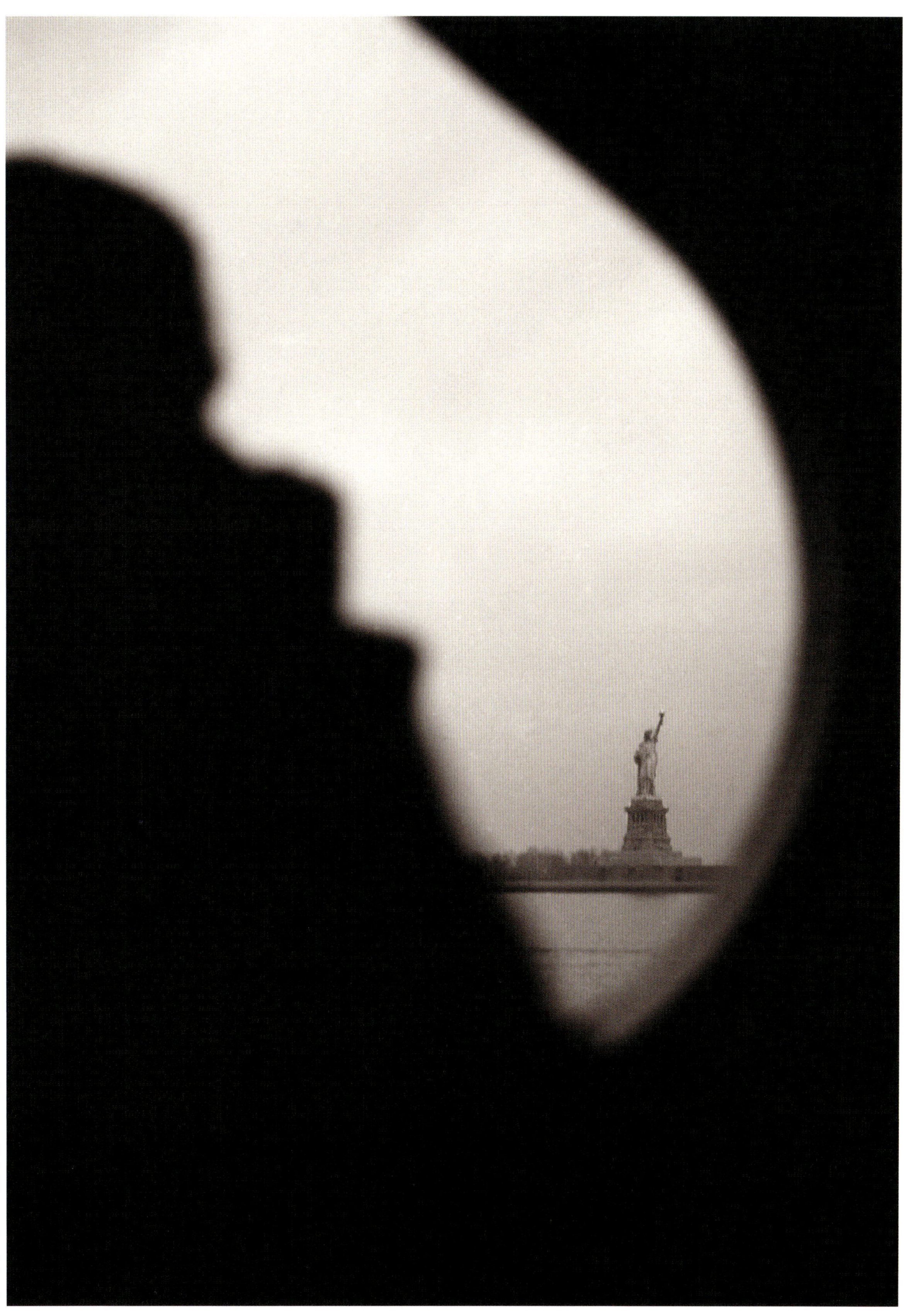

The Honeymoon (Staten Island Ferry), 1992

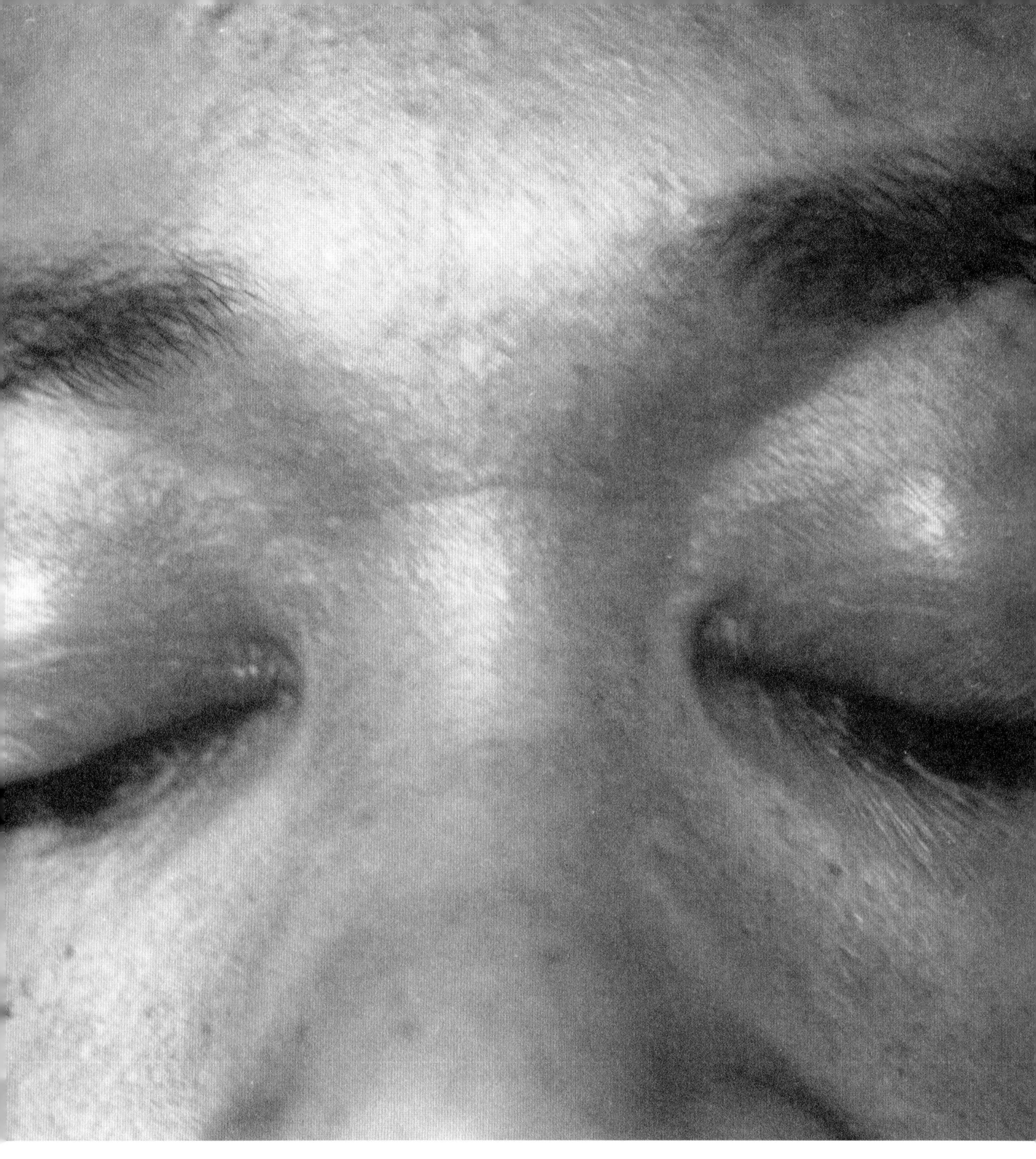

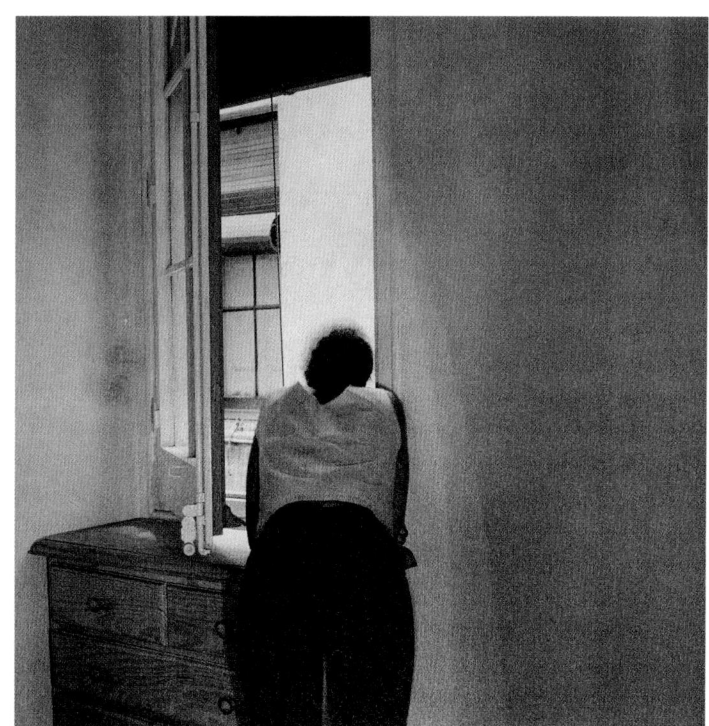

Barcelona, 1988

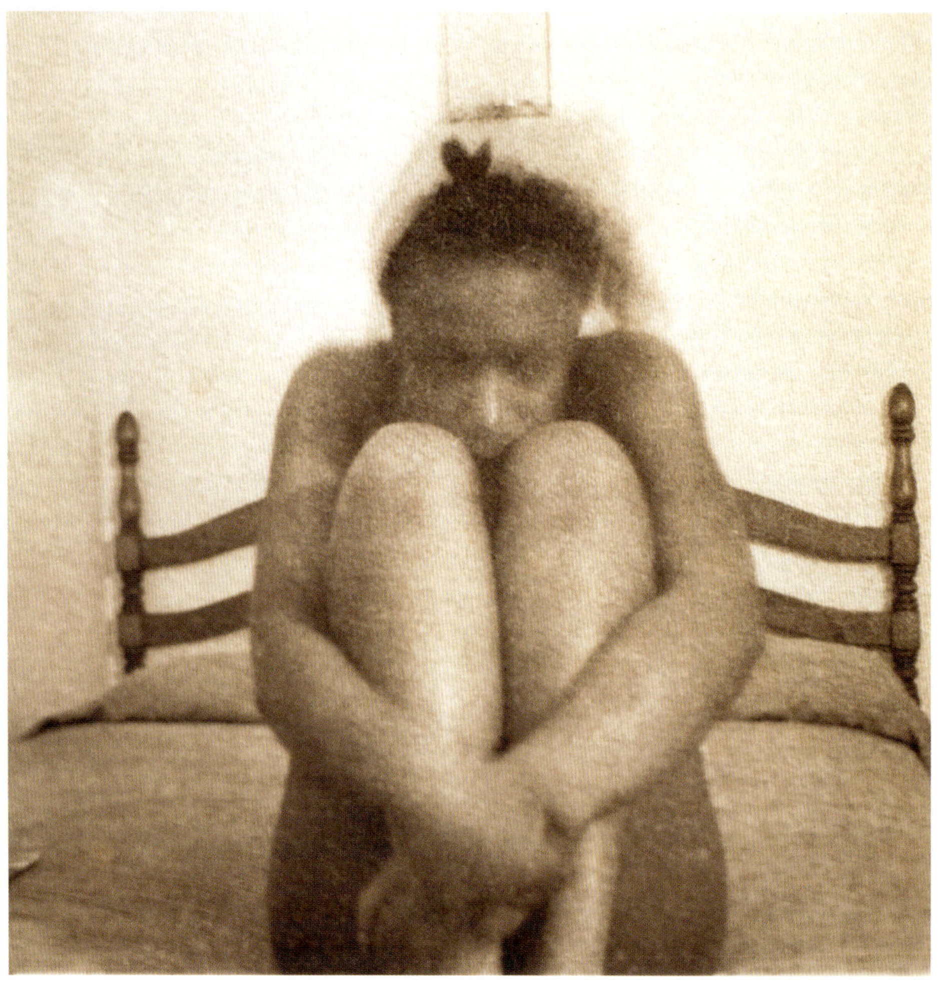

Shame

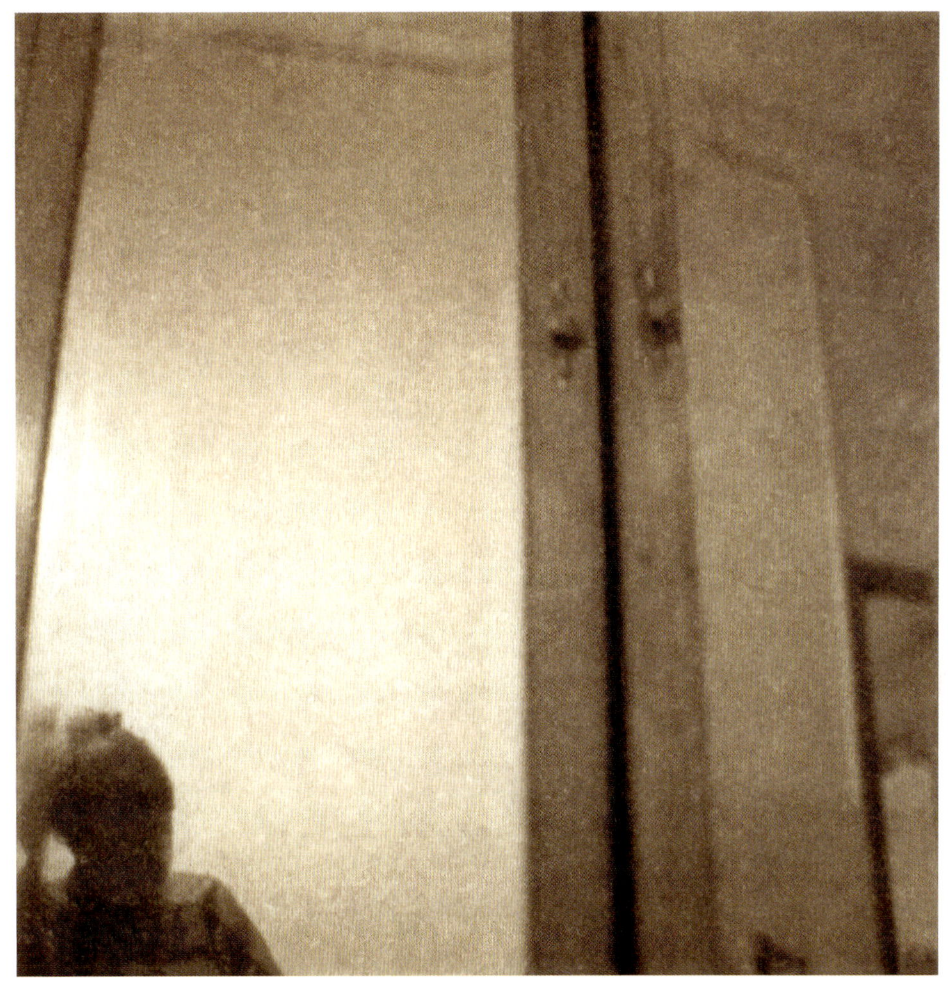

Reflection

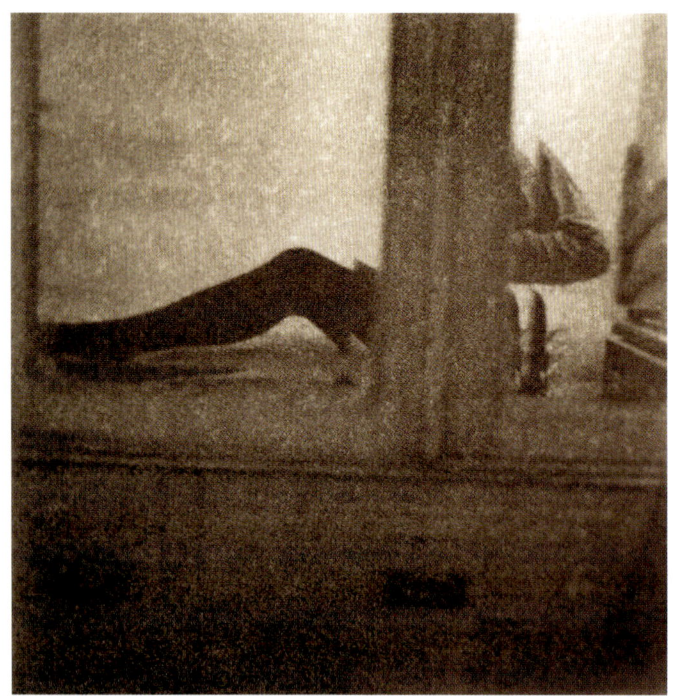

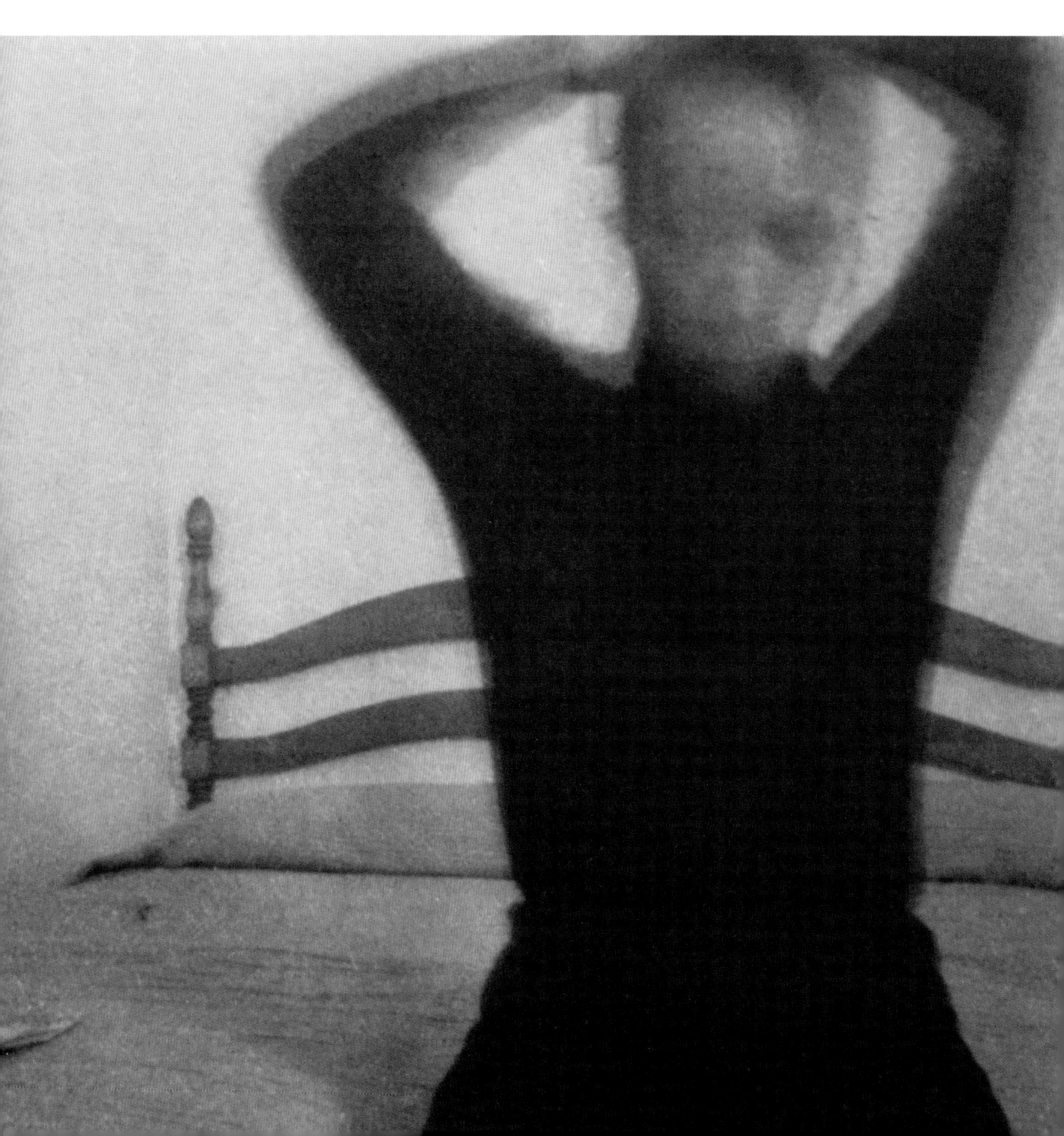

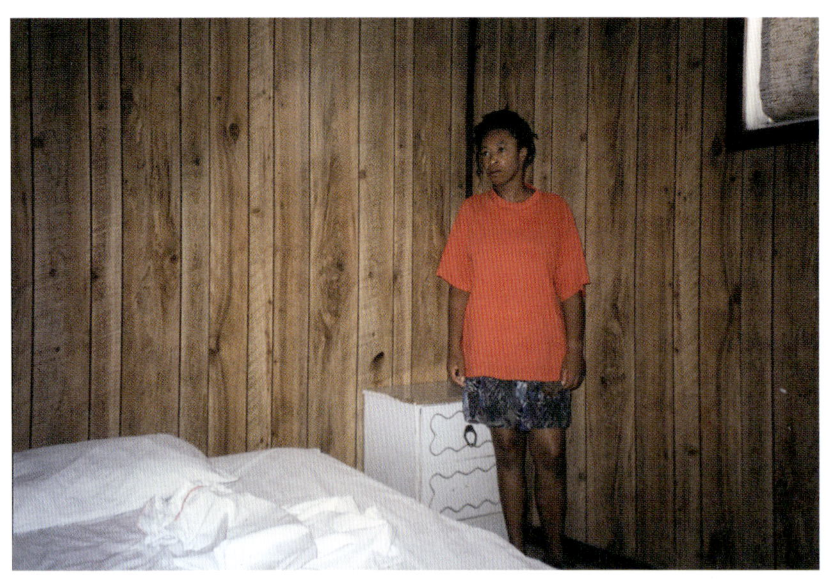

Amy in Wood Panelling

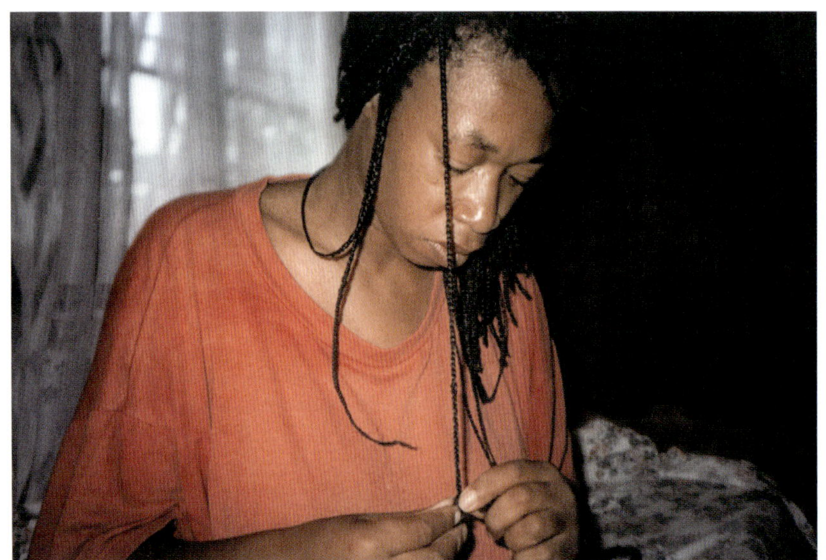

Grooming

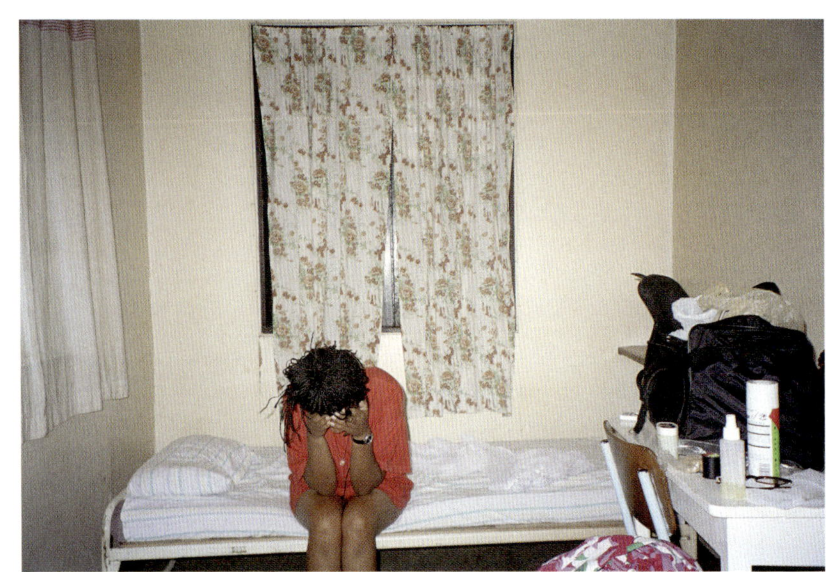

Alone

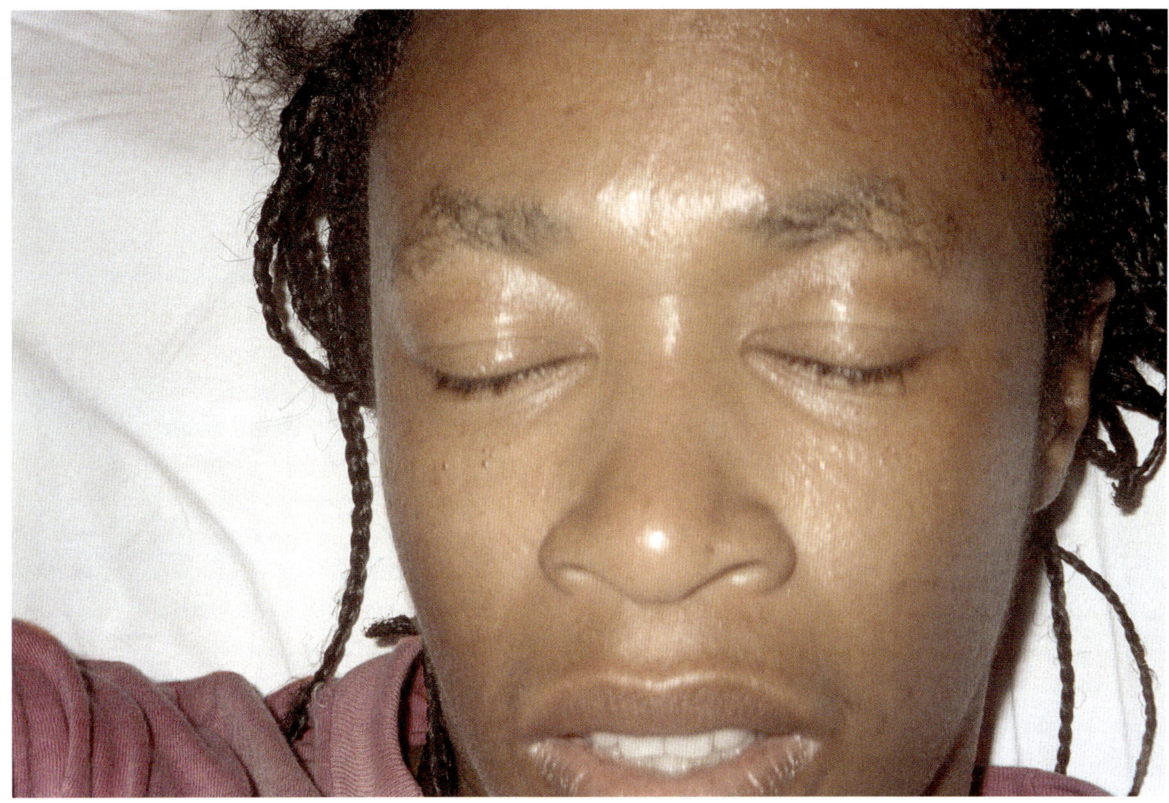

Sleeping (Caracas)

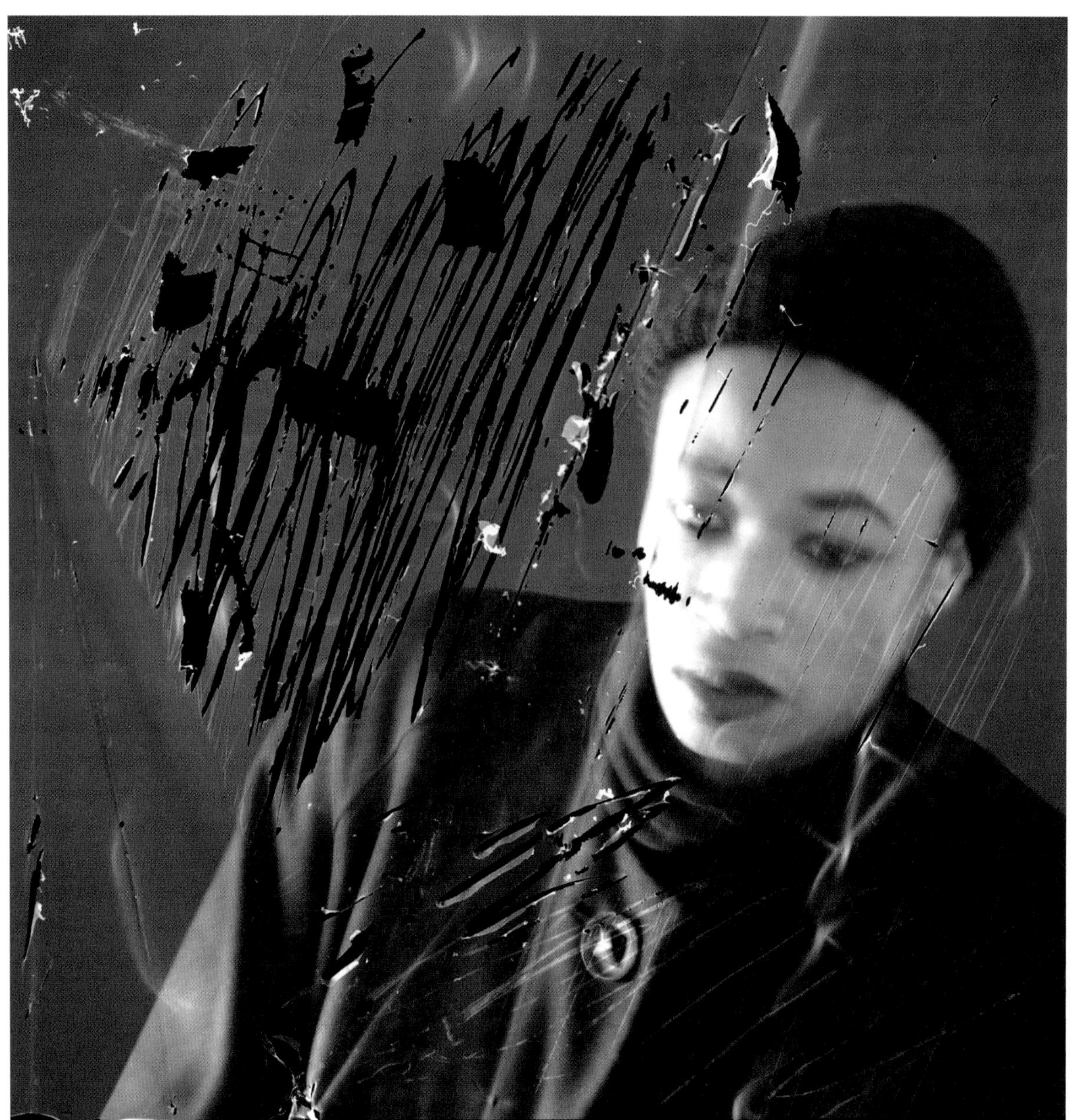

Self Portrait in Wool Hat & Polo Neck [Scratched]

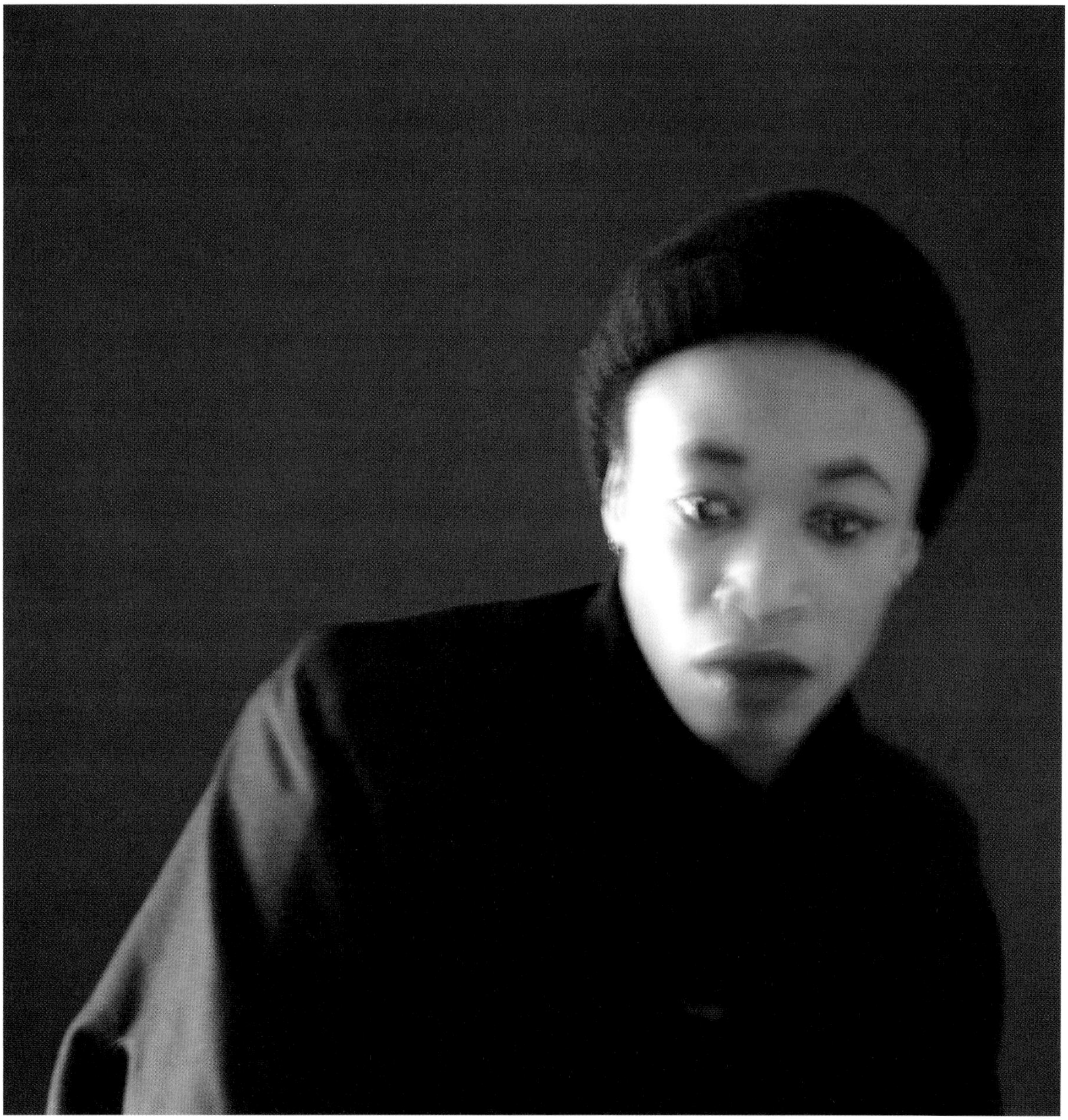

Self Portrait in Wool Hat & Polo Neck

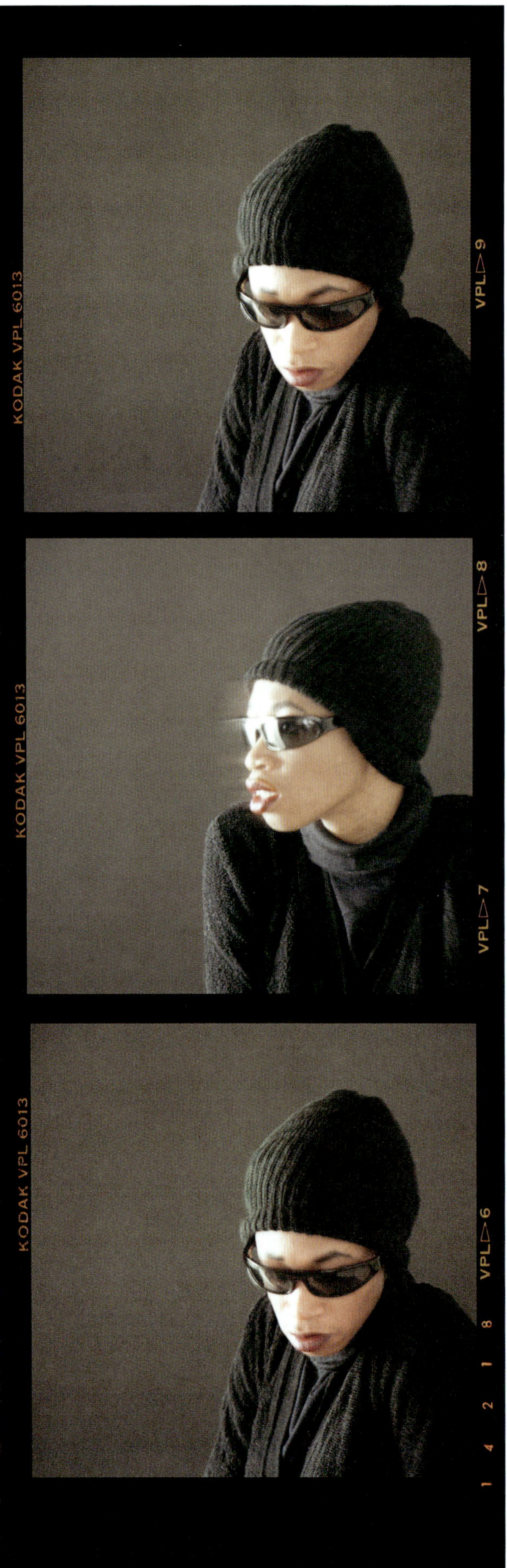

Self-Portrait in Black Ski Hat, 1988

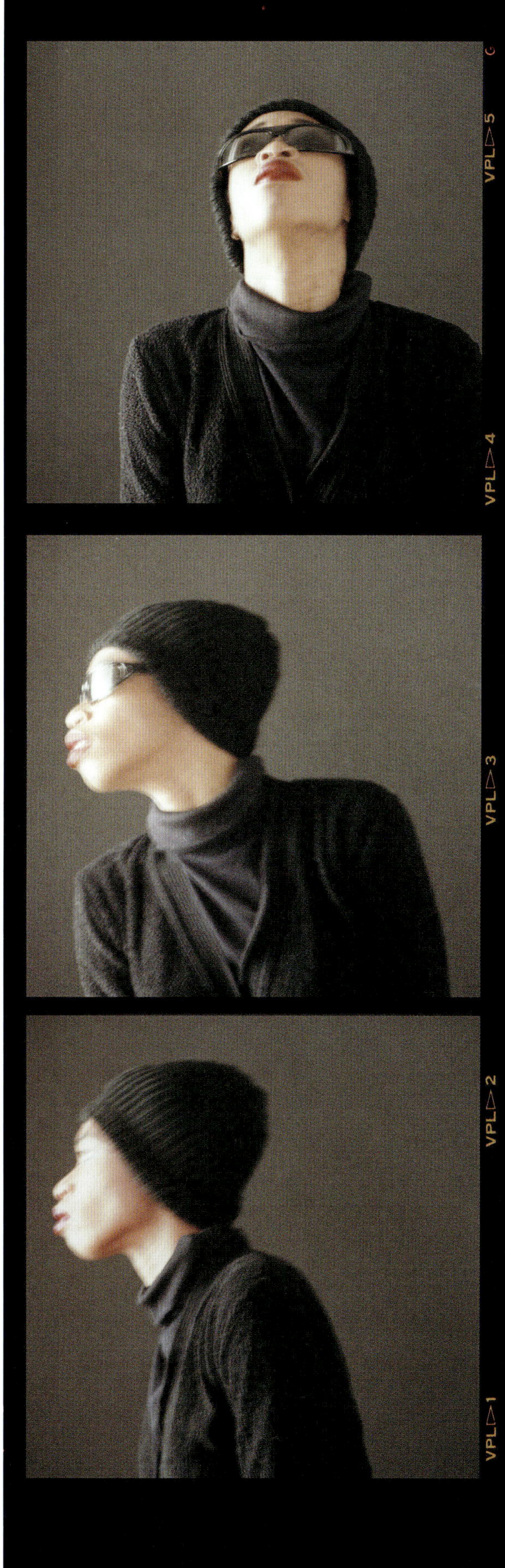
VPL▷5
VPL▷4
VPL▷3
VPL▷2
VPL▷1

Santa Maria (Cowboy & Angels) Top

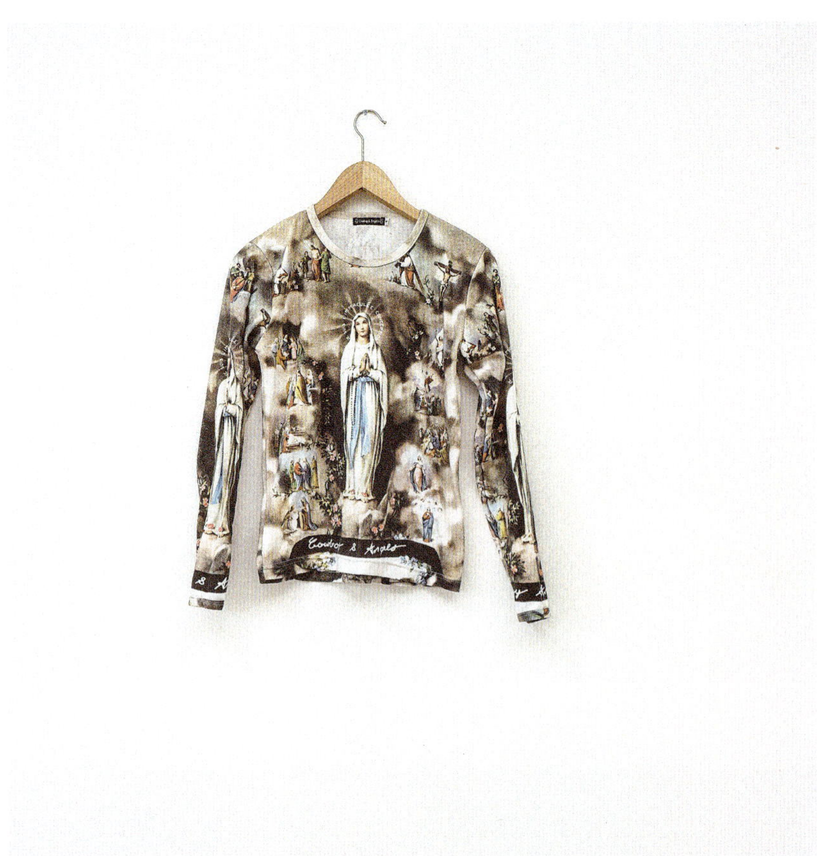

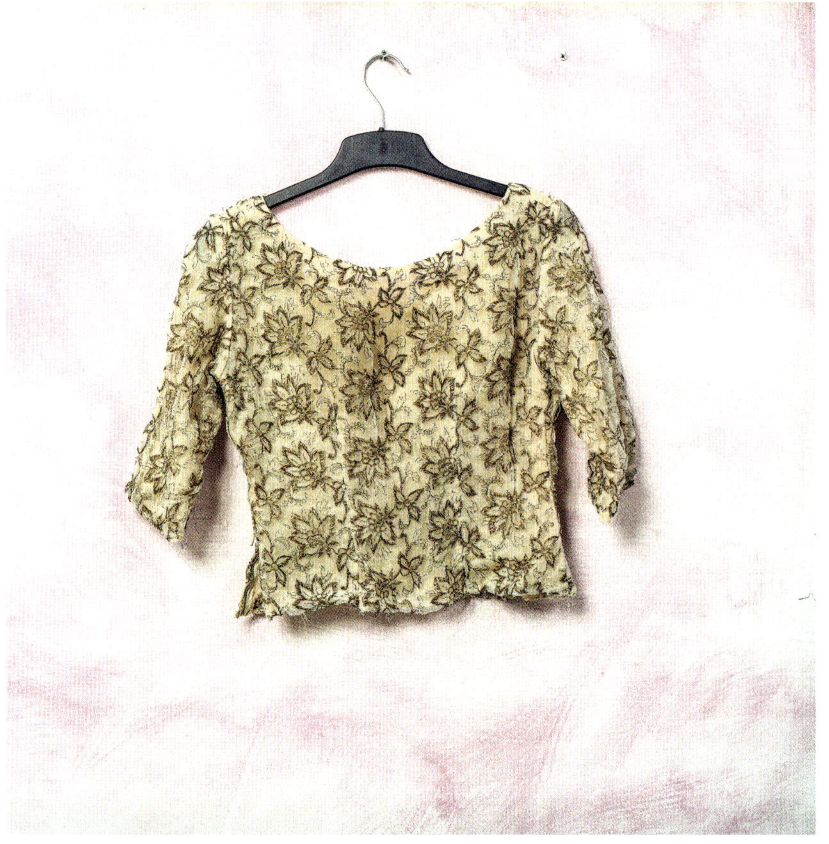

Cream-Gold-Brocade

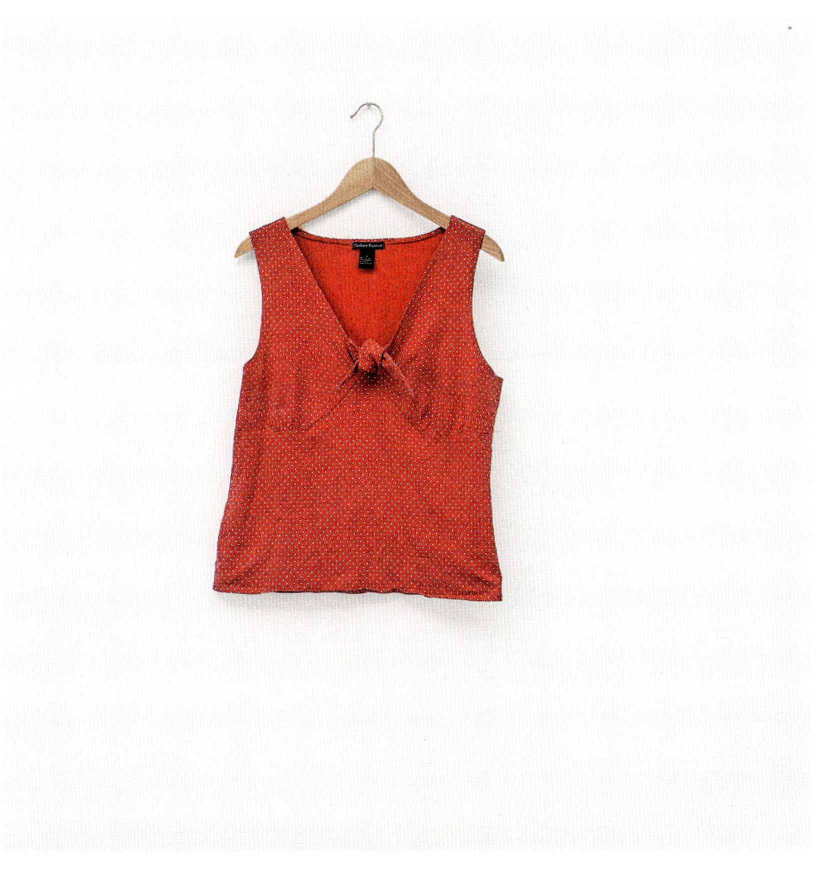

Red Sleeveless Top

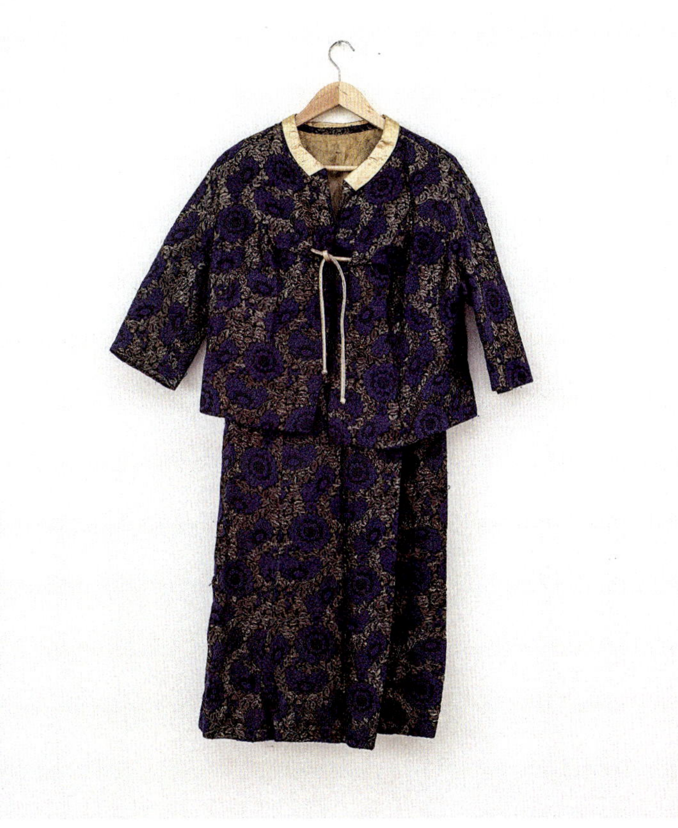

Blue & Gold Twin-set with Gold Lamé Collar

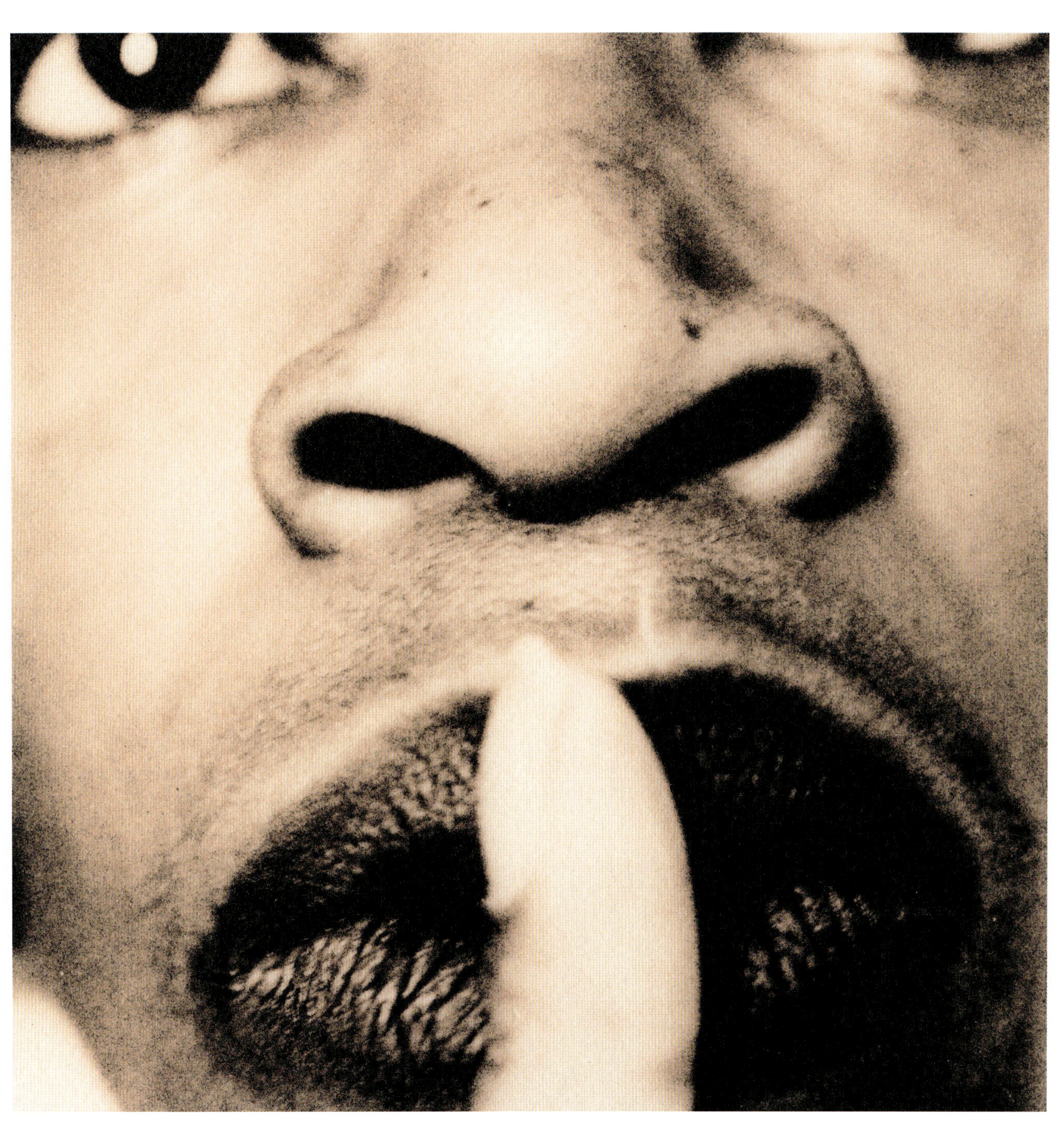

Silence (II)

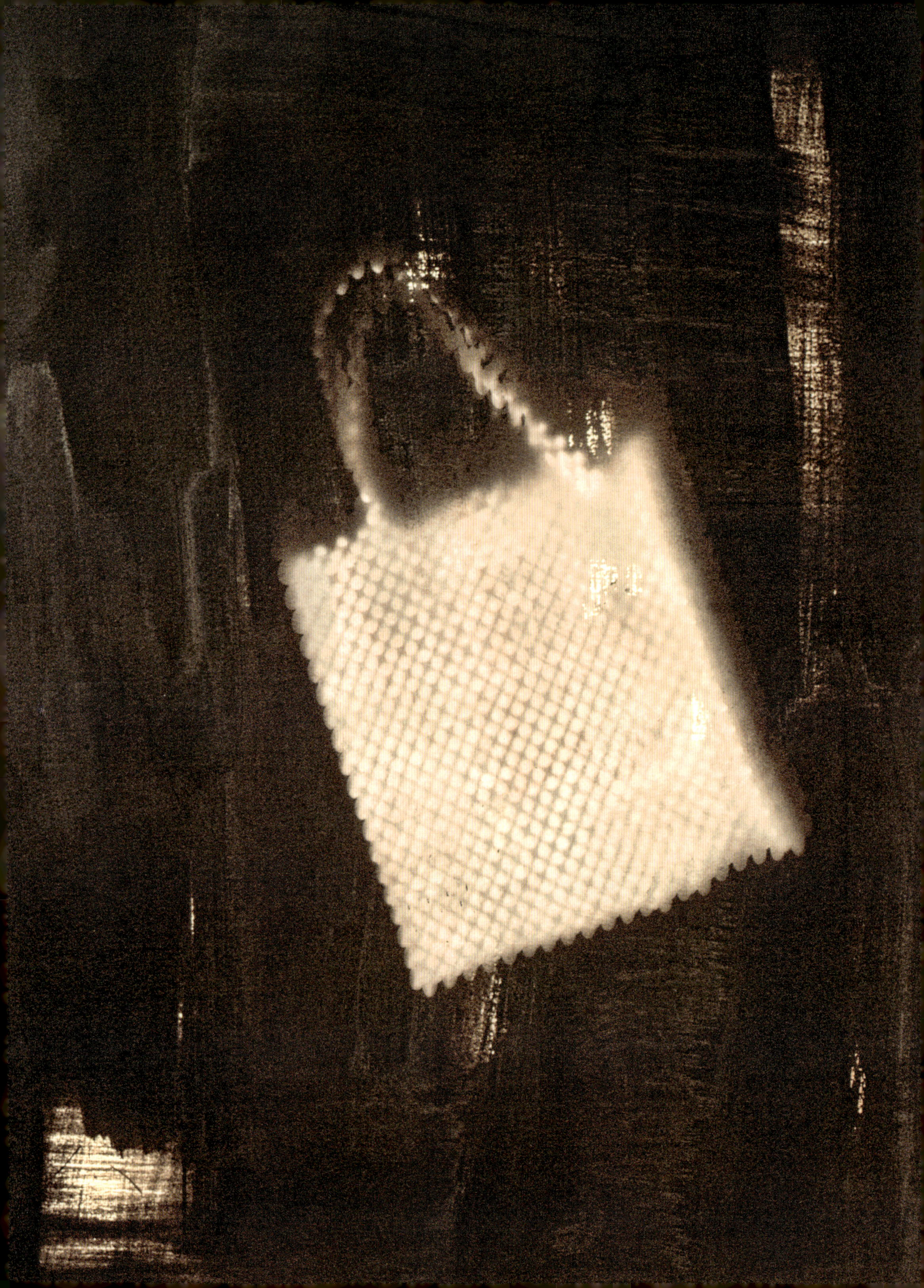

Kate Bush

Between Photographer and Subject

Joy Gregory has been an indelible presence within the community of Black artists who changed the conversation in British art of the 1980s and beyond. Over four decades, she has advanced the language of artistic photography while imbuing it with a subtle politics that argues passionately for both natural and human diversity. Experimental and experiential, her work has consistently emerged from, and been underpinned by, an ethos of collaboration with her photographic subjects. Thus, informed by multiple voices and viewpoints, Gregory's art reveals complex truths rather than predetermined ideas about human life and history.

Gregory's artistic contemporaries include Sonia Boyce, Keith Piper, Donald Rodney, Maud Sulter, Roshini Kempadoo, Brenda Agard, Issac Julien, Barbara Walker, Eddie Chambers, Maxine Walker, Dave Lewis and – slightly more senior – Ingrid Pollard, Sunil Gupta, Mitra Tabrizian, Rotimi Fani-Kayode and Lubaina Himid. In the post-pandemic 2020s, the work of many of these artists is being given overdue institutional attention. As each individual artist's history is being reappraised, it is illuminating to consider what makes Gregory's work distinctive within the context of British art and photography of the era. Her artistic trajectory has been in many ways, unusual. And while always central to the group in terms of the energy and generosity of her collaborations, with hindsight, curiously, her work was omitted from several of what art history would now deem 'landmark' exhibitions of Black British art in the 1980s.[1]

* All unattributed quotes from Joy Gregory in conversation with the author, 27 February 2025.

While at the Royal College of Art – the first Black woman to be accepted onto the Masters in Photography in 1984 – Gregory met Keith Piper who was studying environmental art. In 1986, Piper proposed her work for inclusion in a show his friend and Blk Art Group comrade Eddie Chambers, was in the process of selecting. Chambers was to famously dismiss Gregory's work as 'not Black enough'. That remark, oft quoted, reveals how her work has had from the beginning a distinctive quality that set it apart from many of her contemporaries in the Black Arts Movement. Against the backdrop of widespread racism in Thatcher's Britain, in the art world, 'we were all', Gregory remembers, 'in the same space, fighting the same battles' around issues of visibility and exclusion. Artists like Eddie Chambers, Marlene Smith and Keith Piper of the early Wolverhampton-based Blk Art Group (1981–84) had begun to create unapologetically bold, political, sometimes combative work, delivered in the form of graphic image and text or expressionistic montage and assemblage. Their volume was loud, intended to make people sit up and listen. In comparison, Gregory's voice was soft: 'My work was ethereal and my message difficult to place.'[2] By 1990, however, the series *Autoportrait*, a sequence of dramatic, exquisitely printed, performative self-portraits, was to establish her as a leading voice in Black British art. She has said this is the moment that politics enters her work, and the first time she thought about race in relation to representation. However, I would suggest that from the very beginning her work has been attentive to both aesthetics and politics: but its political meaning, expressed in a personal, often nuanced way, was easy to overlook in the clamour of the time.

Beginnings

In 1981, when Gregory, despite her love of painting at school, elected to study not Fine Art, but commercial photography at Manchester Polytechnic, she set off on her unique path. 'Even though photography was not really seen as an art form, even at that stage, it was a rich medium in my mind and I really wanted to understand it and learn how to make it work for me.' Her course prepared its students for work in fashion, advertising or editorial photography. While Gregory learnt those languages, she also devoured the photo-scientific element of the course. She was to experiment endlessly in the darkroom, surrounded in chemistry,

1 Such as Lubaina Himid's *Thin Black Line* (1985–6) in the ICA concourse, or *Testimony* at Camerawork in the summer of 1986, a survey of Black women photographers including Brenda Agard, Ingrid Pollard and Maud Sulter. Nor was she included in the touring *D-Max* exhibition (1987–88), or the following year, *Intimate Distance* at The Photographers' Gallery, which presented a group of Black women photographers including Ingrid Pollard, Sutapa Biswas and Maxine Walker.

2 Joy Gregory, email to author, 28 February 2025.

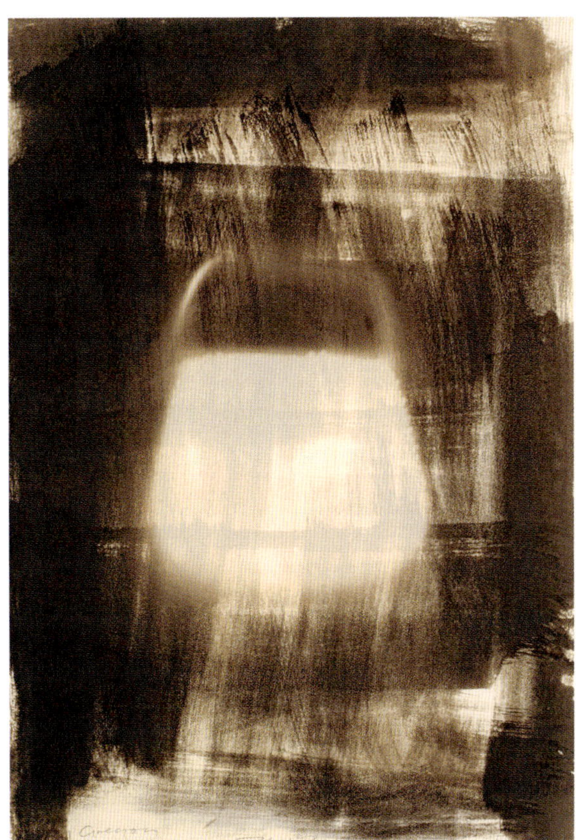

Black Bead

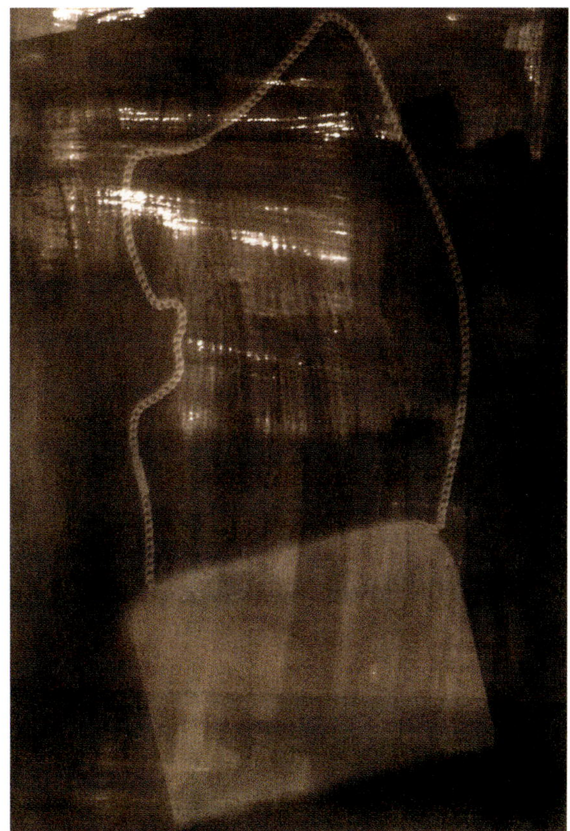

Maggie Thatcher's Handbag

exploring the alchemic transformations that lie at the heart of the medium. The possibility of making something appear from nothing is an idea that has continued to captivate her. This period of study gave her an intricate understanding of both early Victorian printing methods such as salt and cyanotype, as well as the latest developments in modern colour photography. As soon as she mastered a technique, she would experiment with it, breaking the rules she had just learnt. Her deep technical knowledge of all aspects of the medium, most especially printing, has freed Gregory to reimagine photography as an expressive medium with a material quality comparable in some ways to painting. Her use, for example, of viscous emulsions such as liquid light which can be brushed onto the surface with gestural fluidity, or her choice of papers of varying tactility, contribute to this painterly feel.

Manchester Polytechnic, one of the very few colleges where one could study photography at the time, had been in the 1970s, a bastion of the black-and-white, social documentary tradition. Alumni include Martin Parr and Peter Fraser, both of whom by the early 1980s under the influence of earlier Americans such as William Eggleston and Stephen Shore, have been credited as the pioneers of colour documentary photography in Britain. For Gregory the classic documentary model – the photographer as privileged witness, roaming the world, capturing on camera a stream of decisive, objectively 'truthful' moments, was anathema. She stayed inside and created her own worlds in the studio. Arguably

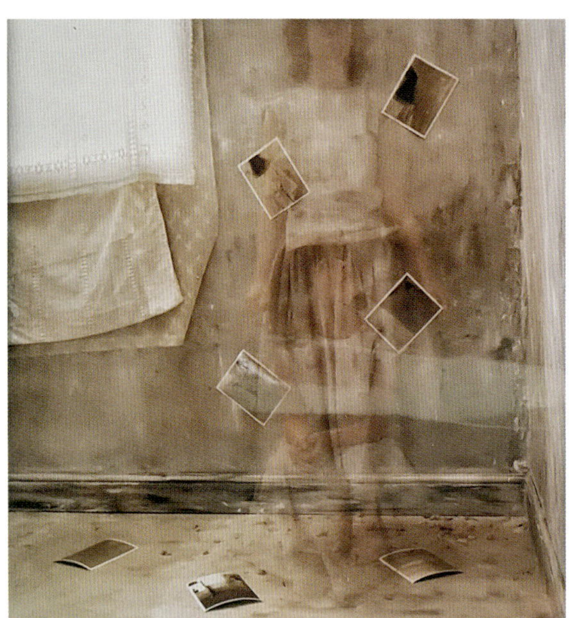

Grey Room [Janet standing]

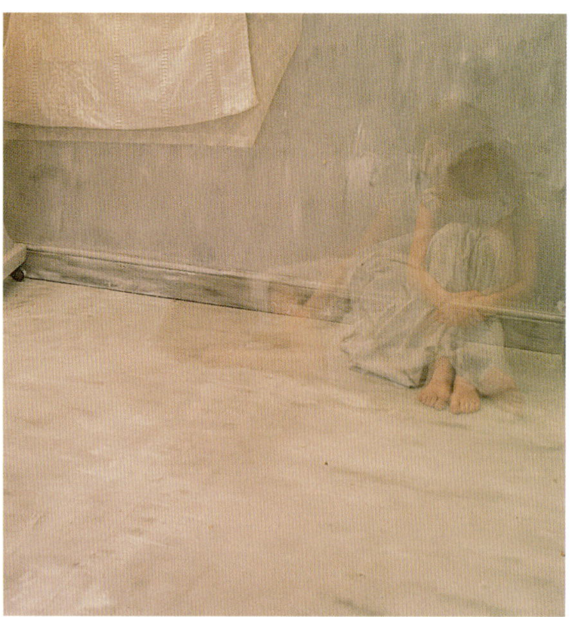

Grey Room [Janet sitting]

however, she was as early an innovator in the medium of colour as the prominent men of British twentieth-century photography. Her series of *Constructed Interiors* for example, crafted from up to thirty exposures, were highly experimental for a young student. Unlike the British colour documentarists, she did not make colour prints from a negative, but contact printed directly from a large format transparency. This gives her images an unparalleled richness of colour and light.

The 1980s was a formative period for Gregory, and when we consider some of the artists who caught her attention at the time it is clear to see how different her early reference points were to her peers. Many Black British artists of the 1980s were looking across the Atlantic to the 1970s, post-Civil Rights generation of African American artists. The work of people like Adrian Piper and Carrie Mae Weems, for example, who were creating conceptual and performative photographic works, were particularly influential in Britain. Gregory, by contrast, was 'focused on the world of commercial art production. I had a fascination for album covers, advertising billboards and editorial imagery.'[3] At the RCA, she studied still life as a genre, writing a dissertation comparing seventeenth-century Spanish still-life painting and contemporary still-life photography. When one remembers the photography she was looking at then, such as the mediative, Morandi-esque still life of Dutchman Peter Ruting or the formalistic arrangements of natural objects by American Olivia Parker, one can see how Gregory adopted certain principles – pared-back compositions, everyday objects the central and sometimes single focus, often arranged flat to the picture plane – before going on to radicalise the very notion of a still life.

3 Ibid.

Gregory's camera-less still lifes have been a constant through her career, from *Language of Flowers* (1986) to *The Handbag Project* (1998–2005) through to the pandemic piece, the *Invisible Life Force of Plants* (2020). I describe these as radical still lifes in the sense that the object itself, the *raison d'être* of the picture, is missing. Only its ghostly trace, a white, lucent centre where it once sat on the paper, is left behind. And moreover, in eschewing the camera these works involve a subtle recasting of the normal power relations between photographer and subject. Where a classic documentarian gazes down the lens, fixing the world as they see it in a frame, by contrast a photogram[4] results from what might be described as a more equal collaboration between photographer and subject. The artist arranges a specimen on the light sensitive paper, and thereafter the plant essentially illustrates itself. In this sense, just as Gregory has always rejected the model of the documentary photographer, out in the world producing putative truths about that world from a place of privileged viewing, there are in these camera-less works an inherent rejection of a masterful gaze. Instead, in visual terms Gregory embraces the variables of the photographic process, excited by what will emerge from the unpredictable interaction of subject, chemical, paper and light.

Language of Flowers (1986), the first and perhaps defining work of this family of camera-less works, carries a political meaning in addition to that implied in its authorial ethos of reciprocity. The titular 'language of flowers' refers to a now-disappeared language from Victorian times whereby lovers and suitors sent each other encoded messages in the form of symbolic bouquets. But where the Victorians chose sumptuous, often exotic blooms, Gregory by contrast catalogues all the unremarkable plants she found growing in her immediate urban locale, from daisy to dog violet. She fixes the image of each 'weed' onto beautiful papers from around the world, thus turning something of supposedly no importance into a unique and unrepeatable work of art. 'Why are certain plants valued, and why are others disregarded?' she asks, adding, 'this piece was not just about race it was about class.' *Language of Flowers* signals the first appearance of what will develop into two of the themes that are explored in Gregory's major works from the 2000s onwards: plant life as metaphor for human life; and the idea of lost or endangered language as symptomatic of the fragility of cultural and ethnic diversity.

4 Or 'photogenic drawing' as William Henry Fox Talbot called them when, in 1834, he invented the technique of sensitising writing paper to light by coating it with silver nitrate, placing an object upon it and then exposing it to sunlight.

The 1990s

The late 1980s and early 1990s was the defining time for so-called issue-based photography. There existed then, a small but national network of photo galleries and community darkrooms, supported – crucially – by medium-specific, state funding. Across race, gender, sexuality and disability, the politics of identity and the politics of representation were the dominant ideas circulating in the independent photography sector. The writing of intellectuals Stuart Hall and Paul Gilroy helped frame and motivate a group of Black British photographers to assert their presence as authors and subjects. Their work was fuelled by the recognition that photography was the visual medium wherein identities had been most overtly controlled and distorted in the mainstream – but where they could also be remade. Gregory's work during the 1990s shared many of the strategies deployed at that time. Negative representations of 'Blackness' that had accrued over decades in the British media, were forcefully challenged for the first time. There was a general flowering of self-portraiture in the impetus to give visibility to Black faces; and there was much imaging of the visual signifiers of racial difference – the Black body, skin and hair in particular.

Gregory, together with Black British women artists like Sonia Boyce and Claudette Johnson, brought a feminist lens to bear on racial inequality. This was most powerfully expressed in her seminal work of the period, *Autoportrait* (1990). She characterises it as: 'My response to the invisibility, beyond the exotic, of Black women in fashion and beauty images ... I wanted to conjure the mood of the catwalk, all fantasy and glamour, a world from which me and my kind had been almost totally excluded.'[5] It comprises a sequence of self-portraits shot from a variety of angles, dynamically framed, unconventionally cropped, and printed – significantly – using a Lith developer. Her intricate knowledge of what was possible to achieve in the darkroom, enabled Gregory to render skin tone and hair texture with great subtlety and expression compared to conventional black-and-white printing. Later in the decade, she went on to make a number of works that addressed the constructed nature of 'femininity'. *Objects of Beauty* (1992–95), for example, is a series of twenty-one kallitype prints, a visual catalogue of objects – hair grip, corset, eyelash curlers – photographed flat to the picture plane in the manner of museological or anthropological photographs. These are the consumer products sold to women by the beauty industry, the tools with which to manipulate our bodies in order to attain an acceptable level of attractiveness.

5 Joy Gregory, *Objects of Beauty (Autograph)* (London: Chris Boot, 2004).

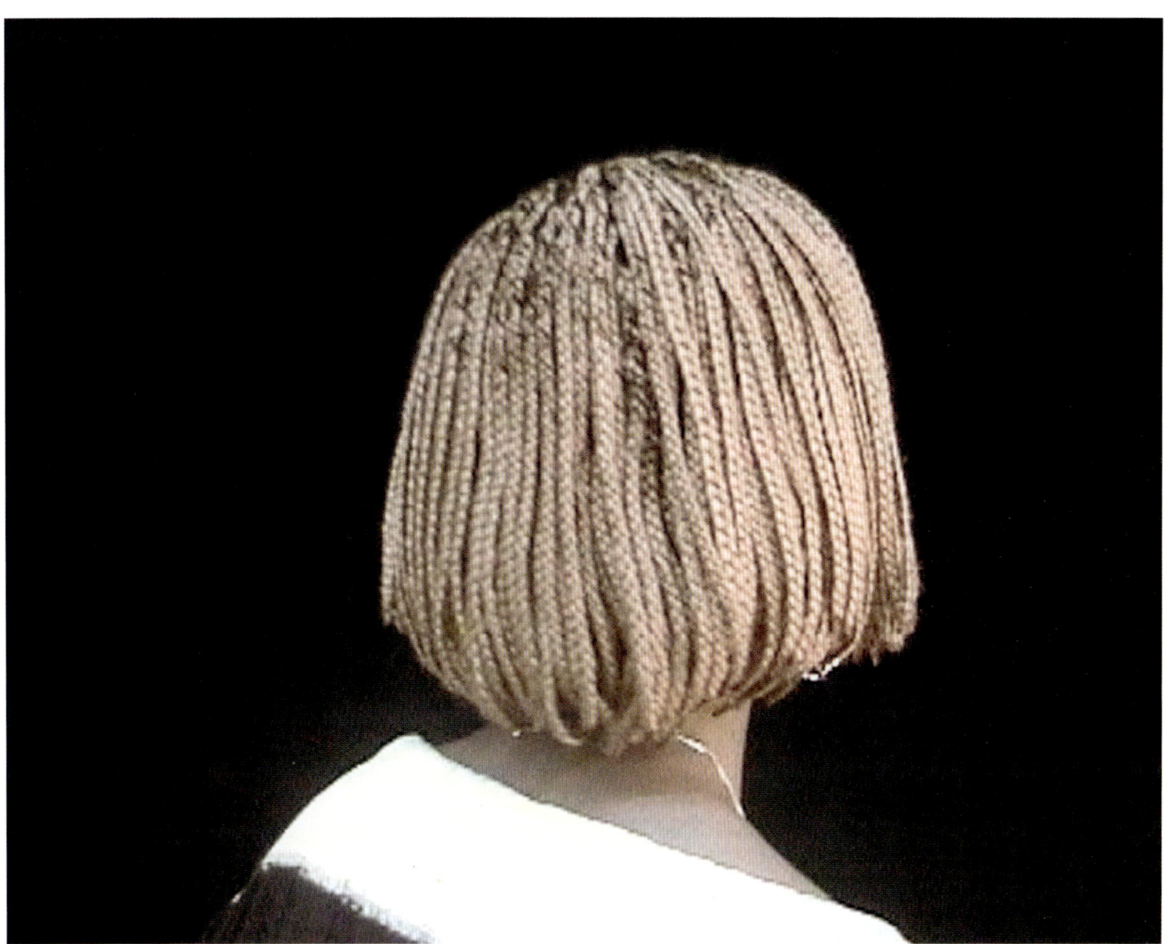

Zara, 1997

By the time of *Fairest* (1997–98), part of *The Blonde*, a playful, multidimensional work incorporating film, photography, and performance, Gregory took her critique of received ideas of beauty into new terrain. She had been struck at the time by how many people of colour she noticed on Europe's city streets suddenly sporting blond hair. She interviewed a cross section of people, women and men, Black and white, Queer and straight, asking them the same set of questions: How would you describe yourself? Why did you decide to go blonde? What emerges – and what is typical of Gregory's empirical methods and undogmatic approach to her subjects – is that, far from the phenomenon being about people of colour mimicking a white ideal of glamour, and therefore 'betraying their race' (as some Black commentators stated at the time), '[t]hese new blondes ... revelled in its artifice.' Gregory found herself identifying 'a positive side of globalisation involving the crossing not only of political and physical borders but also the internal borders of human identity'.[6] *Fairest* is Gregory's celebration of how as subjects, we are not externally defined. We have the power to create our identities as we fantasise and desire them.

6 Ibid.

Later works

With the two recent, magisterial works, *Seeds of Empire* (2021) and *The Sweetest Thing*, (2022), Gregory joins the ranks of senior British artists such as John Akomfrah, Yinka Shonibare, Sonia Boyce, Keith Piper and Steve McQueen who in mid-career are producing era-defining, multi-levelled art that addresses aspects of British colonial history and its legacies. They work to give form and expression to specific diasporic histories which have been excluded from the national narrative.

Gregory, the child of Jamaican parents, grew up in a small English town, a rural background compared to her contemporaries. The natural world has always held meaning for her; the wildflower meadows around her home a place of escape, the medicinal plants her parents used to salve and soothe, a source of fascination. From *Language of Flowers* (1986–2004), botany has served as one of the allegorical routes through which she has addressed questions around colonialism, identity and diversity. She asks: 'Why are certain plants where they are? Why are certain people where they are?' If the imperial drive for enrichment included the trade of plants, deracinated from their natural habitats and dispersed from one continent to another in pursuit of new profits, then plant life has provided Gregory with an apt metaphor for diasporic experience.

The theme of botany finds most complex expression in her major, polyphonic installation, *Seeds of Empire* (2021). The work is structured around a brutal encounter between Hans Sloane, the seventeenth century botanist, collector and physician, and Rose, a woman enslaved in the house where Sloane stayed on a visit to Jamaica in 1687. Through a layering of image, sound and voice, Gregory then contrasts Sloane's botany of empire, with the ancient plant knowledge of African and Indigenous people in the Caribbean: a knowledge that helped them resist their violent oppression.[7] As her camera roams over lush and verdant gardens in Jamaica, Windrush generation friends talking to Gregory over the telephone recall their yearning for their abundant gardens back home: sources of emotion and comfort compared to the grey and chilly England that they found in the 1960s. The fundamental interconnectedness of humans with nature, of people with place, and of biodiversity with cultural diversity – these are important truths which are characteristically, in Gregory's art, expressed through careful attention to the voices of others.

7 Represented for example in Gregory's photographs of the manchineel tree, its deadly apple-like fruit sometimes served by enslaved people to unwitting plantation owners (*Plants of Resistance, Manchineel Tree I, II, III*, 2021). Or the White Cotton tree, its buoyant wood and silky seeds providing all manner of life support, from medicine to bedding, soap to shelter.

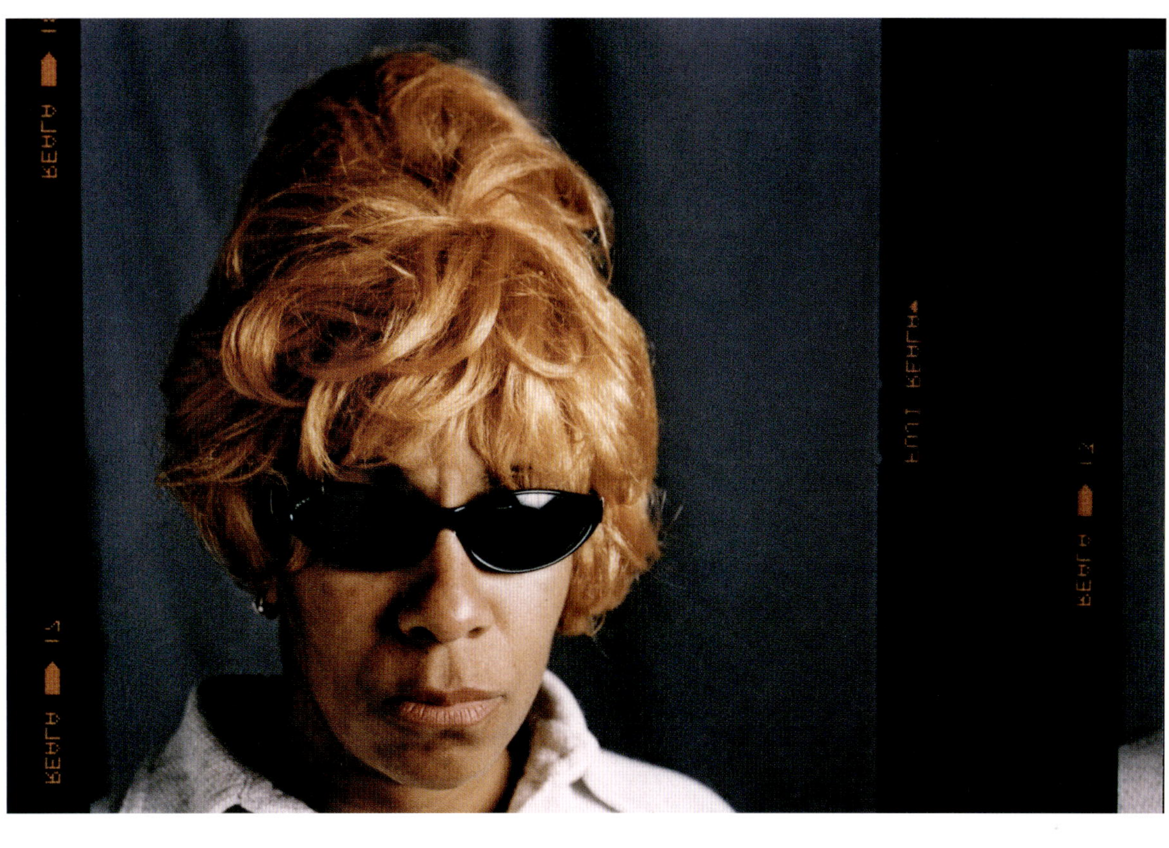

Ingrid (The Blonde)

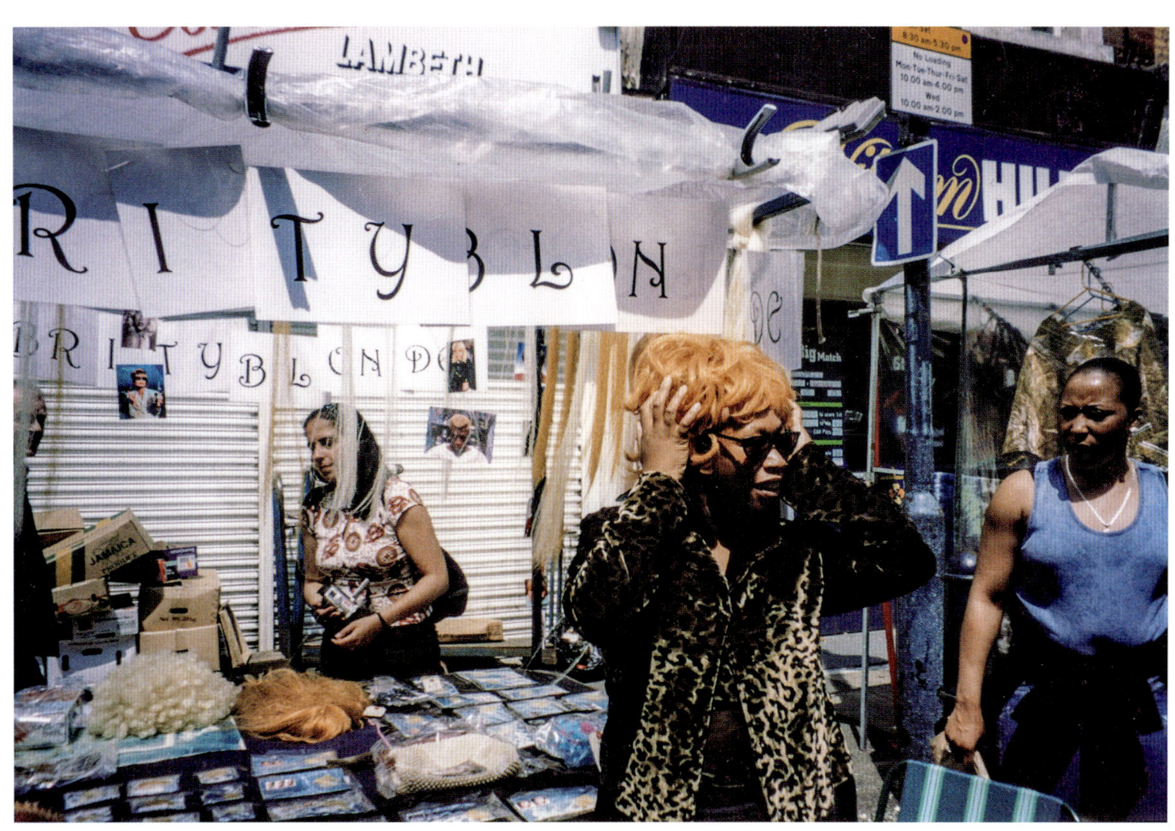

Stockwell Siren, Celebrity Blonde, 2003

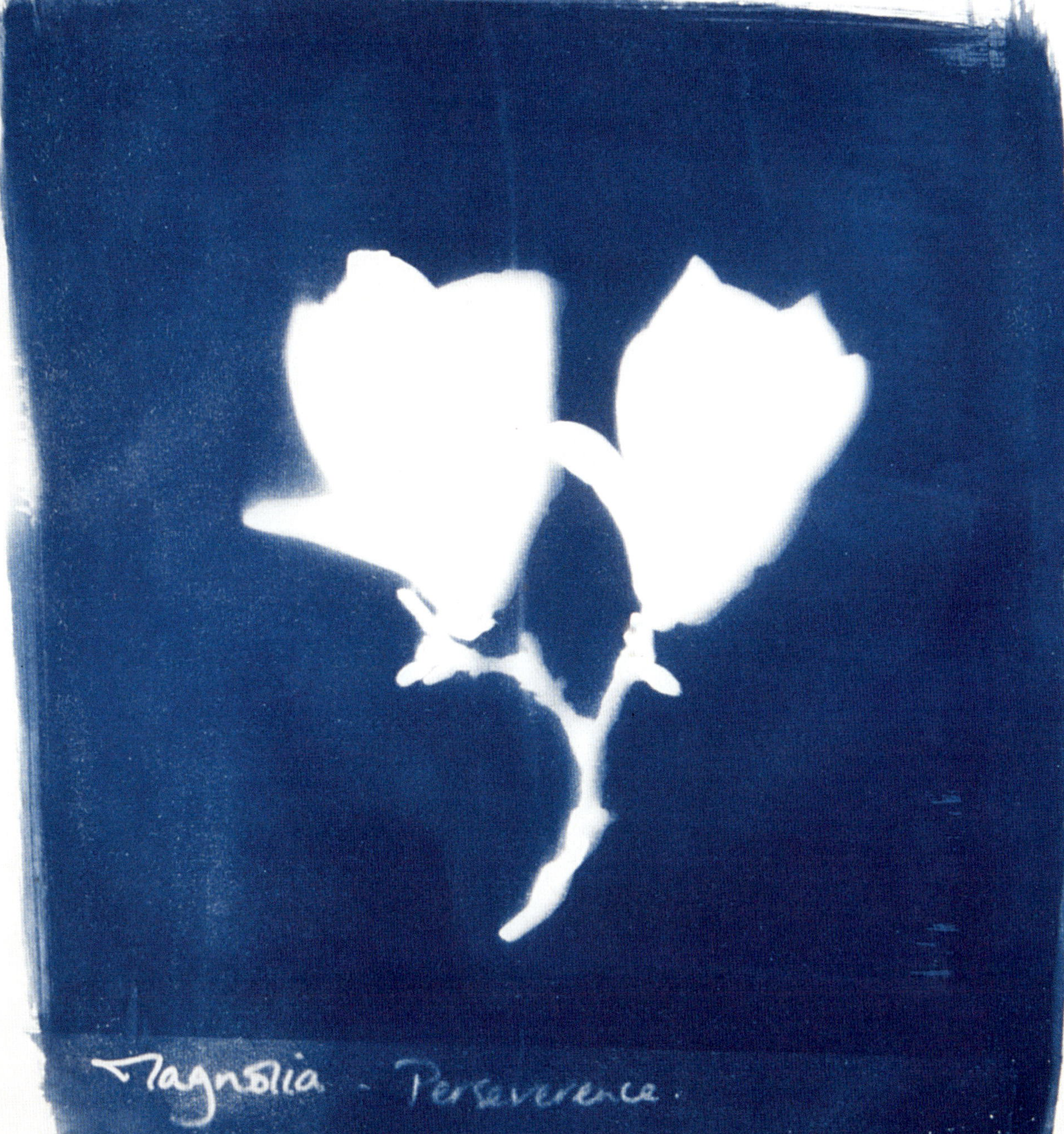
Magnolia - Perseverence.

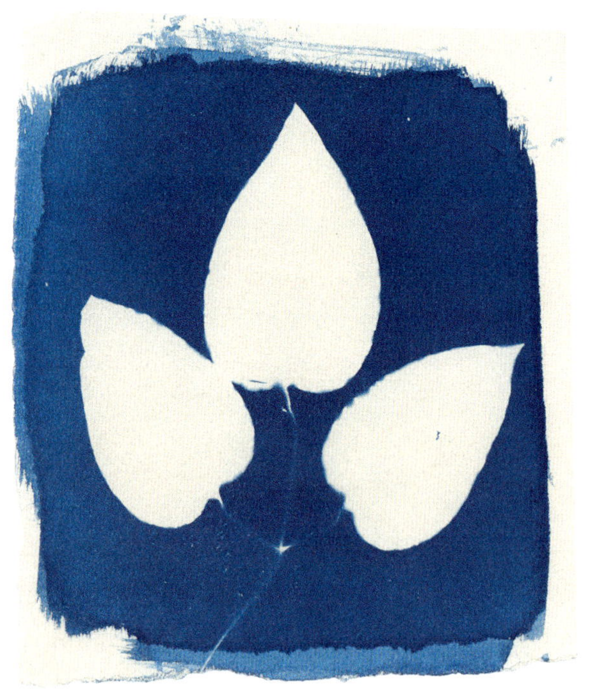

3 Lime Tree Leaves

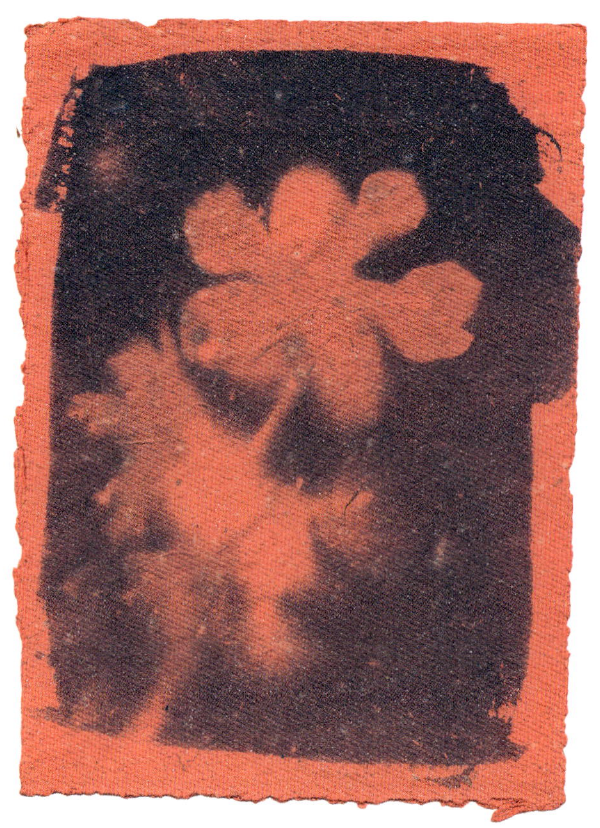

Peony

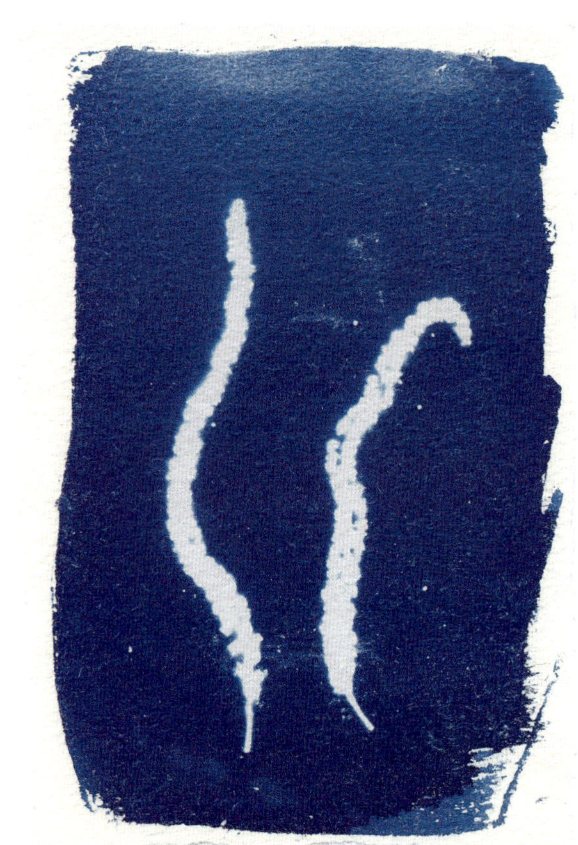

Catkins

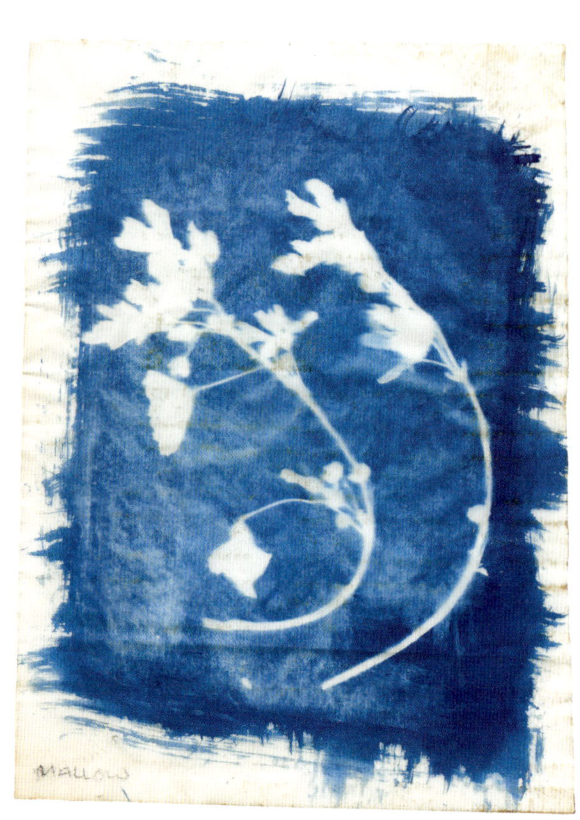

Mallow

Chickweed

Carnation

Dandelion

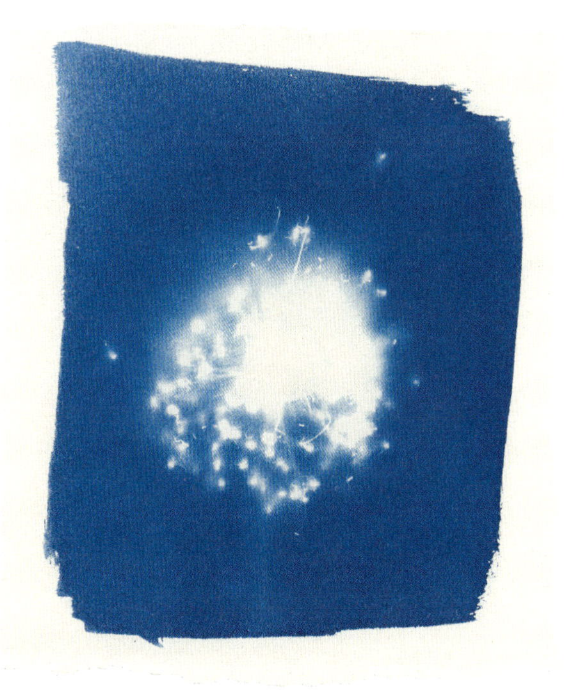

Puffball

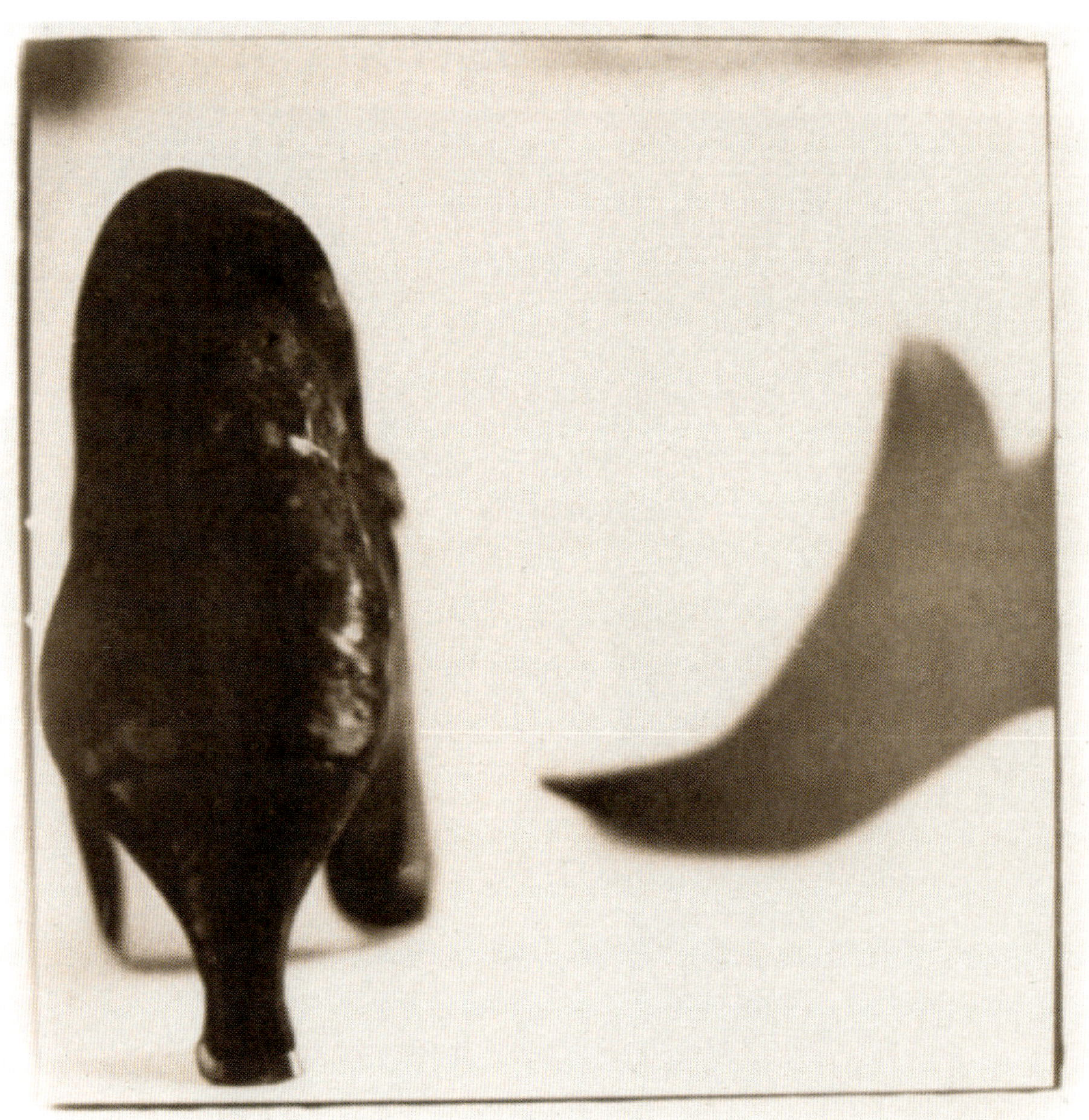

Shoes

Stockings

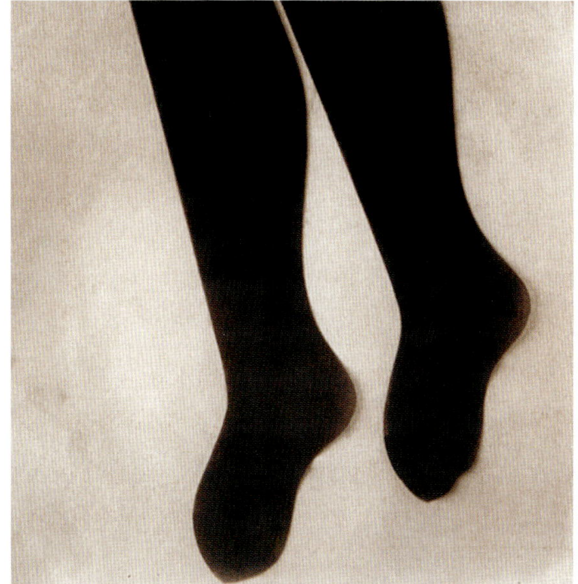

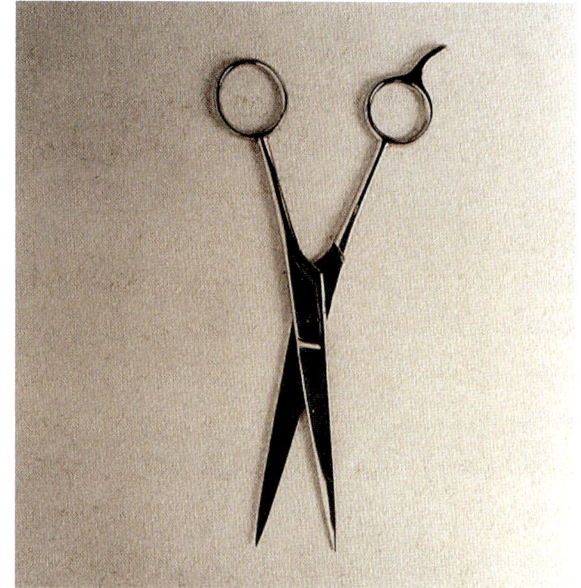

Scissors

Bustier

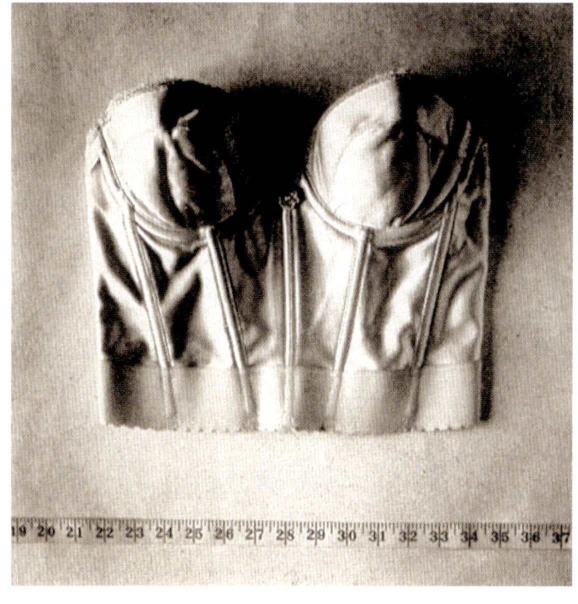

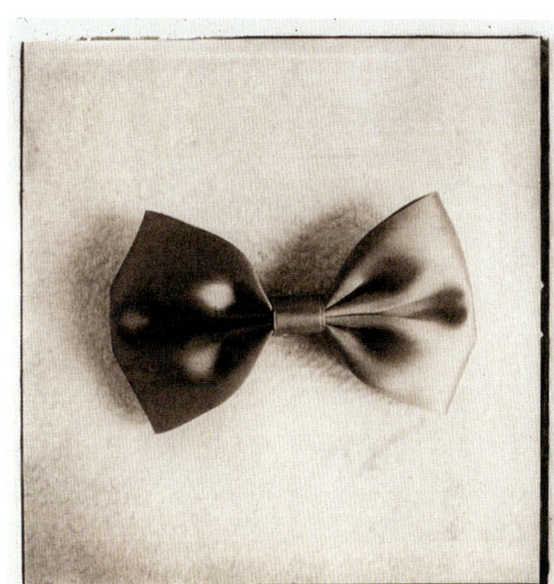

Bow

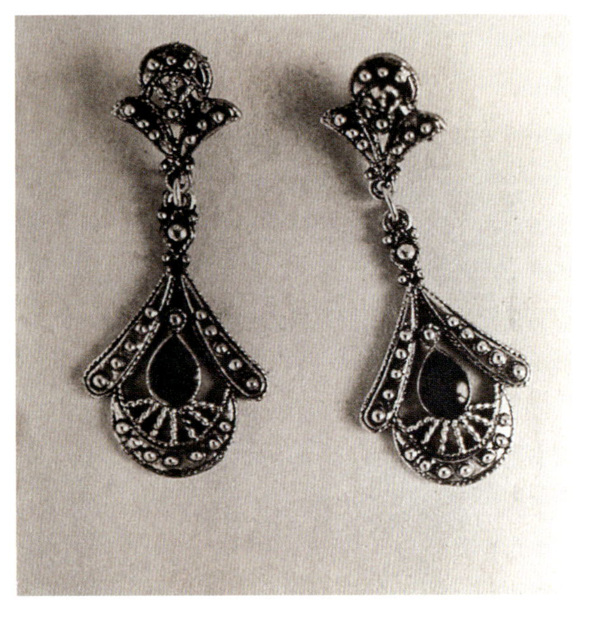
Earrings

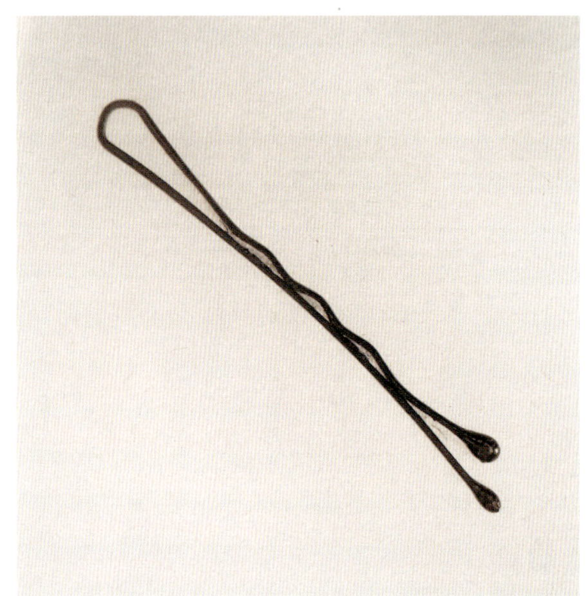
Hairgrip

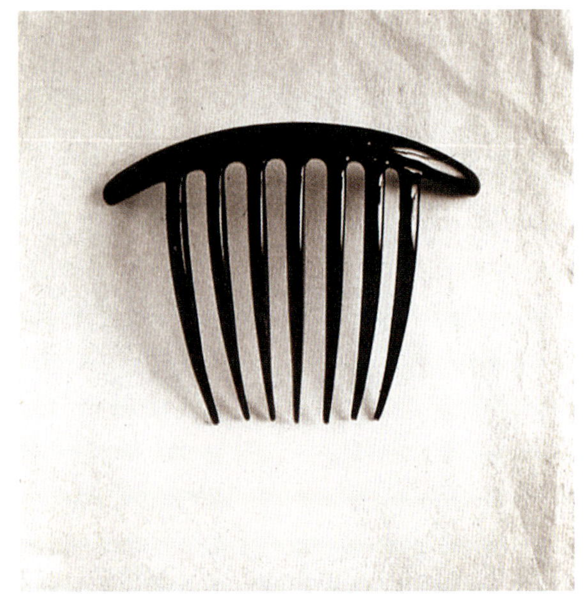
Comb

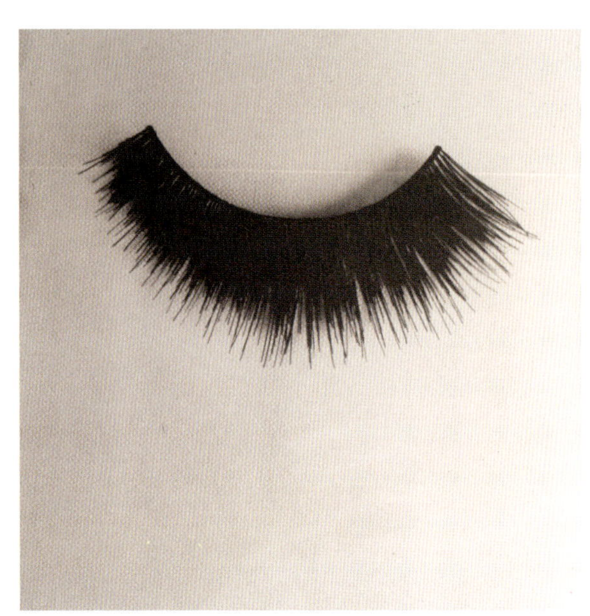
False Eyelashes

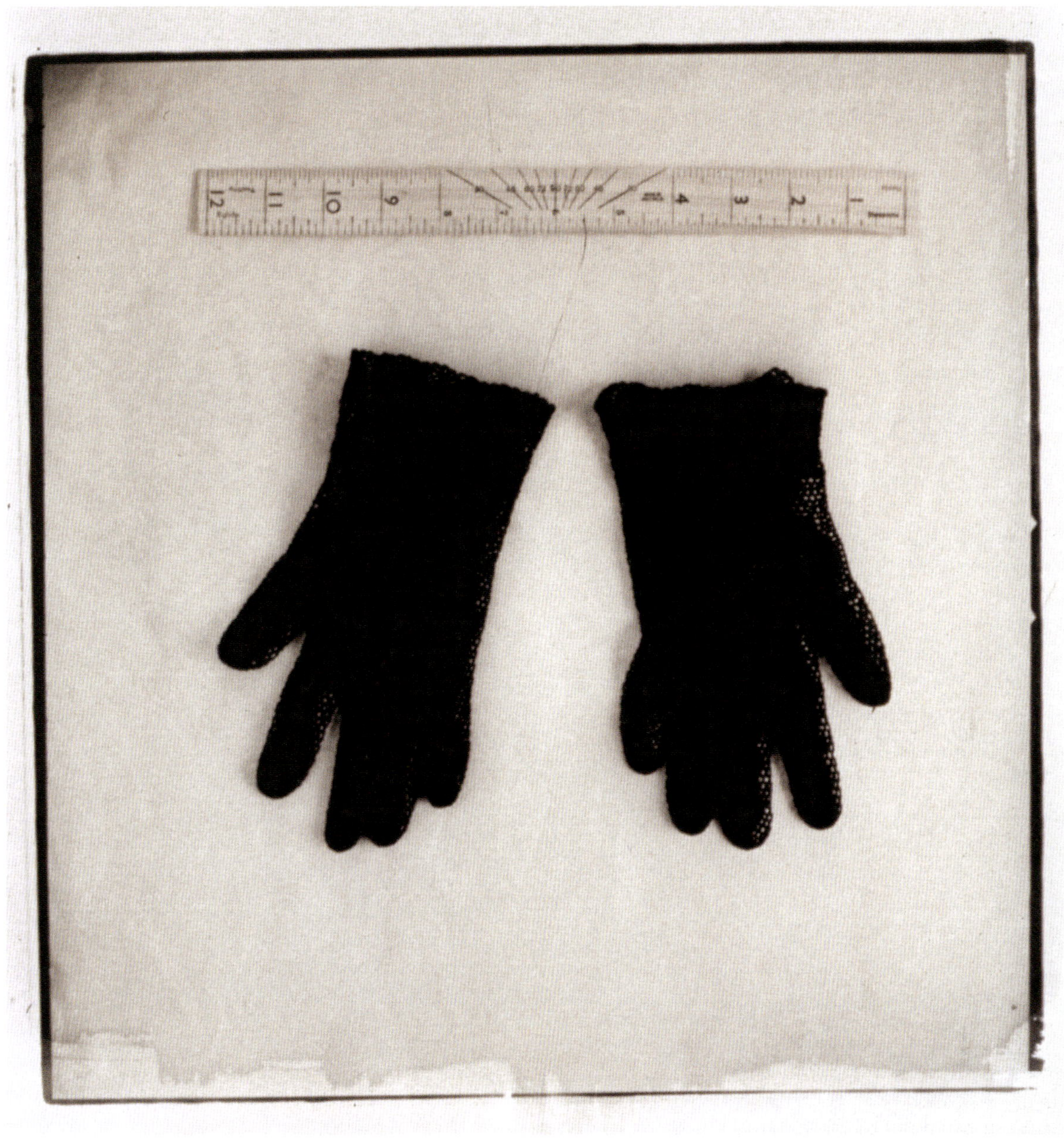

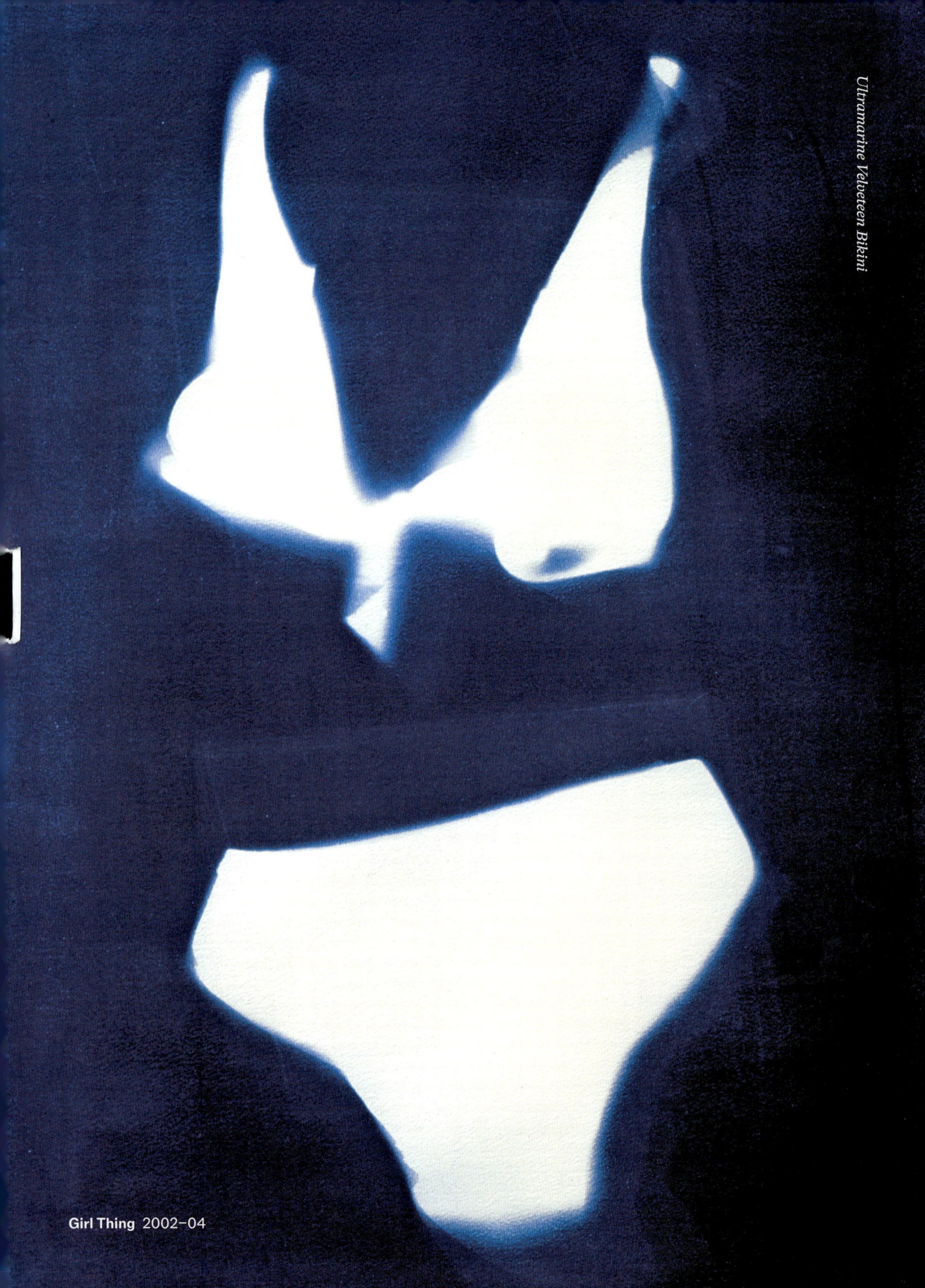

Ultramarine Velveteen Bikini

Big Haired Barbie

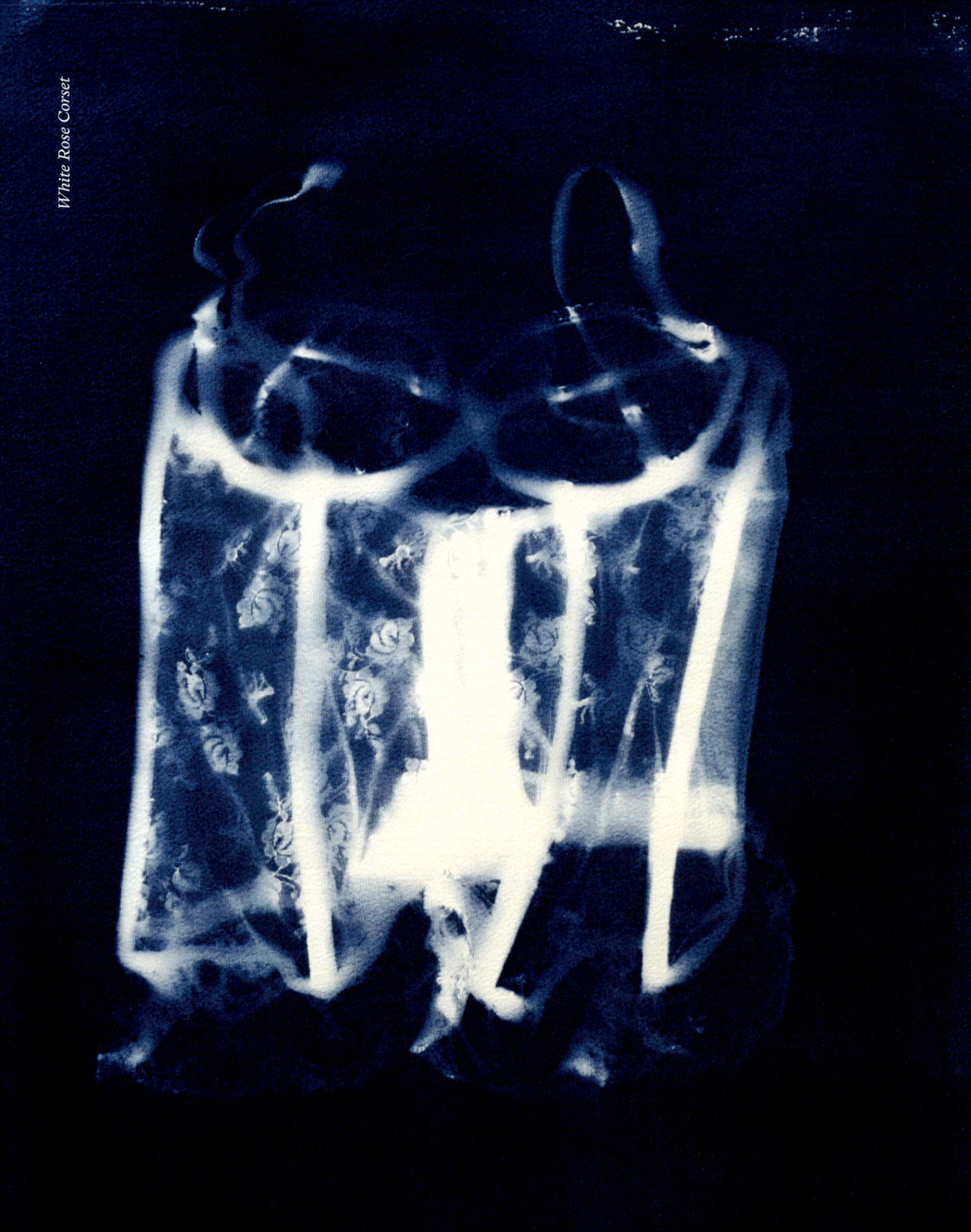

White Rose Corset

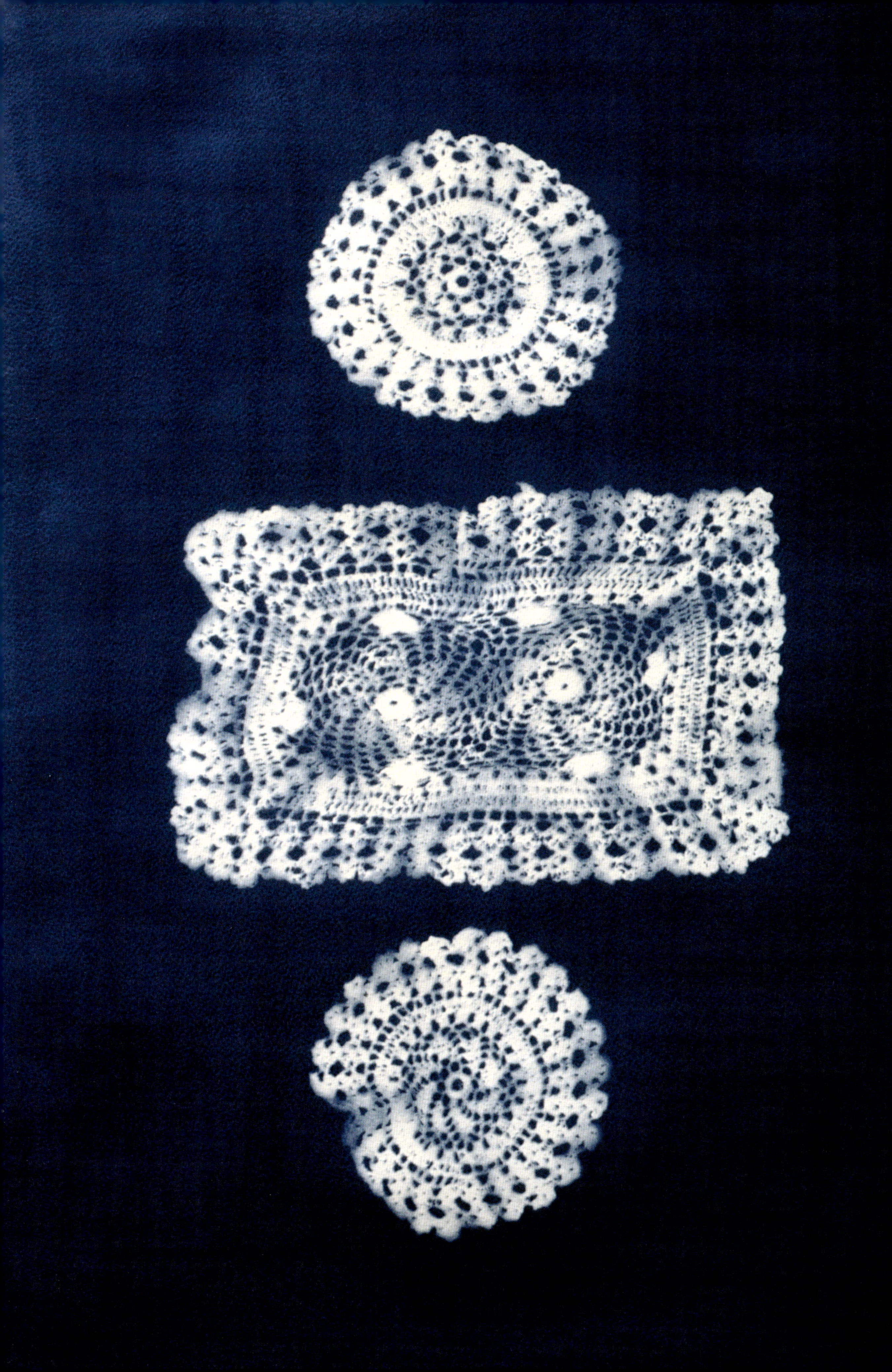

White Lace Dressing Table Doilies

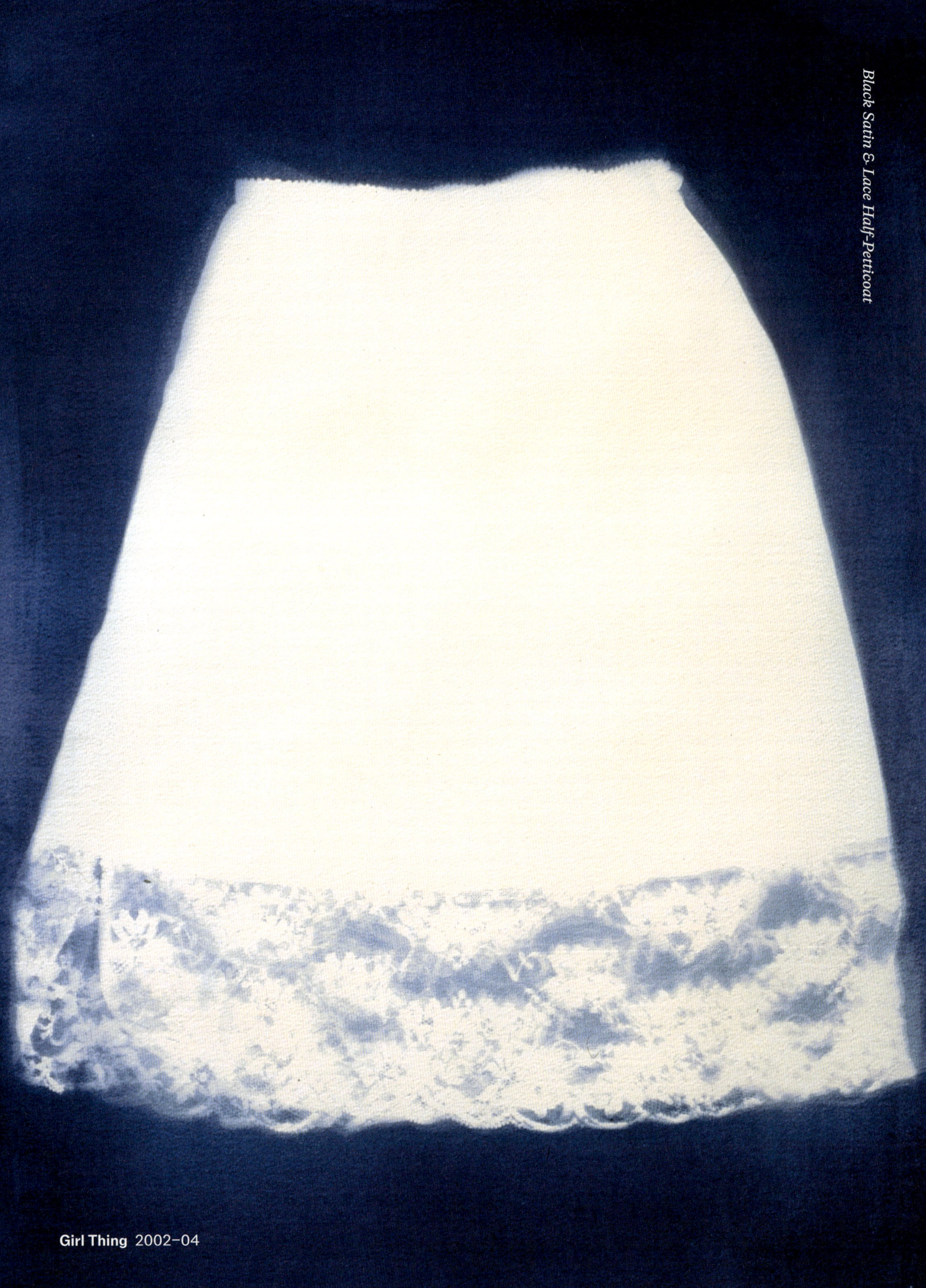
Black Satin & Lace Half-Petticoat

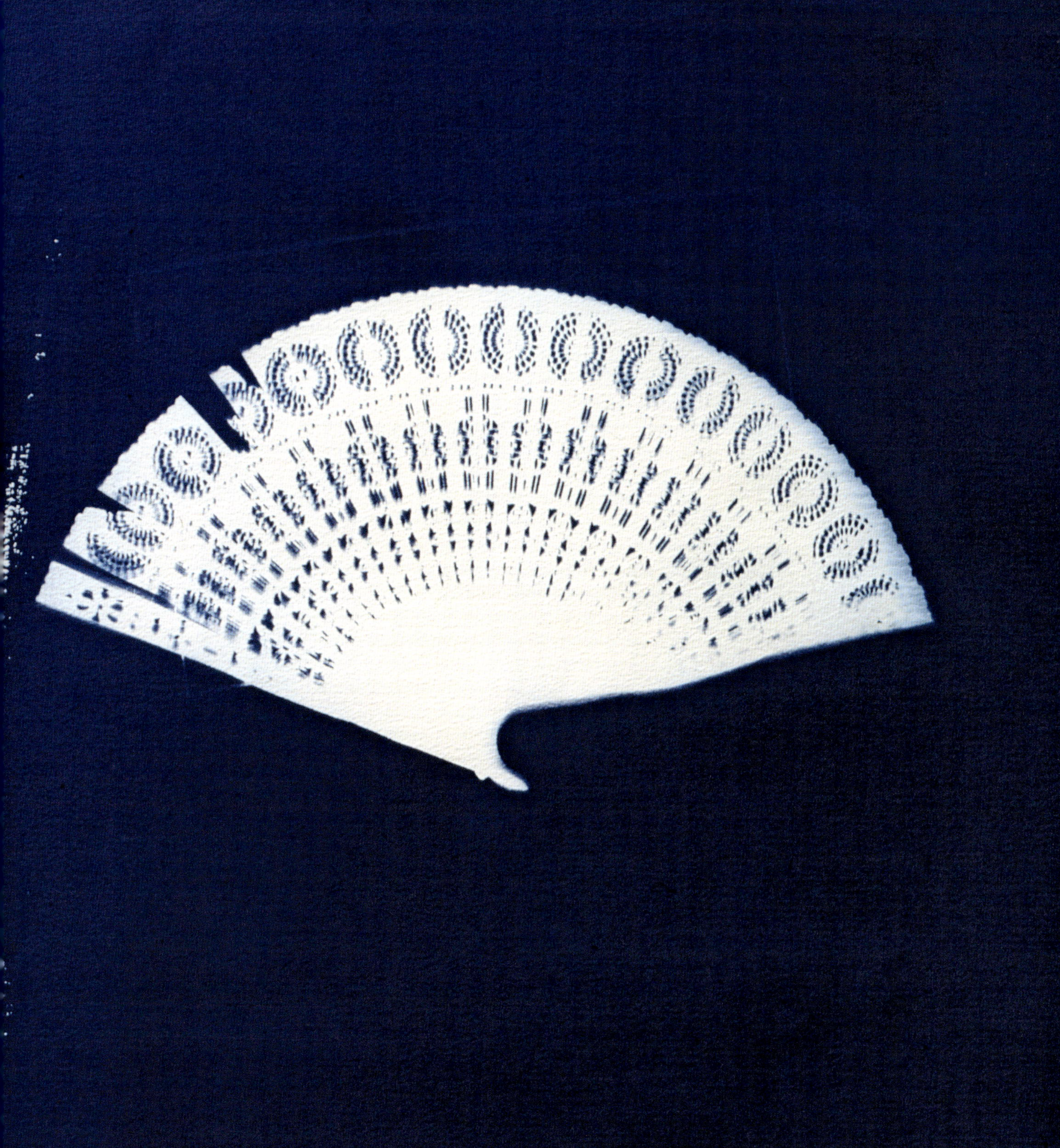

Wooden Fan

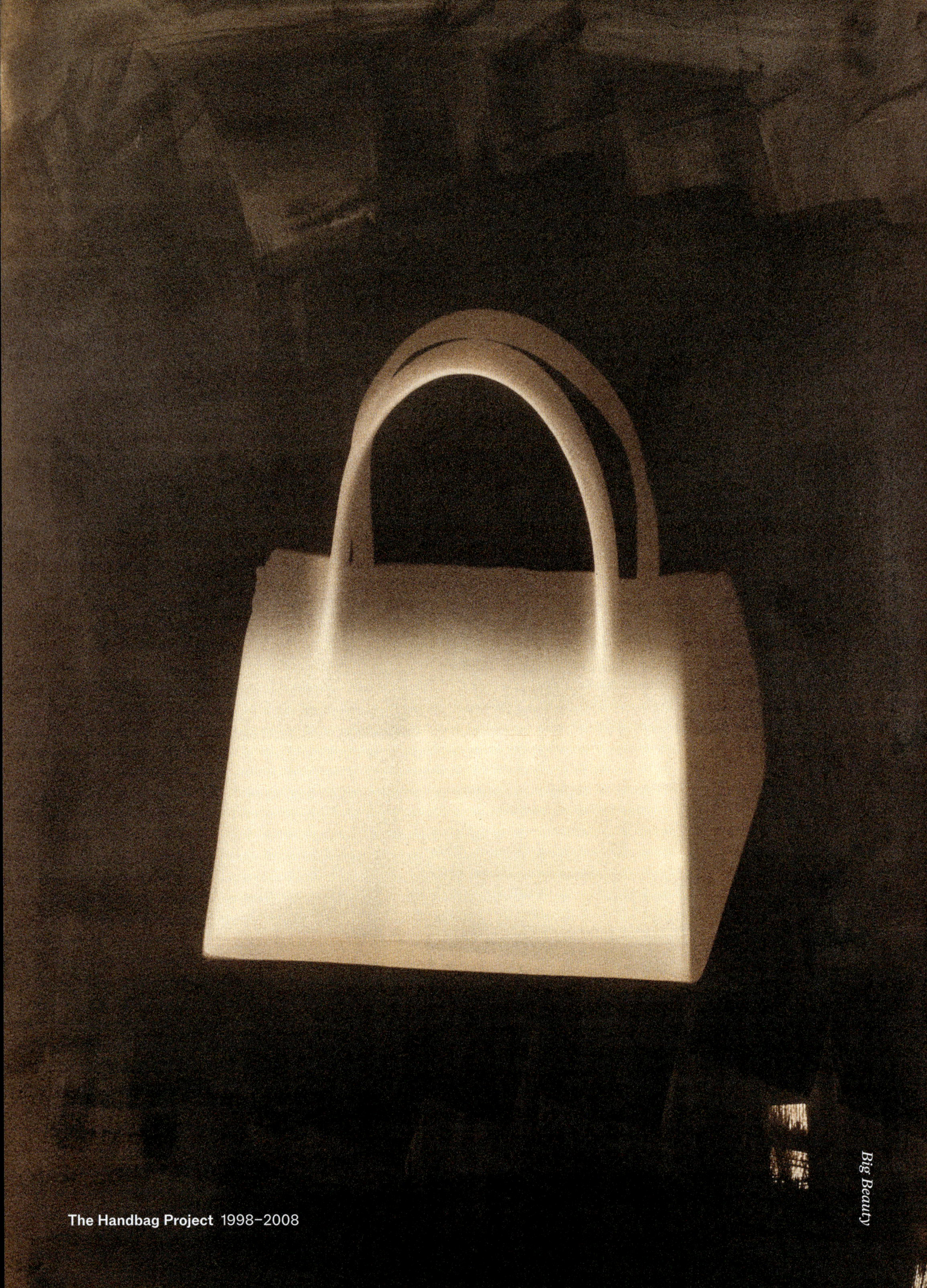

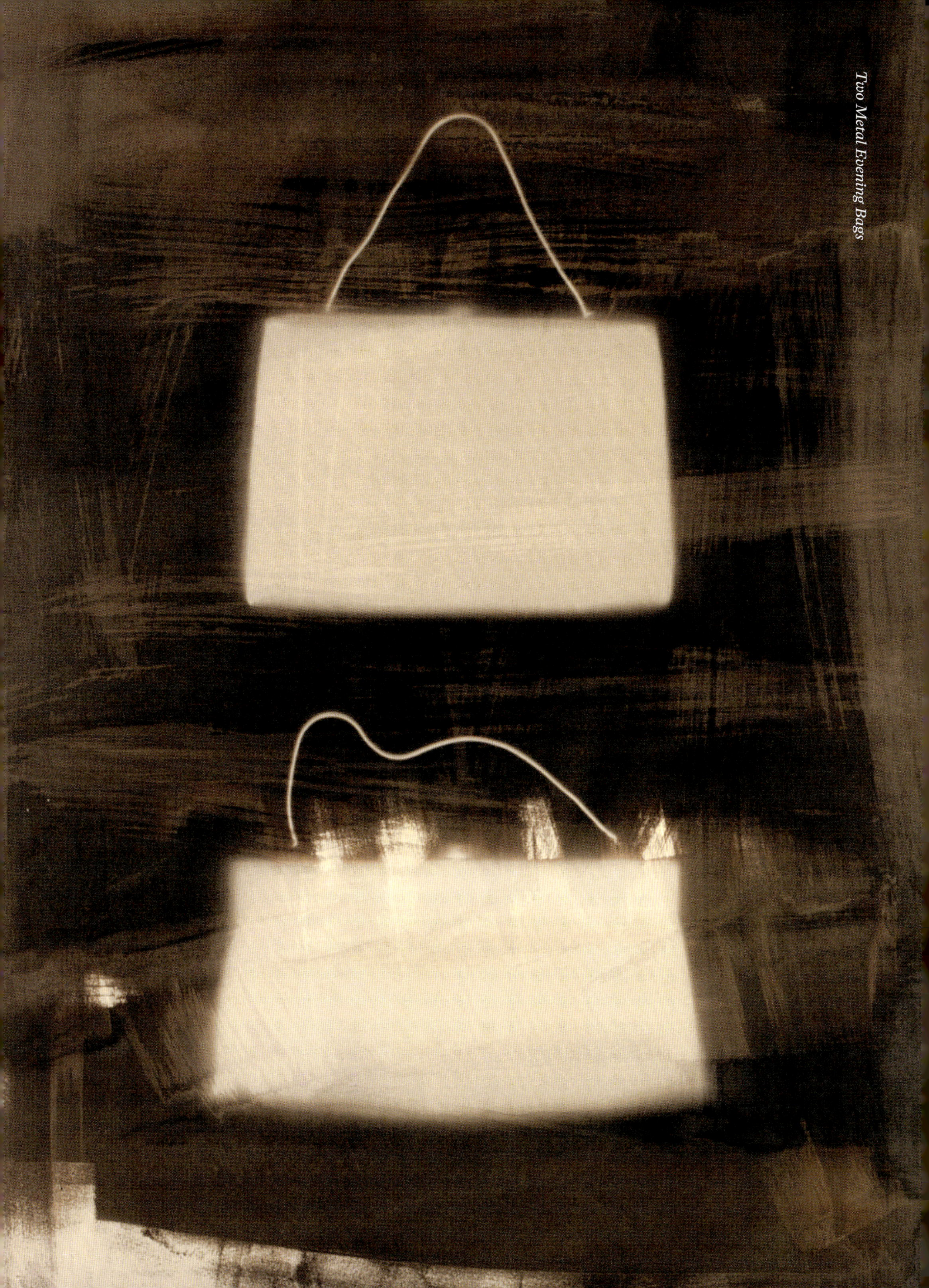

Two Metal Evening Bags

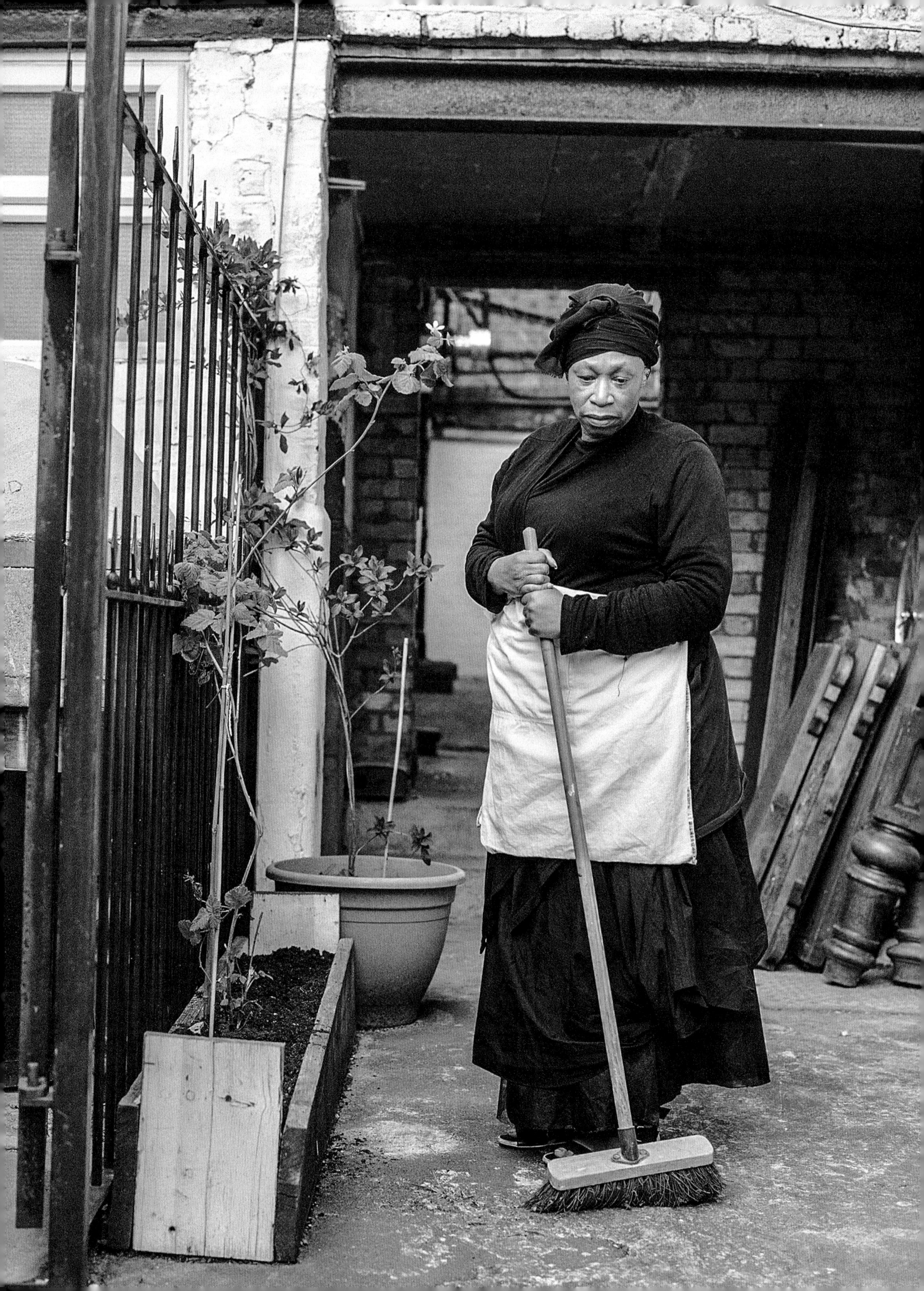

A *Retracing* *of Steps* *and Recalling* *of Voices*

Rohini Malik Okon

Multilayered and deeply evocative, Joy Gregory's recent film works reveal an evolving project of retrieval and recollection. Manifesting through archival research and working closely with communities as participants rather than subjects, her concern is with unearthing and recapturing histories that are in danger of being lost whilst continually experimenting with, and pushing the boundaries of, photographic processes. Working cyclically, she often returns to certain themes and is particularly interested in individual and community narratives exploring connections to the land.

Gregory's haunting and poetic film installation *Seeds of Empire* (2021) takes its cue from her interest in Jamaican plant knowledge and traditional medicine. Underlying this work is a desire to expose how the movement of plants across the globe in the seventeenth and eighteenth centuries was often entwined with the forced migration of enslaved people. Botany as a colonial enterprise involved commodifying local plants and labour while erasing Indigenous knowledge and ecological practices. Gregory's research led her to the figure of Hans Sloane, a seventeenth-century physician, collector and botanist out of whose vast collection both the British Museum and the Natural History Museum were established, and which was built on wealth derived from the transatlantic slave trade. Sloane travelled to Jamaica in 1687, where he recorded and collected hundreds of specimens of plants, many of which had been transported from Africa while others were Indigenous to the island.

Seeds of Empire includes the moving-image works, *Observations: A Little Breeze* and *Observations: Rose*. Taken from a text in Hans Sloane's natural history journal *A Voyage to Jamaica* (1688), in which he charts the weather on a daily basis, a series of meteorological observations form the textual element of *A Little Breeze*. The visual element of this piece evokes Rose, an enslaved woman suffering with depression who lived at the house where Sloane stayed and who features in another of his journals, where he recorded his brutal and non-consensual medical treatment of her. Shot with Super 8 film in a muted palette, the artist herself inhabits Rose as a still and solitary figure in interior scenes reminiscent of seventeenth-century Dutch paintings, imbued with a sense of empathy and dignity in contrast to Sloane's 'objective' observations. The compelling cello soundtrack, composed by Philip Miller with whom Gregory closely collaborated, suggests another layer of unspoken narrative.

Observations: Rose features a series of stills of seascapes and landscapes, luminous and presented in rich colour, from the fecund abundance of rural Jamaica to town gardens and the Royal Botanical Gardens in Kingston, then back across the sea to the Palm House at Kew Gardens. Here the textual element features Sloane's observations of Rose; the violence of his medical impositions at odds with the convivial tone of the recorded telephone conversations we hear throughout the piece. These exchanges between Gregory and a range of people, including family members who had emigrated from Jamaica to Britain, hint at a sense of cumulative personal local knowledge where everyday narratives become amplified by being shared. We encounter recollections of loneliness, darkness and the cold, of first coats and boots and paraffin heaters and a bodily longing to return 'home' to a Jamaica remembered as vibrant and lushly green and warm.

Across the two films, Gregory disrupts any sense of a linear narrative by juxtaposing historical and contemporary experiences and inviting us to consider multiple perspectives simultaneously. Drawing on her research into plant knowledge amongst Indigenous and enslaved people in the Caribbean, *Seeds of Empire* is part of the artist's ongoing endeavour to reanimate archival collections and bring to the surface unheard voices, exploring new ways of acknowledging individual memories and shared histories of displacement, movement and migration. From the transplanting of seedlings between continents to the disappearance or adaptation of language through time, she is keen to highlight how the links between community, the natural environment and local knowledge either endure or are lost.

Gregory's current film project brings together the threads of her long-term research spanning the last twenty years on language endangerment and the connection between language and landscape. At its centre is her ongoing work on the lost N|uu language of the San people of the Kalahari and her relationship with their remaining descendants. Her interest in language, and its deep connection to identity and to the land, started when she was travelling in the Caribbean undertaking research

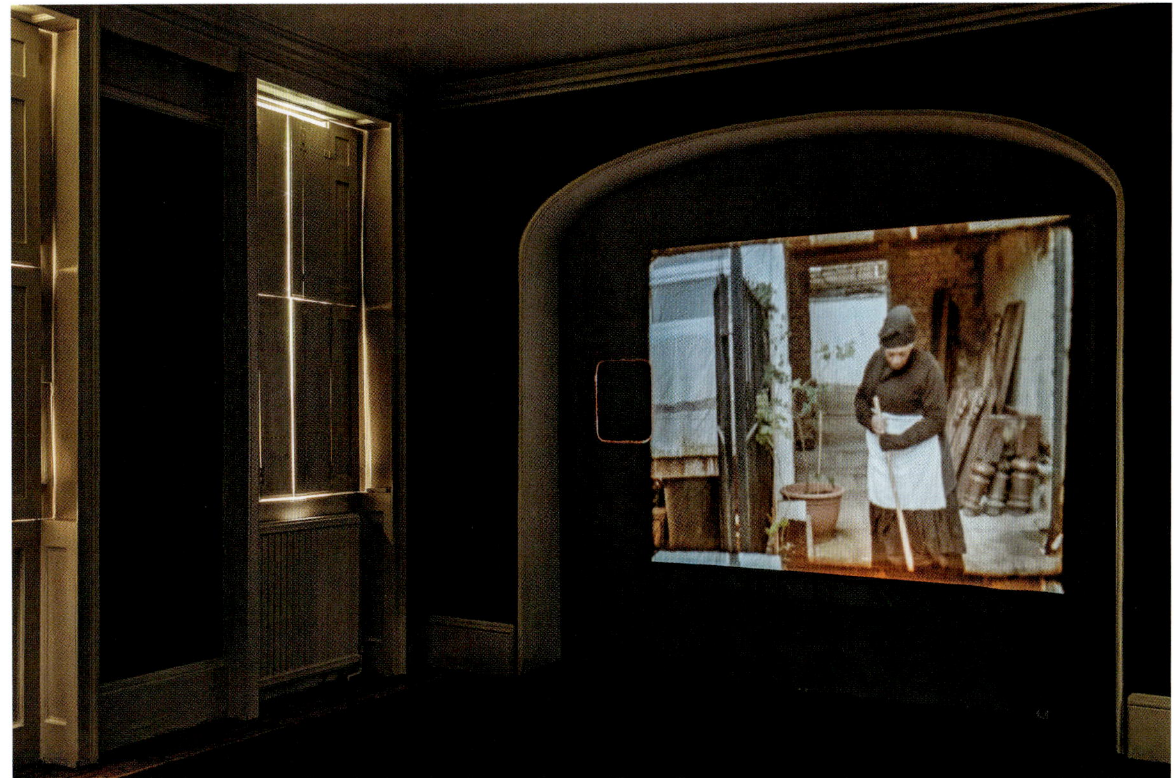

Observations: A Little Breeze, at Danielle Arnaud Gallery, 2021

for *Memory and Skin* in the late 1990s. Being awarded a NESTA fellowship in 2002 gave her the time and the freedom to begin to explore language endangerment in different contexts, and she has described as life-changing her attendance at a conference on endangered languages in Western Australia. Here, her encounter with the deliberate erasure of Indigenous languages amongst Aboriginal communities had a profound impact on her practice, enhancing her sensitivity and sense of empathy and changing the way she worked collaboratively with people. It was after hearing a paper at the conference on N|uu, one of the oldest languages of humankind and known for its click consonants, that Gregory made her first visit to the Kalahari in 2004 to meet with the last few remaining speakers. In 1974, the Apartheid government declared N|uu extinct, but in 1991 land claim activists found twenty-seven people who still spoke the language, including some who could sing the songs, and used this as the main evidence in a court case against the government to win the rights to the land.

Over time, Gregory built relationships with individuals across different generations – there were eight remaining speakers when she embarked on her research – and in particular with sisters Ouma |una and Ouma Khies, who had undergone the abhorrent dehumanising experience of being 'exhibits' in the 1936 Empire Exhibition in Johannesburg. The sisters have since passed and Gregory is acutely aware of the poignancy that for their great grandchildren N|uu is no longer their mother tongue. The material she has collected on her visits back and forth to the Kalahari

A negro woman of his called Rose,

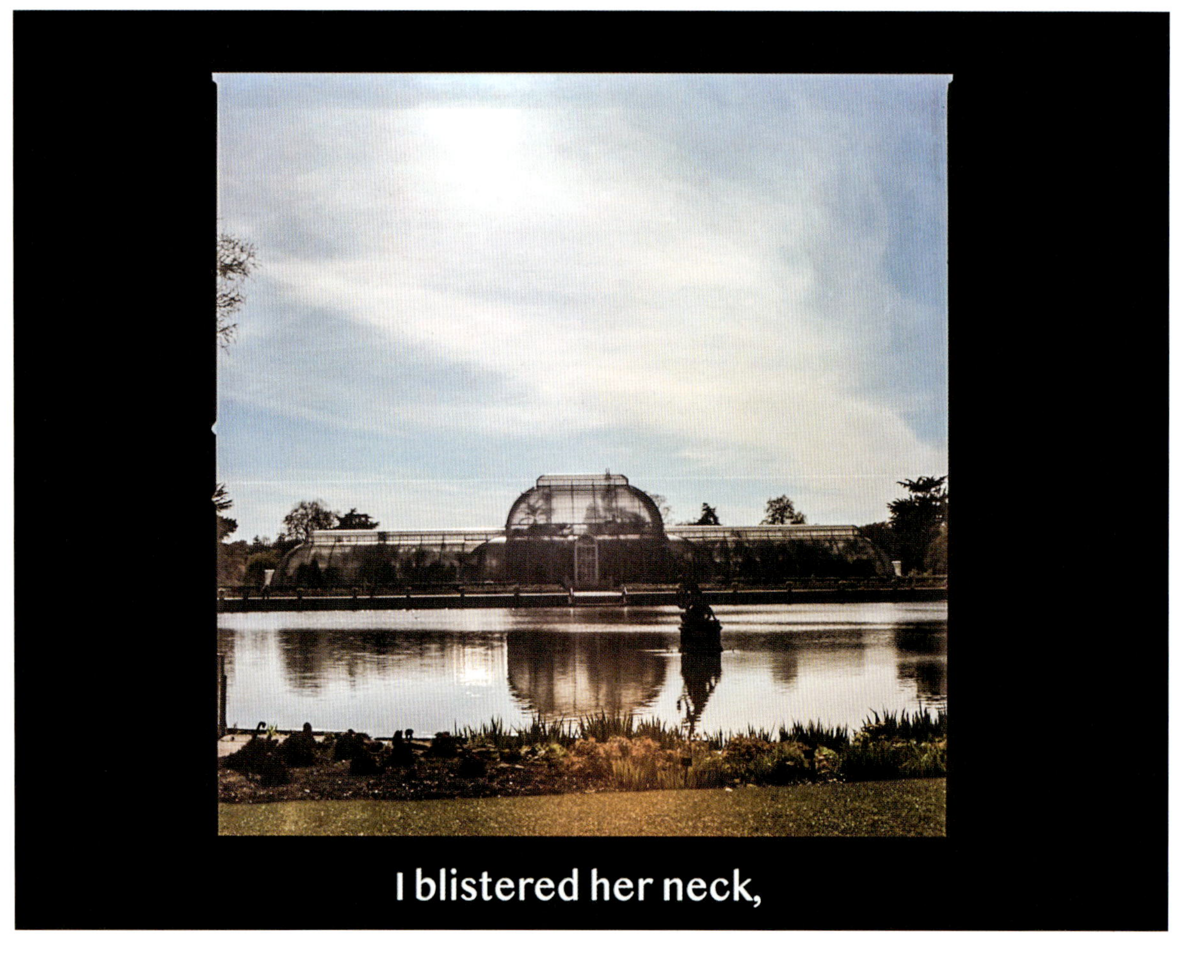

has been gathered through a process of collaboration and exchange over many years and includes recorded conversations, photographs, stories and sounds as well as local plants. Her quietly beautiful and evocative photographic series *Kalahari* (2005–25) documents the expansive plains, troubled skies and red earth of the desert landscape while alluding to centuries of Indigenous knowledge seeped into the ground.

In addition to this landscape series, Gregory has amassed a plethora of images capturing the remaining members of the San community, individually and in small groups where details of homes, clothing and everyday life suggest the intimacy and ease of participants, not subjects, and are at complete odds with the photographs from the 1936 exhibition of Ouma |una and Ouma Khies in which they are objectified as anthropological specimens. Attuned to how this community has been misrepresented or had their representation taken away from them, she acknowledges her responsibility in representing their lives, history and culture.

The new film will retrace Gregory's steps and give an insight into why she is making this work centred on the Kalahari. Approaching it as a form of visual letter or a mapping exercise, she proposes to take viewers on a journey back through her research process, where she gathers material and then lets it brew, percolate, distilling it to find the essence of the work she seeks to make. Ultimately Gregory is interested in looking at the common threads that connect the community in the Kalahari with the experiences of the descendants of Indigenous and enslaved people in the Caribbean, as well as the impacts of colonialism on the younger diasporic generation in Britain.

Drawing on research she has undertaken into her family history in Jamaica, she will consider different registers of loss and displacement while also highlighting resistance and resilience as she contrasts her own sense of identity, in terms of relationships with land, language and Indigenous culture with that of the San. The connection between the San and their land is deep and centuries old, but they have lost their identity associated with the N|uu language, while Gregory's experience of loss relates to being the descendent of an enslaved person and not knowing her history back more than a few generations.

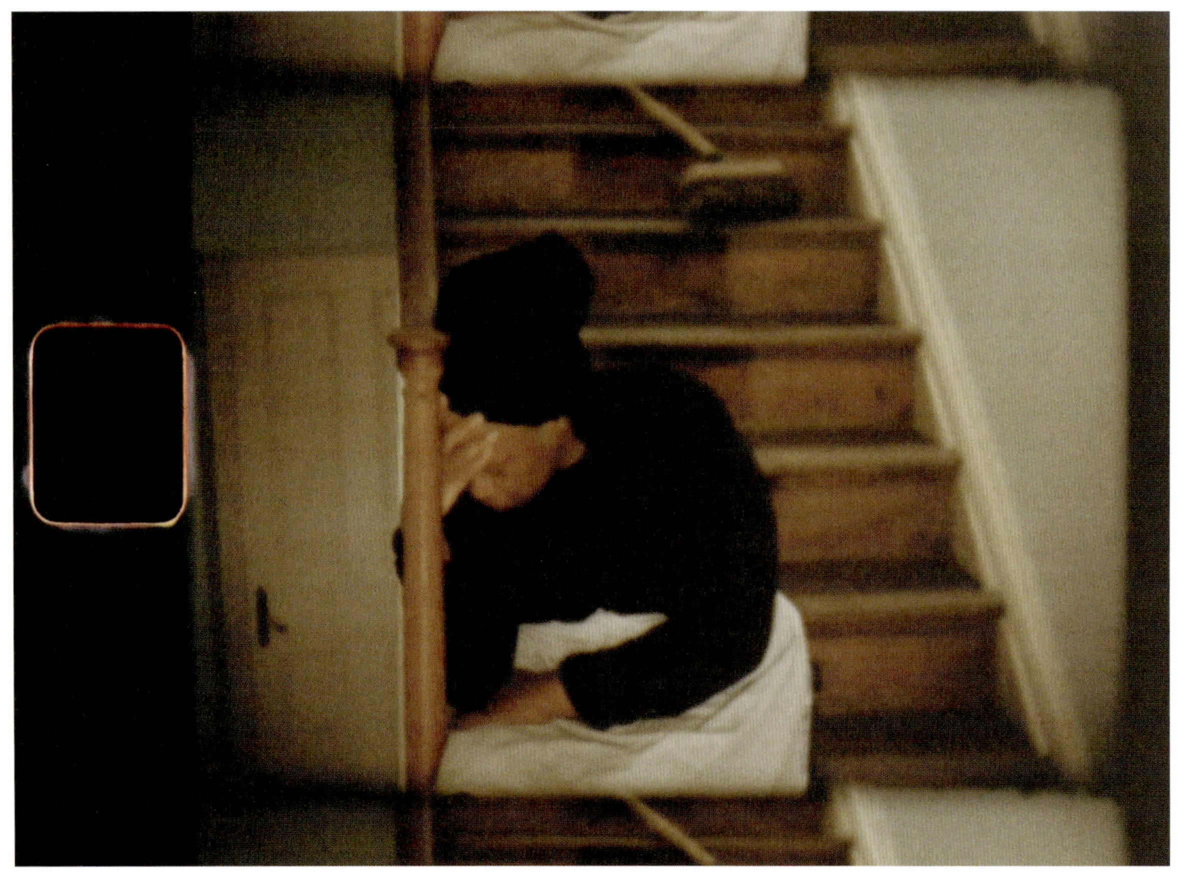

The Staircase (Little or no breeze)

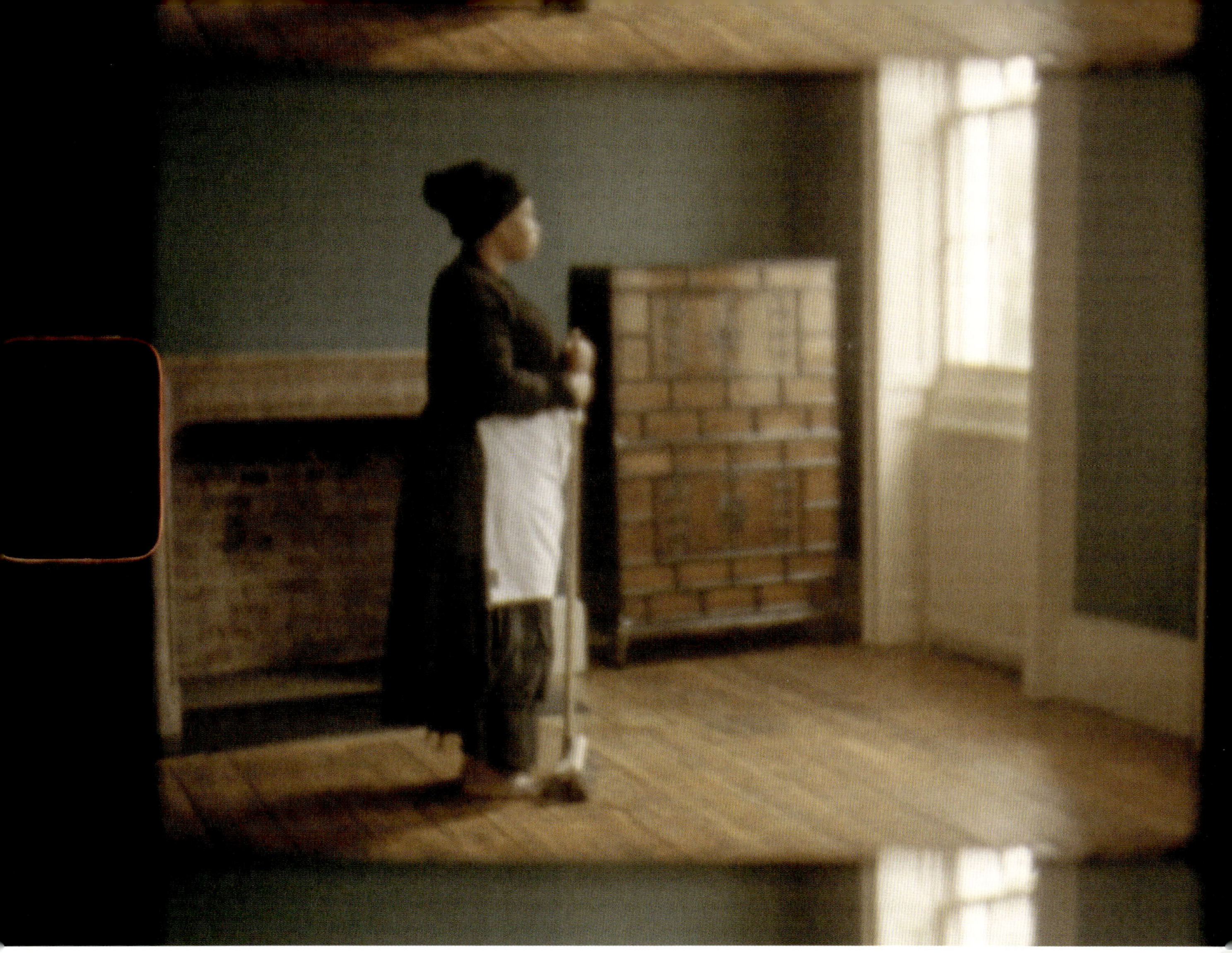

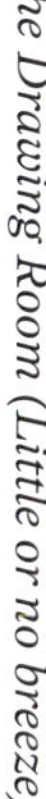
The Drawing Room (Little or no breeze)

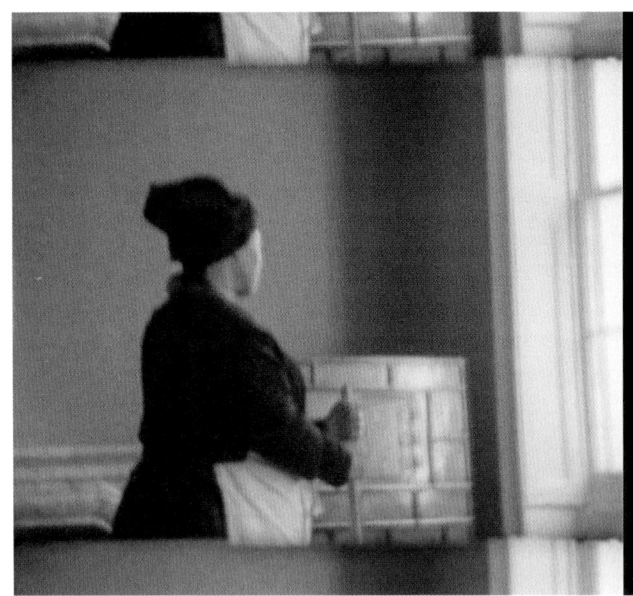

5. A moderate Sea Breeze, hot between the Sea and the Land Breeze, the Breeze blows at at *Port Royal* all night.
6. A moderate Sea Breeze.
7. A moderate Sea Breeze.
8. A moderate Sea Breeze, very hot, and few people perfectly well, Looſneſſes in the night common.

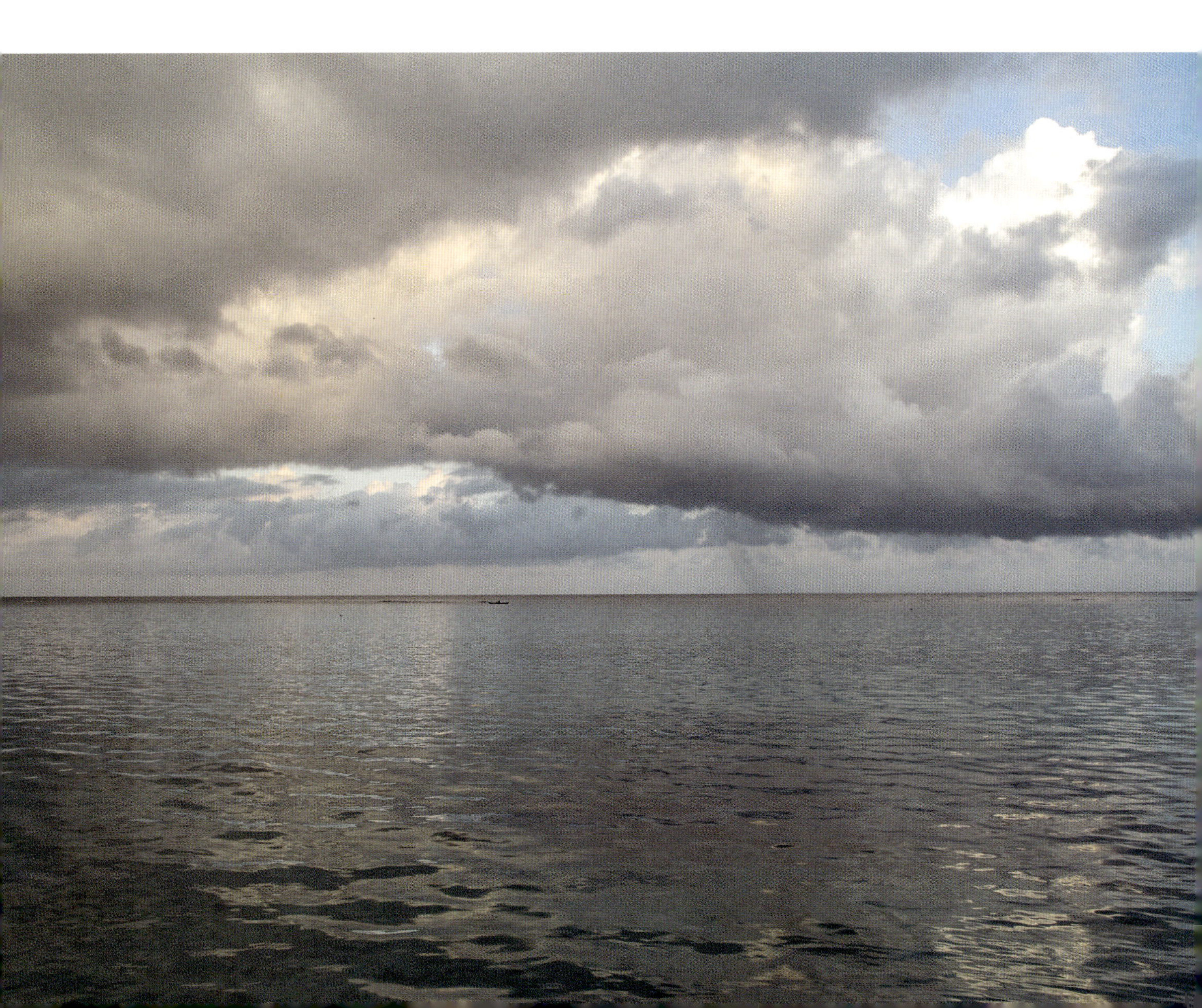

Girl in Red Dress

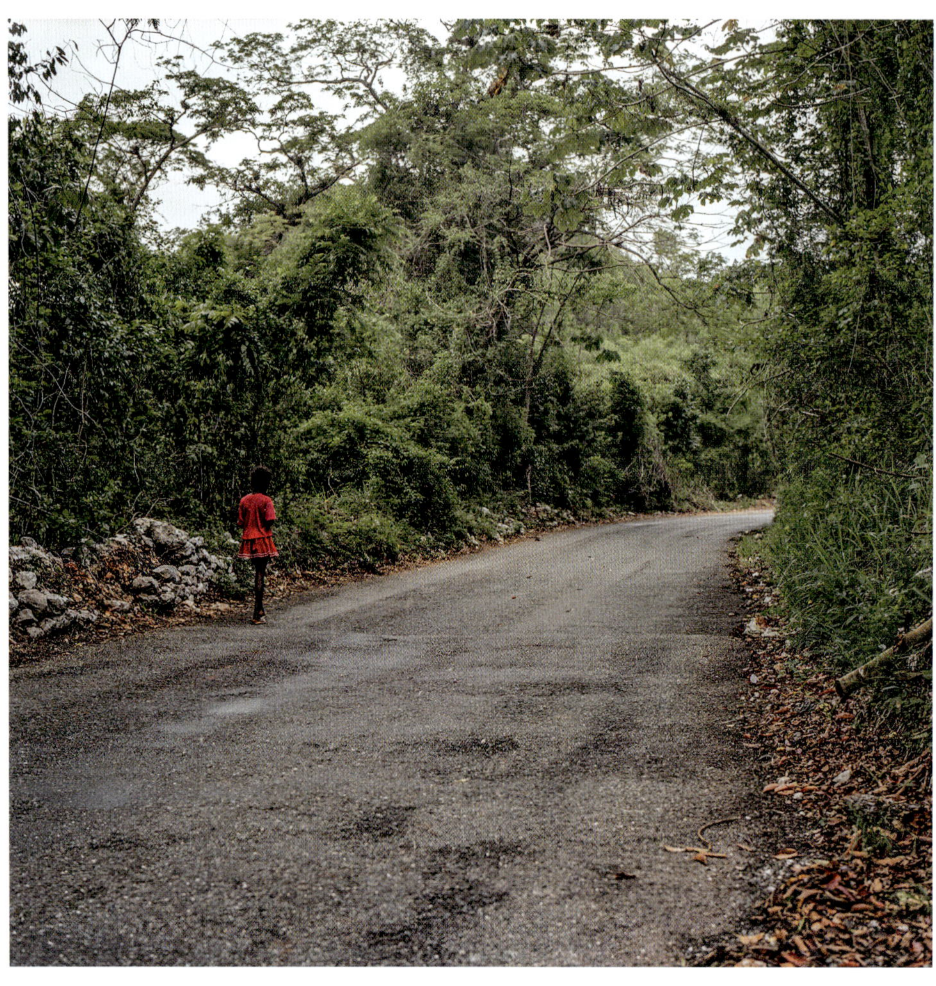

Canefield, Spanish Town

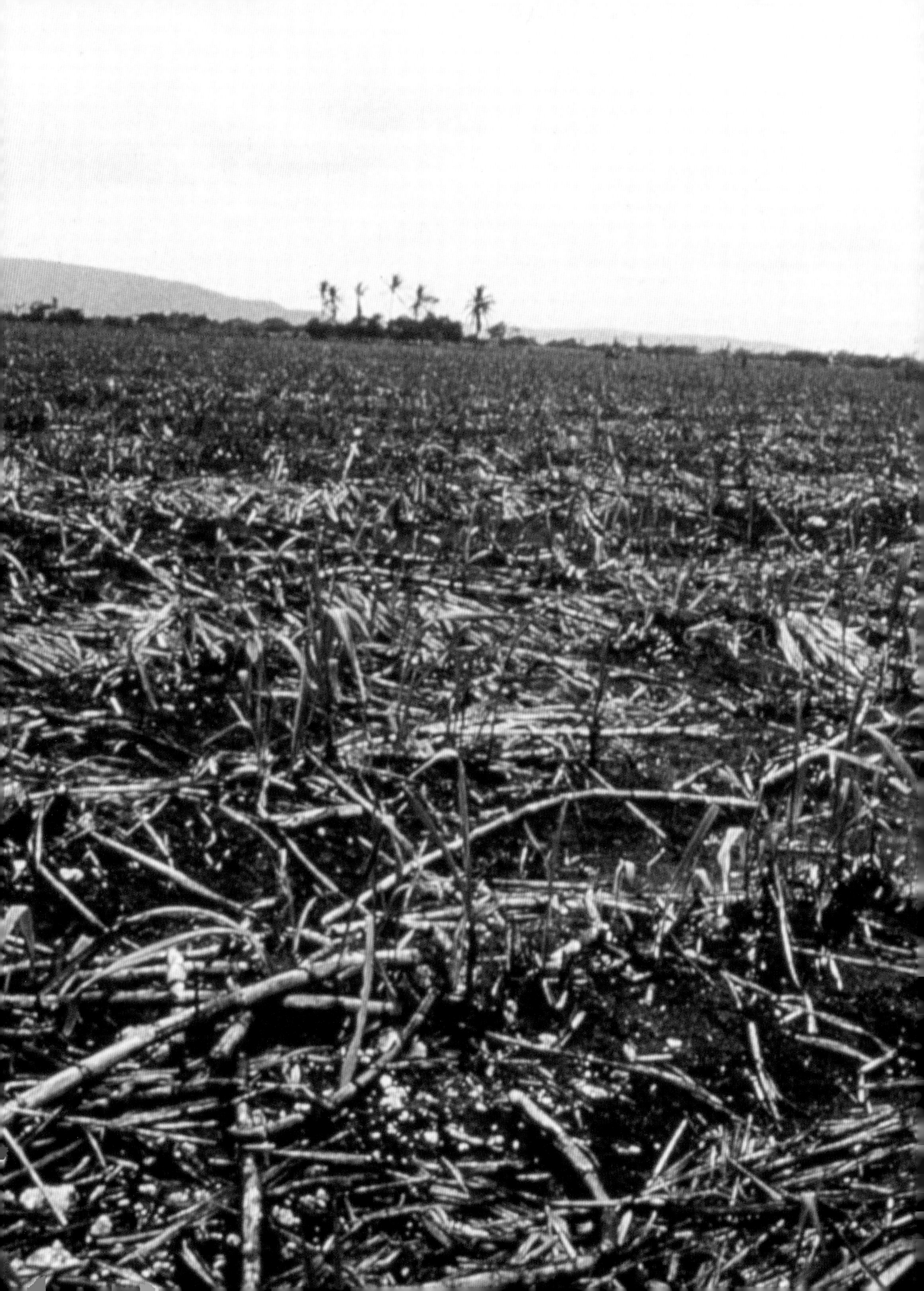

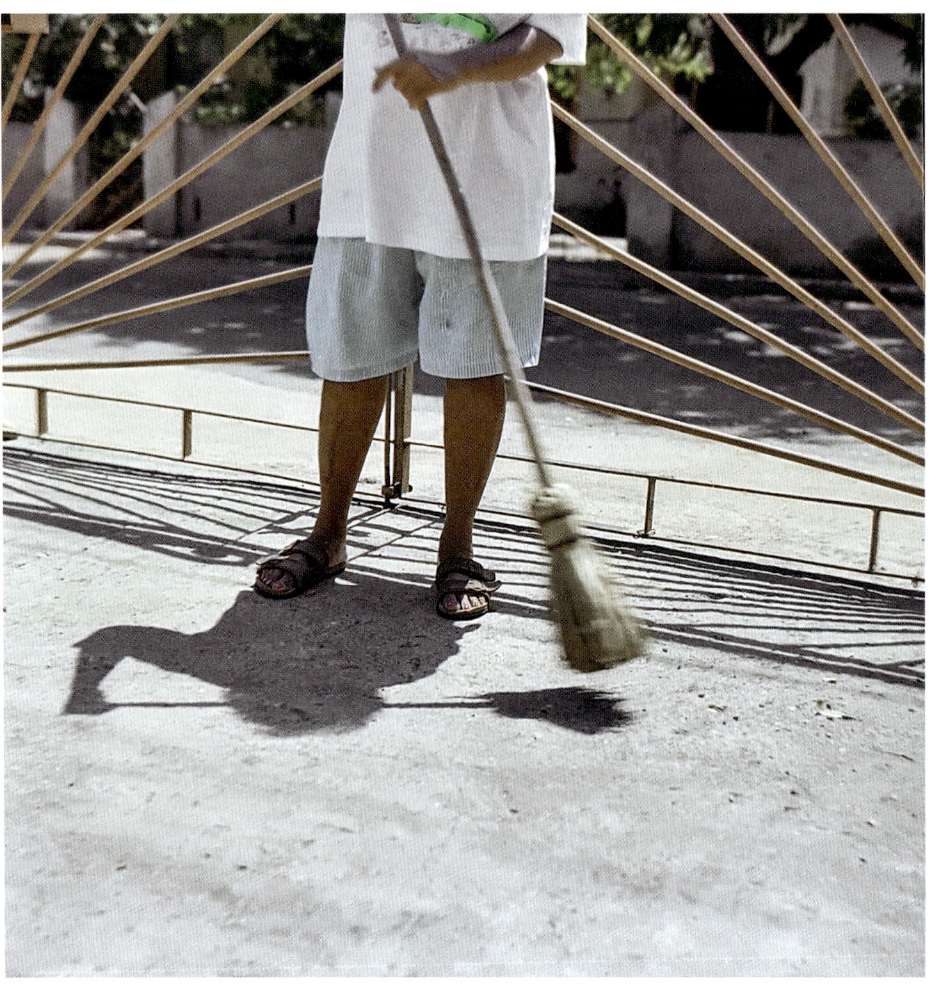

Junie Sweeping, Kingston

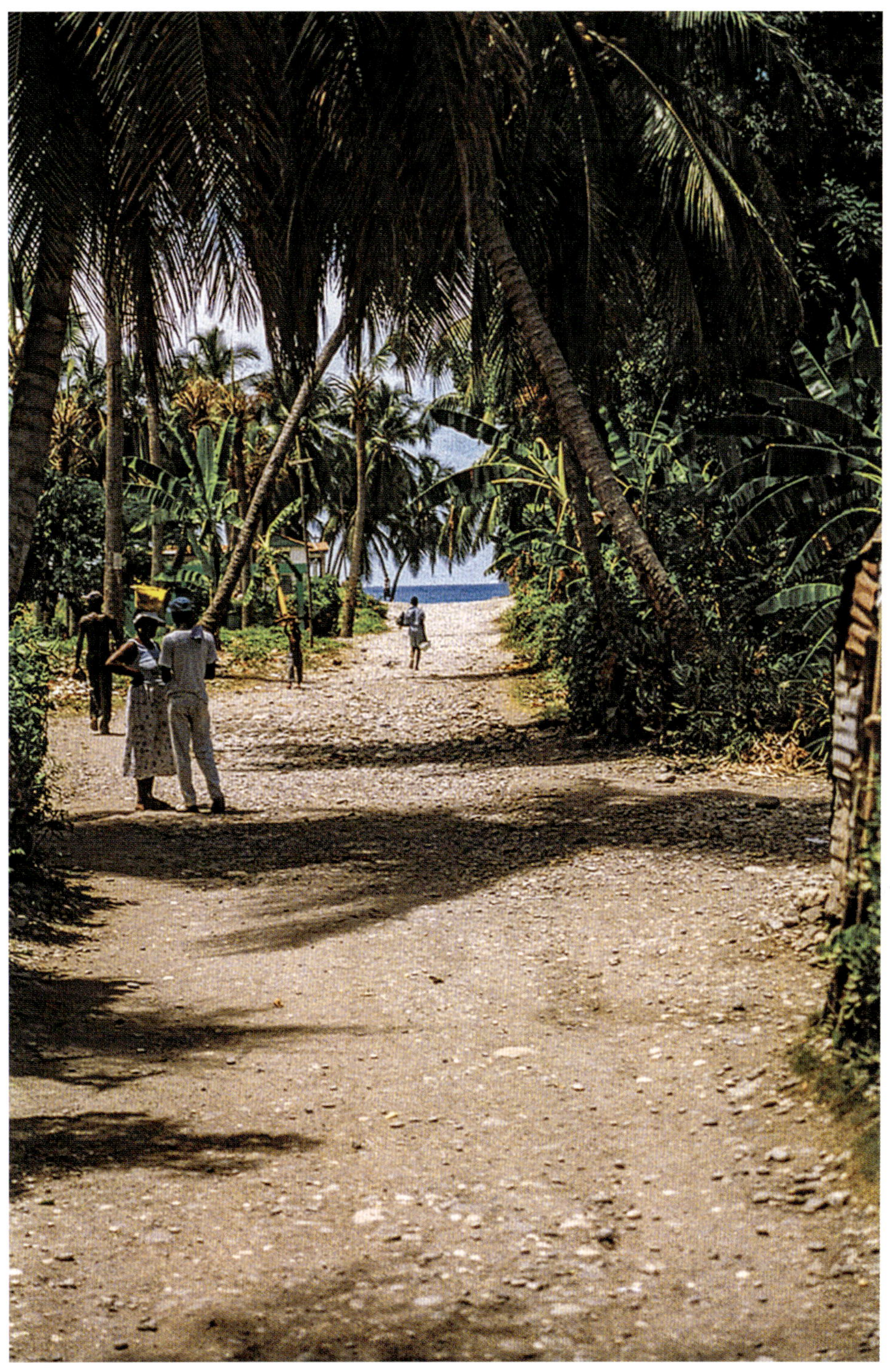

Native Beach, Jacmel, Haiti

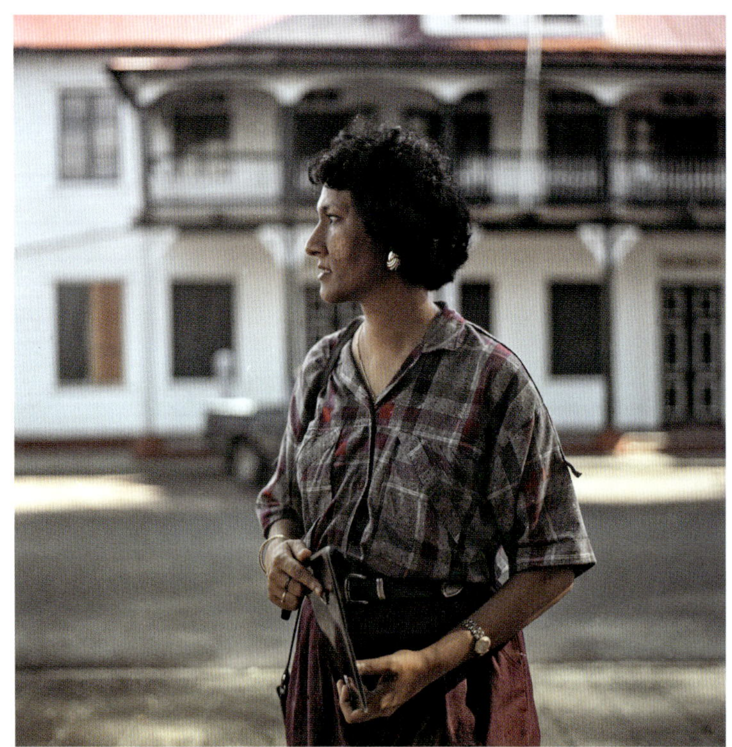

Sheila Ketwaru, Paramaribo, Suriname

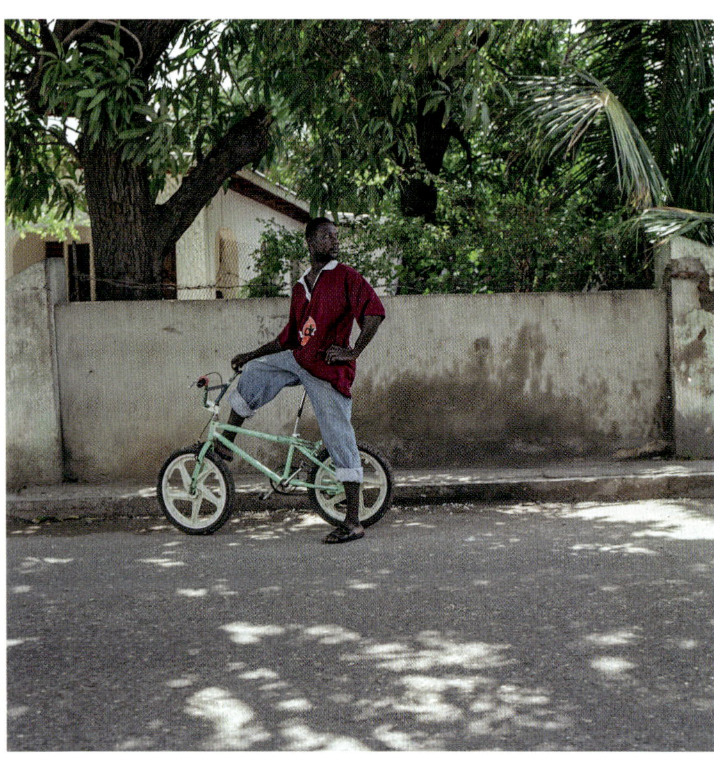

Man on a bicycle, Kingston, Jamaica

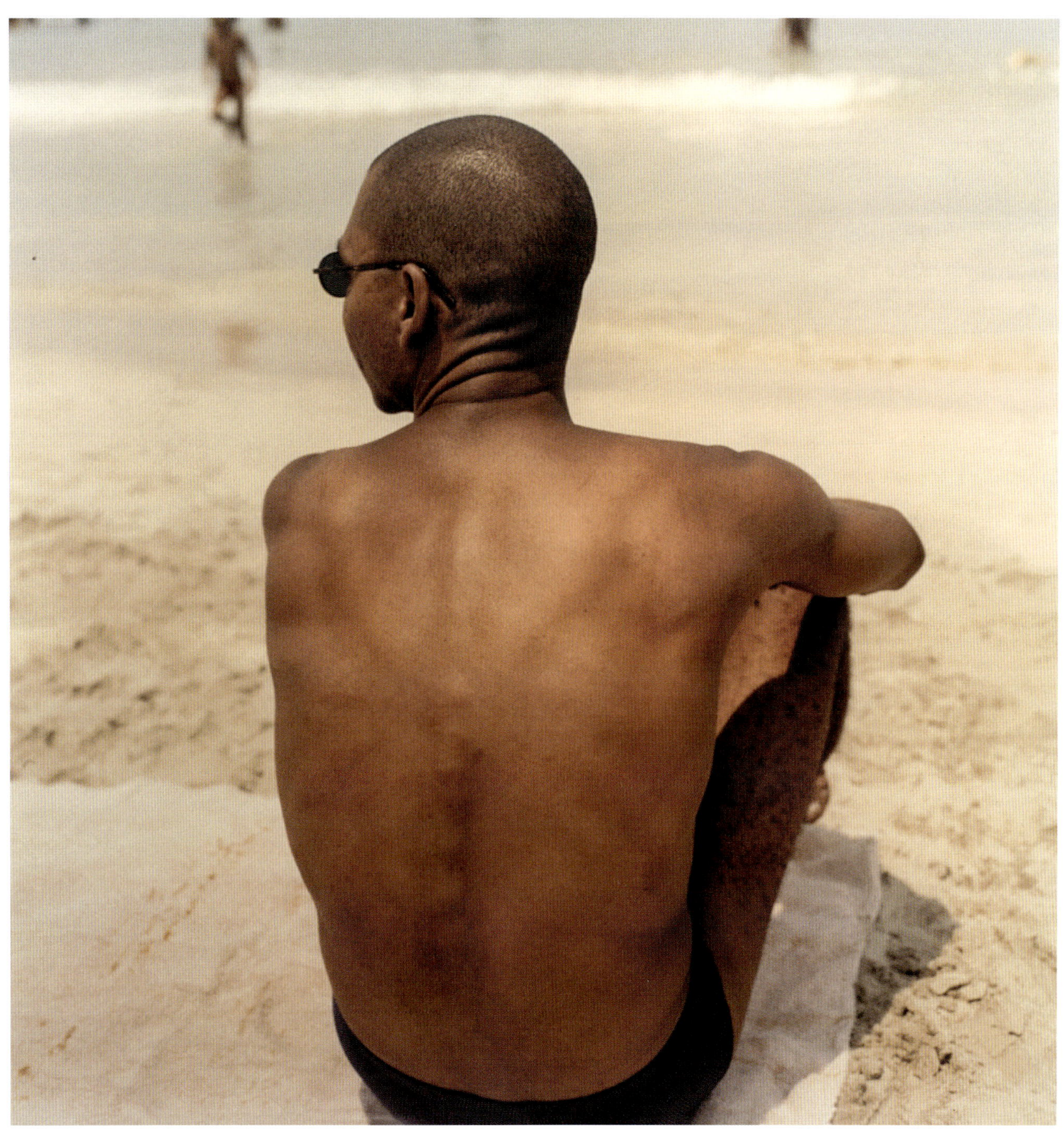

Indra and Christine

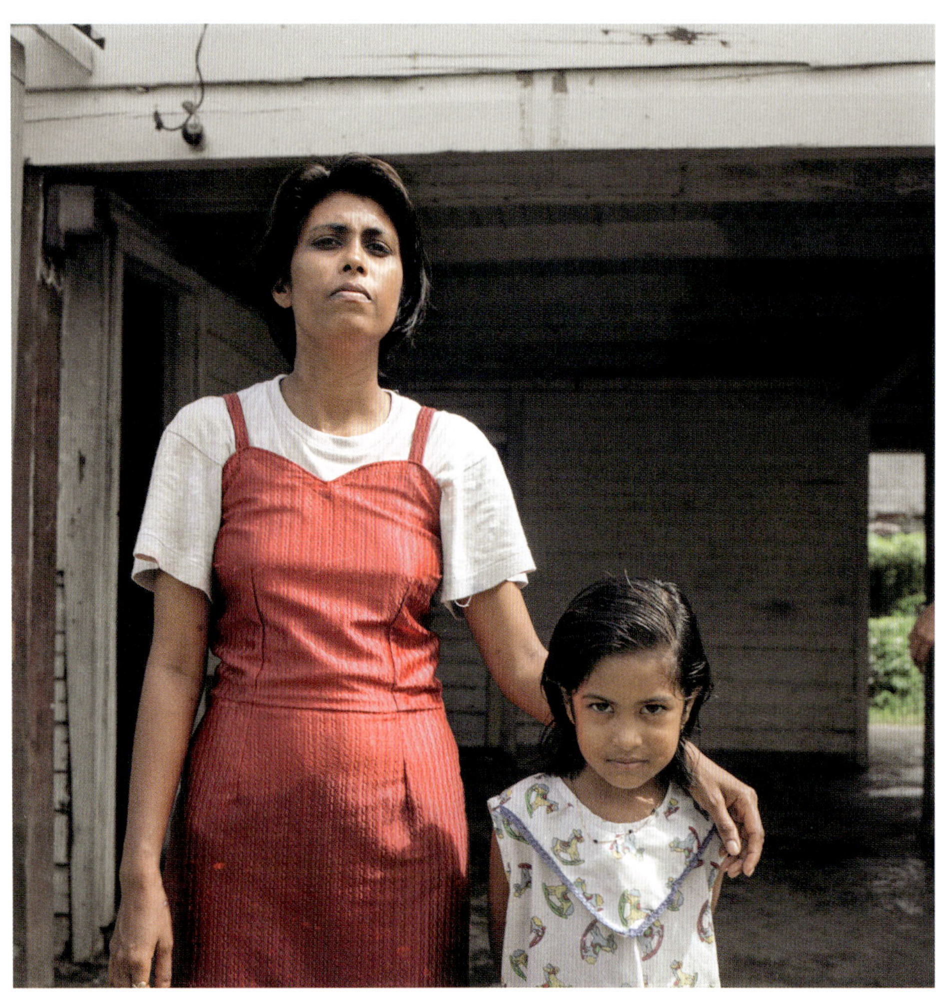

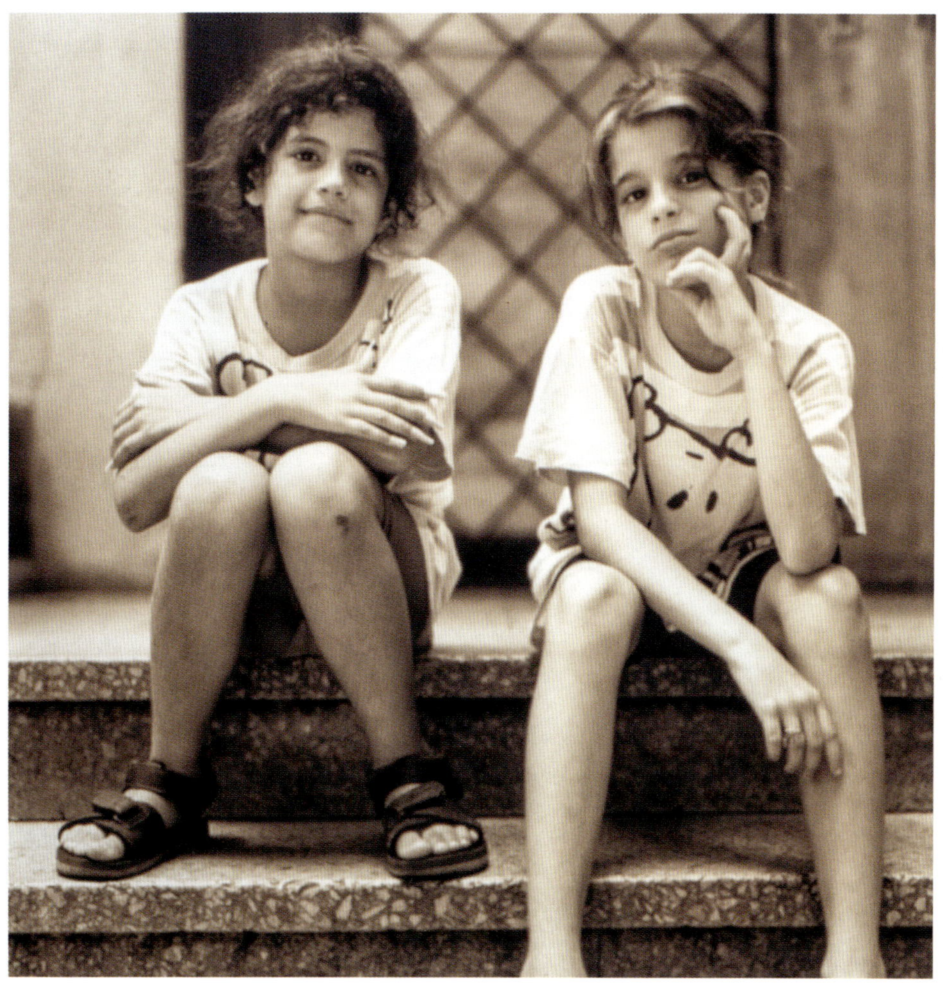

Rocio and Romina

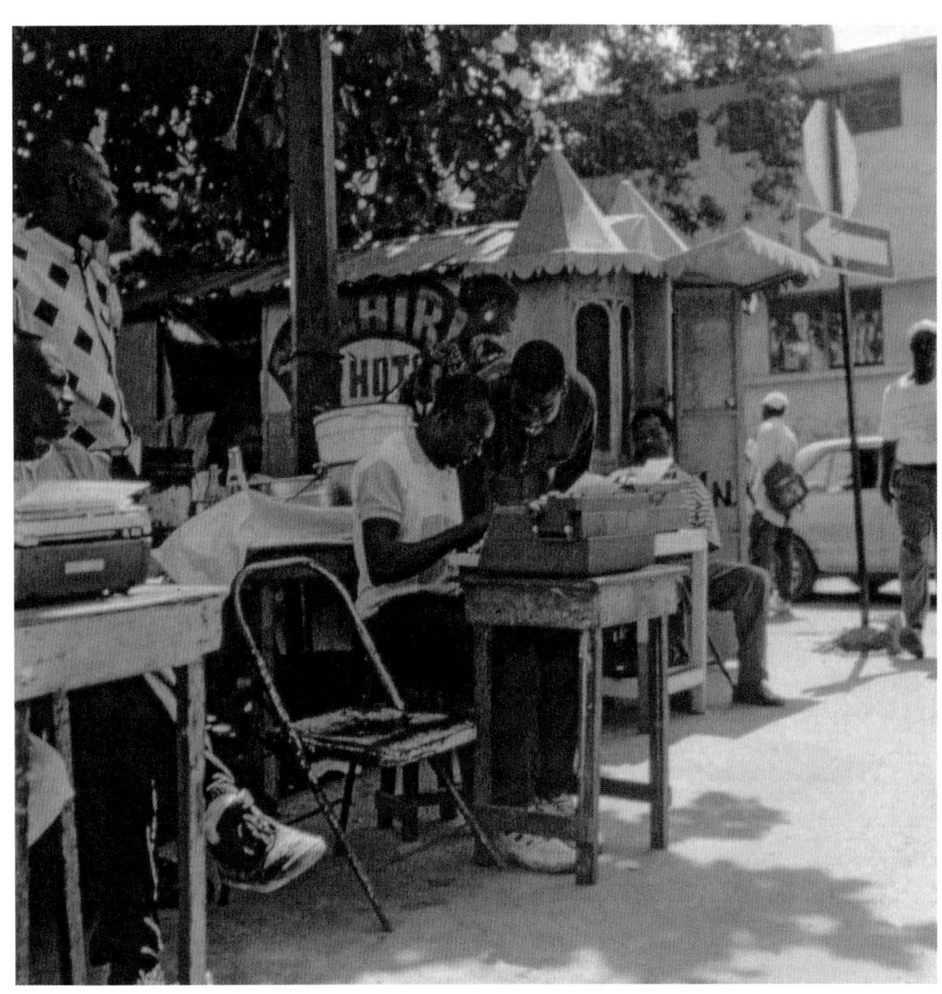

Typing Pool, Port au Prince

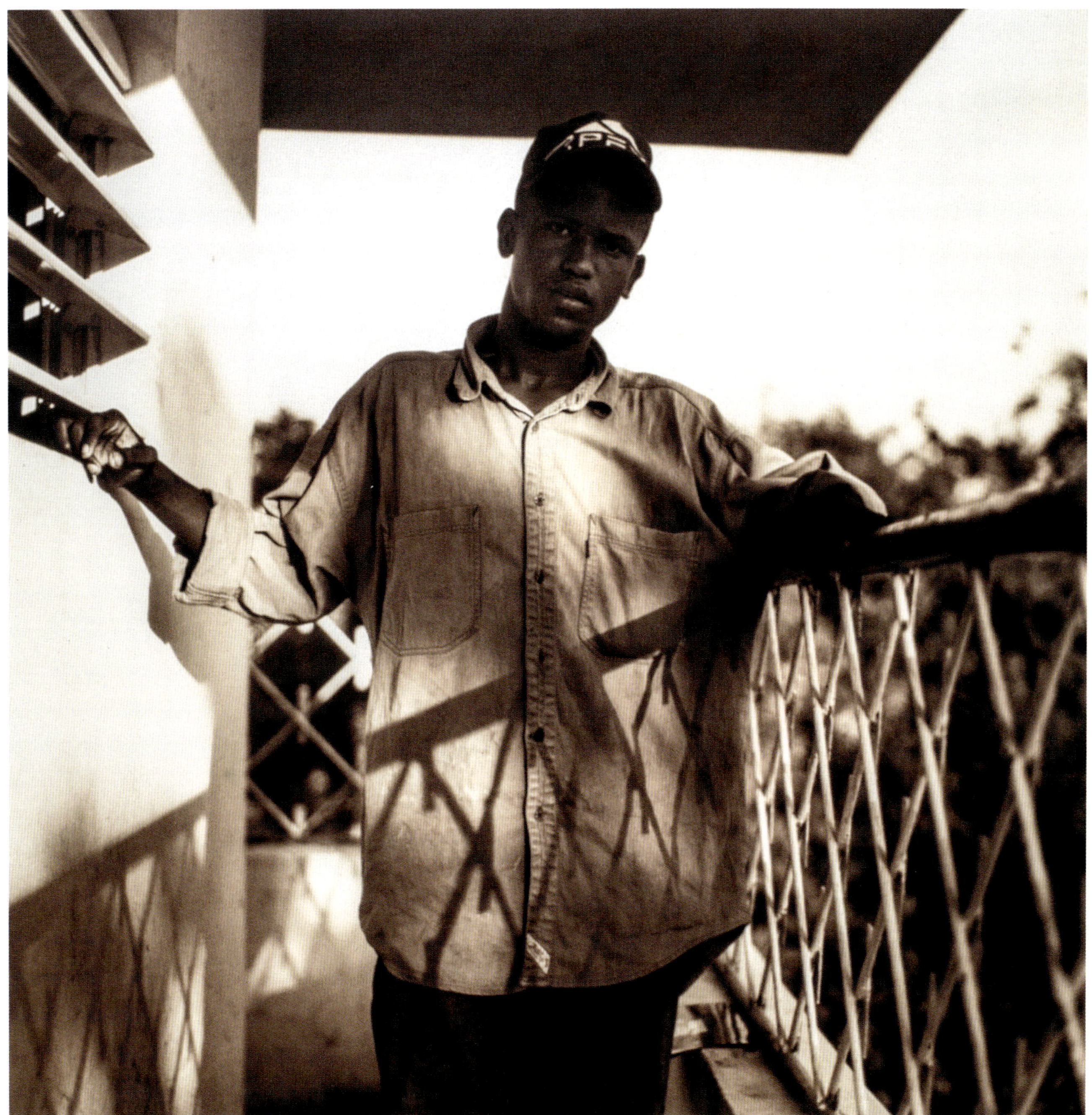

Carlos

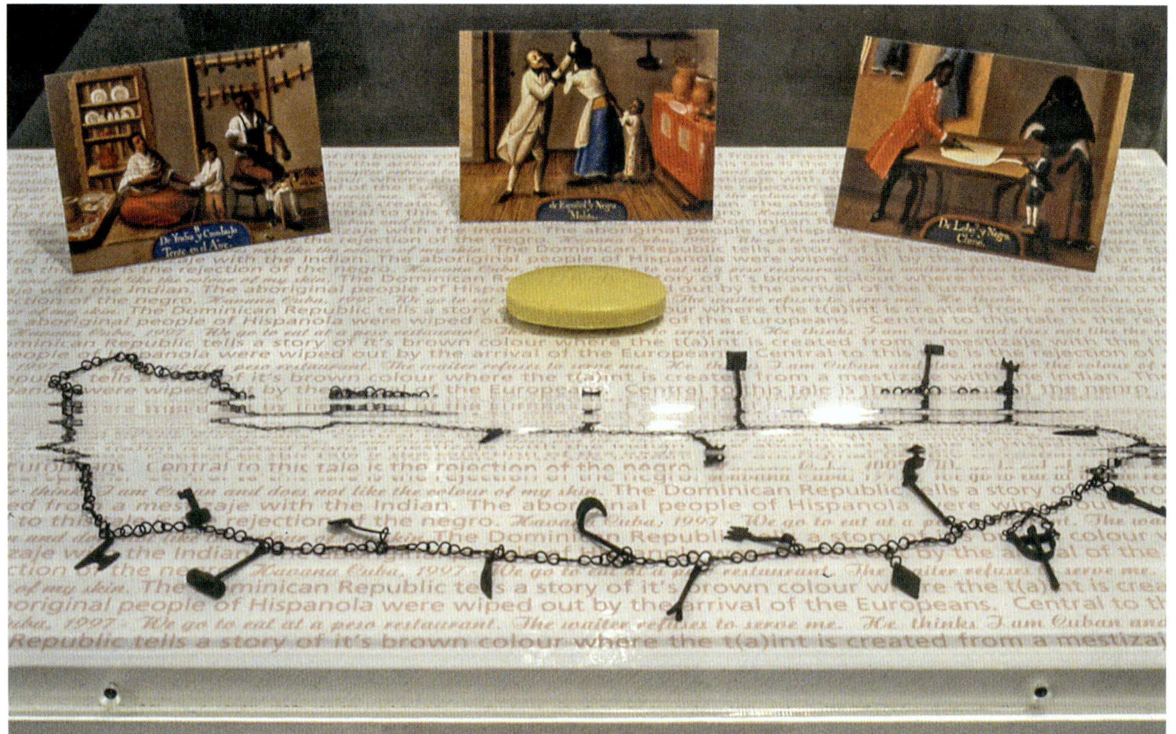
aboriginal people of Hispanola were wiped out by the arrival of the Europeans. Central to th
Republic tells a story of it's brown colour where the t(a)int is created from a mestiza

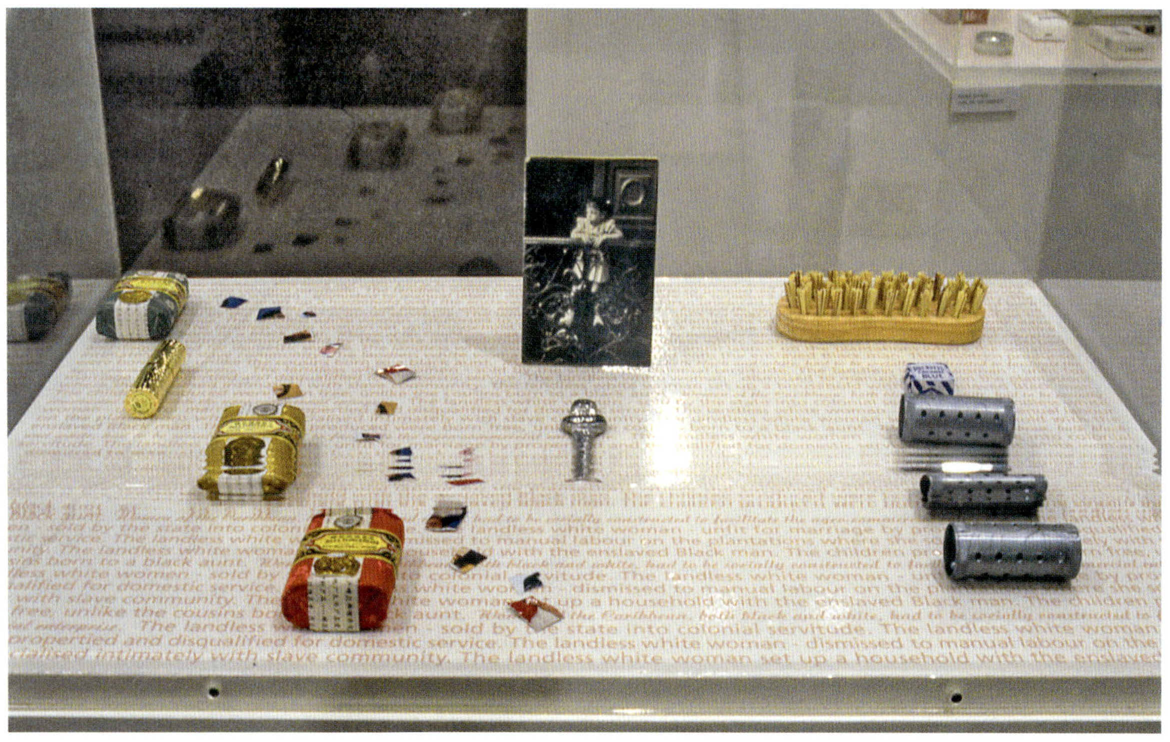
propertied and disqualified for domestic service. The landless white woman - dismissed to manual labour on the

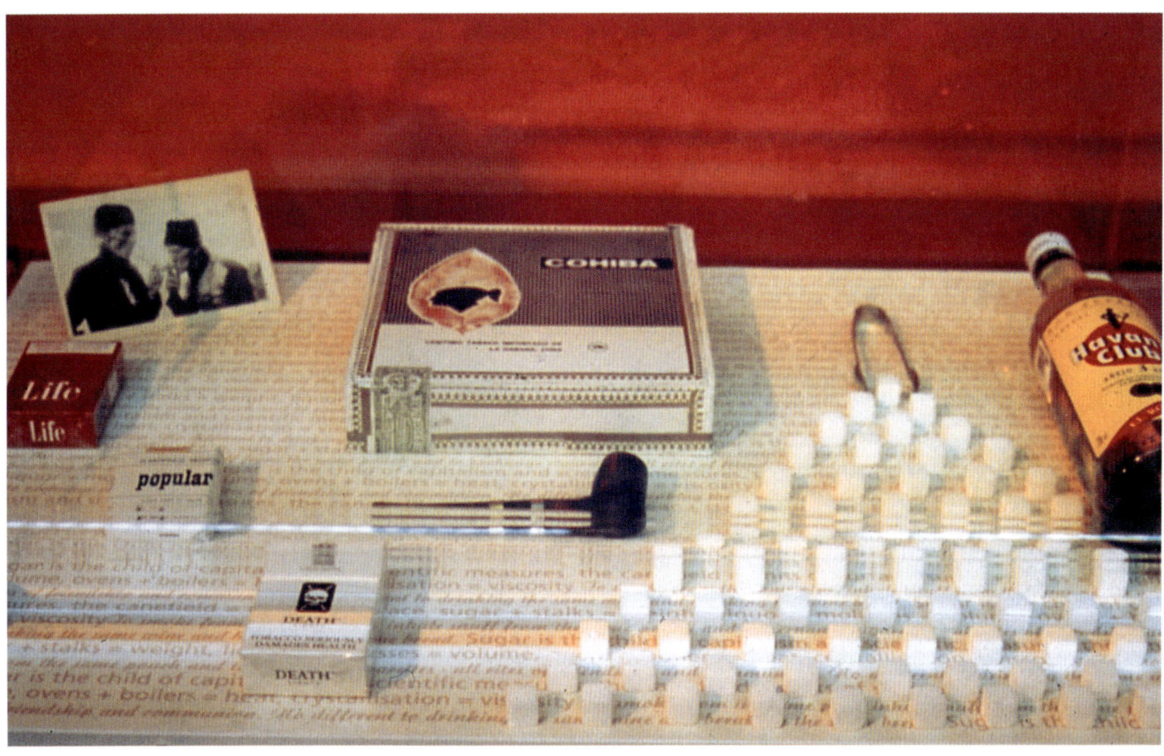

Sugar and Tobacco

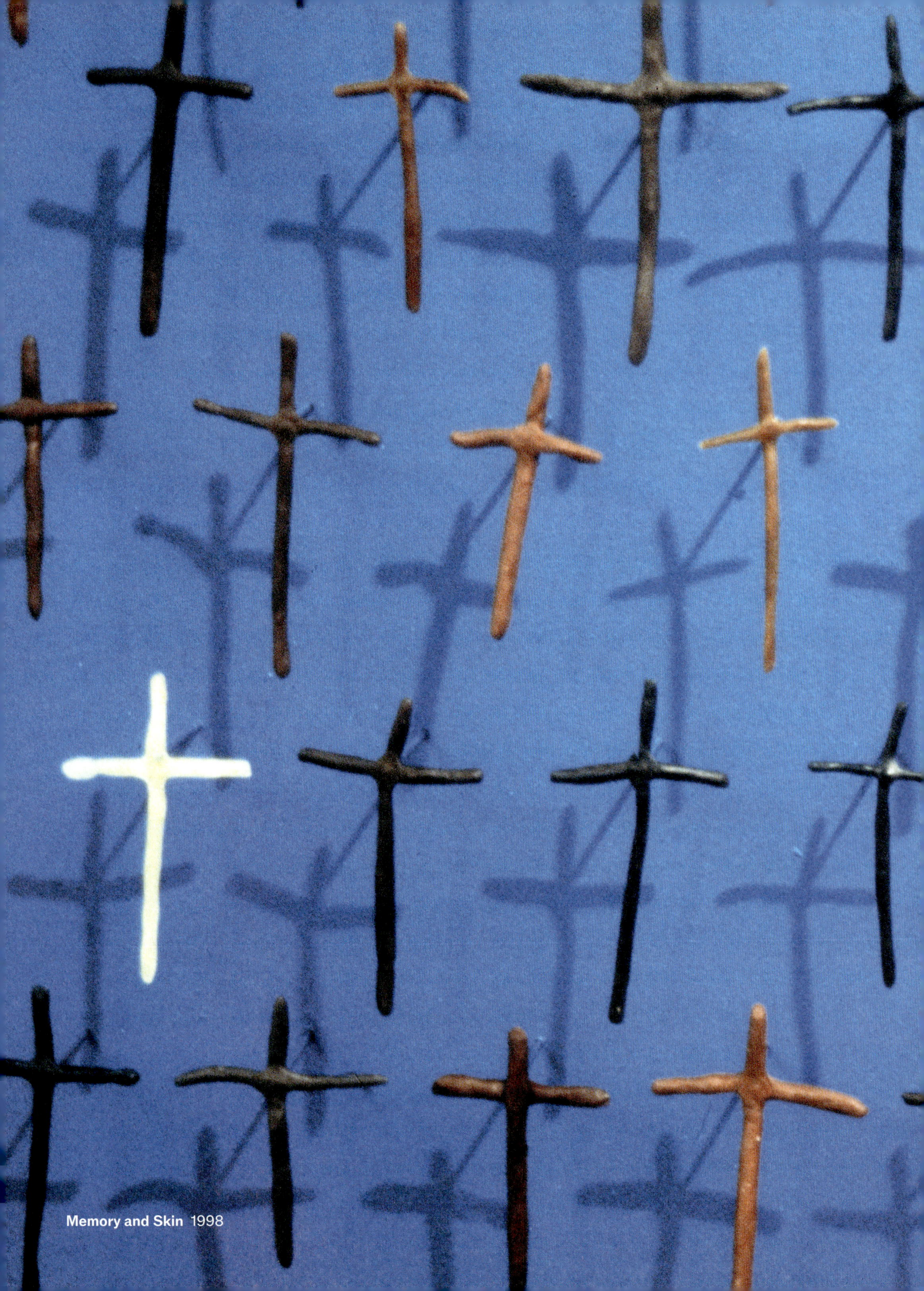

Memory and Skin 1998

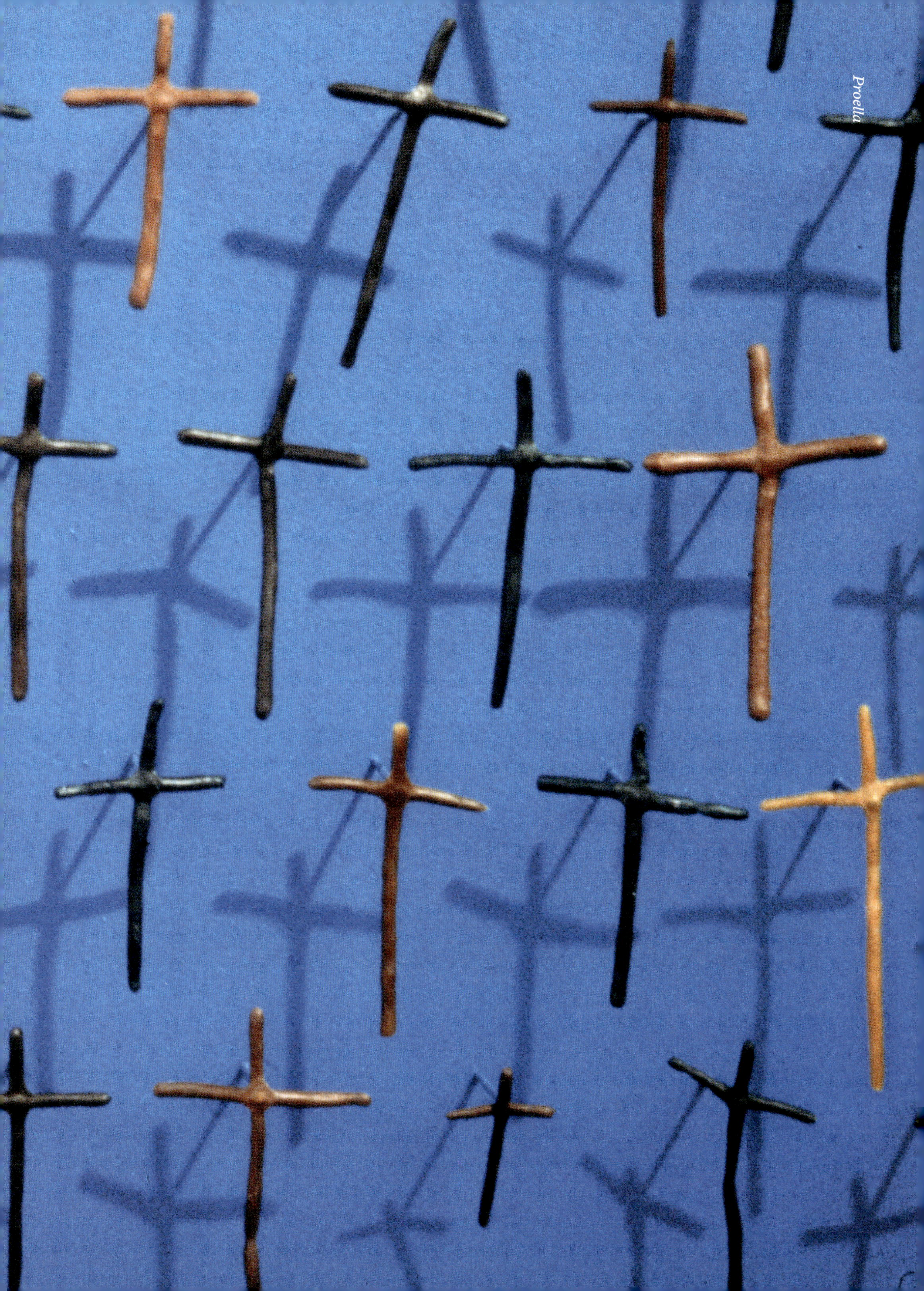

Proella

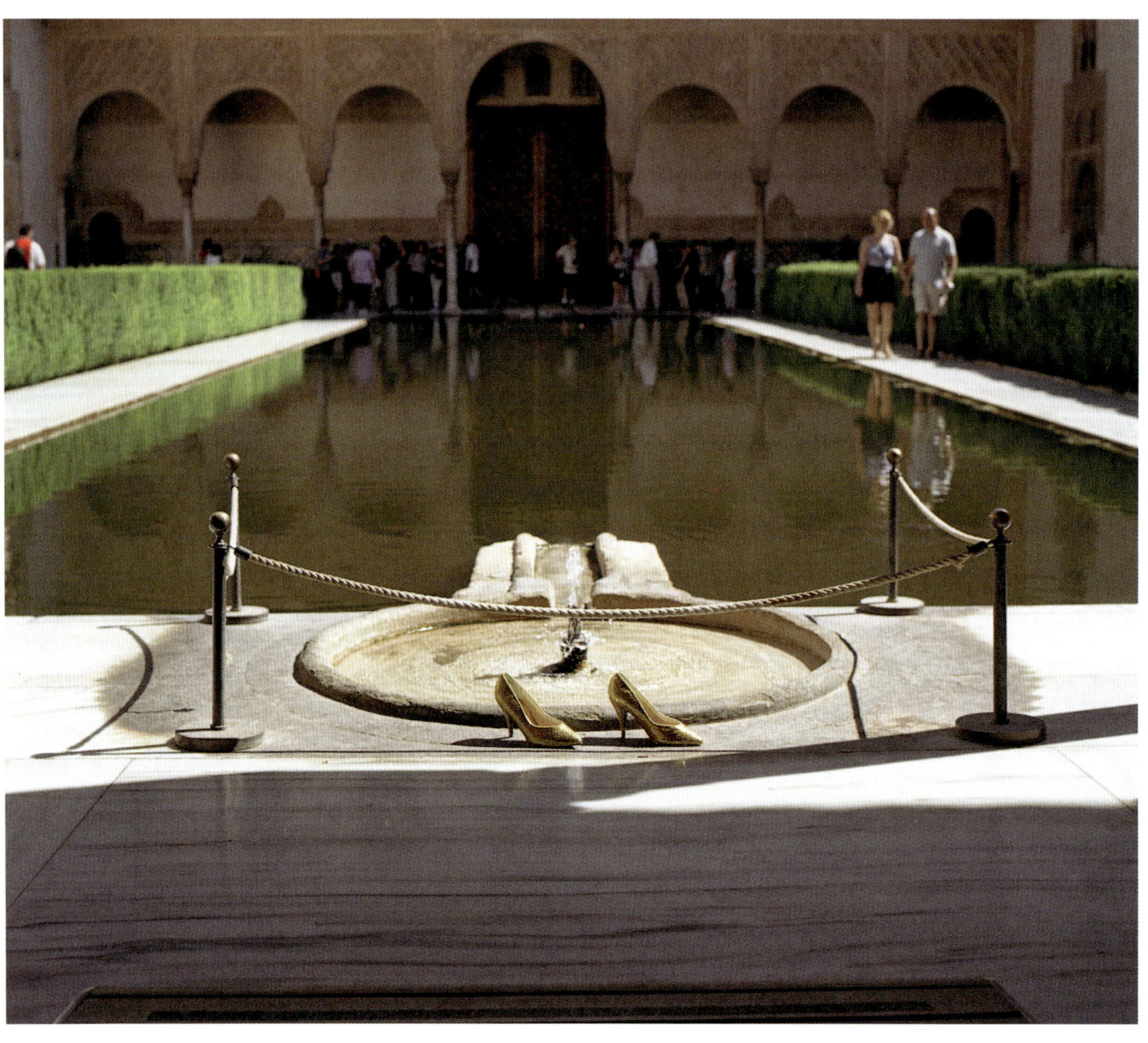

Patio, Alhambra

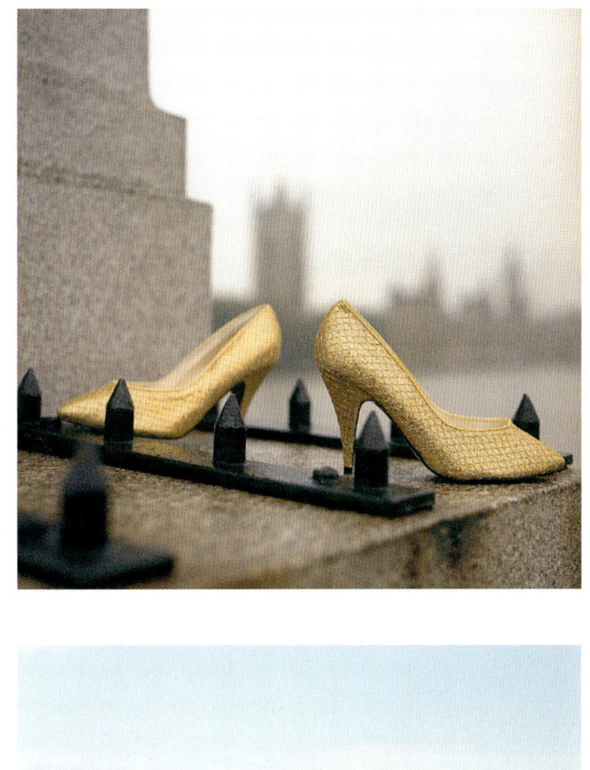

Palace of Westminster, London

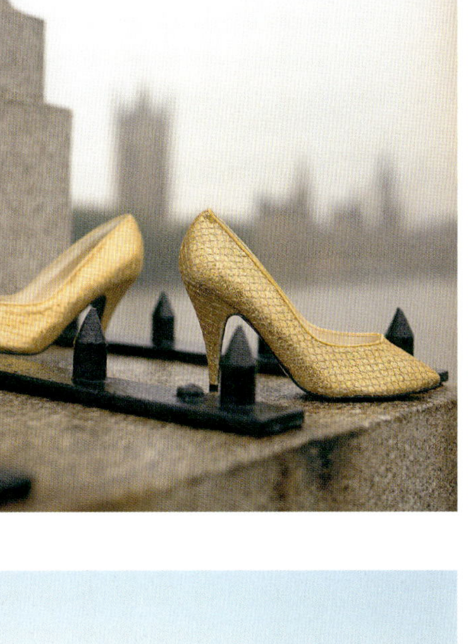

UN, Geneva

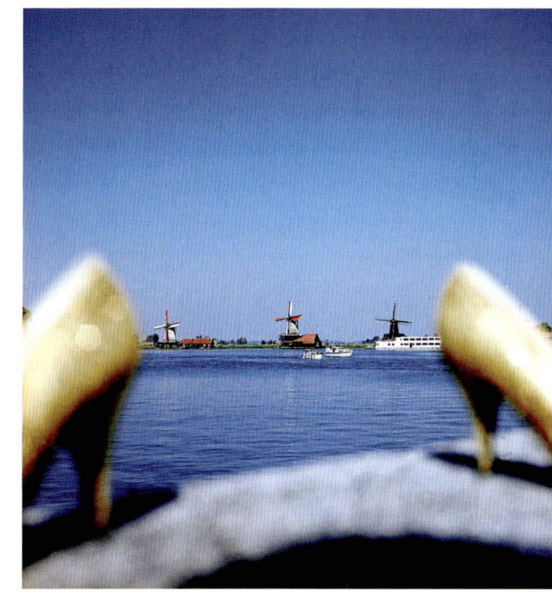

Realto Bridge

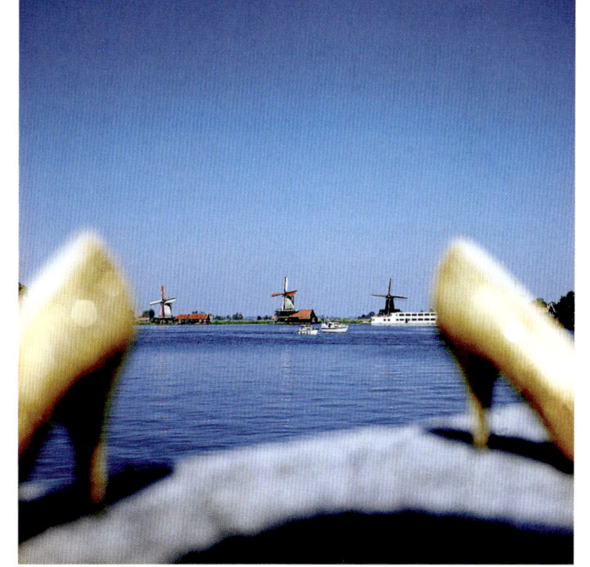

Zaanse Schans

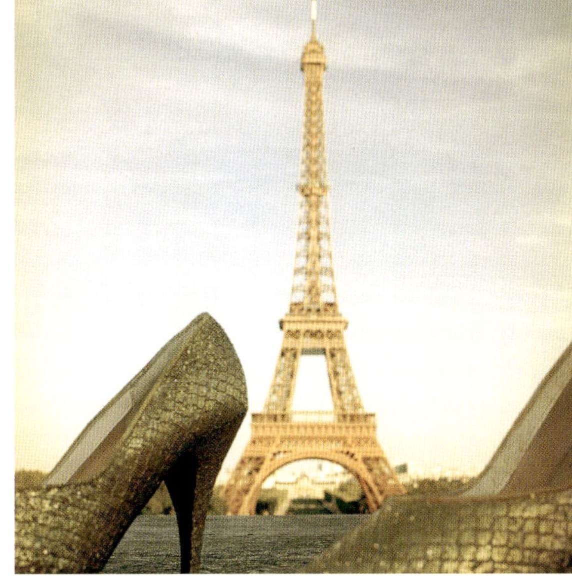

Eiffel Tower, Paris

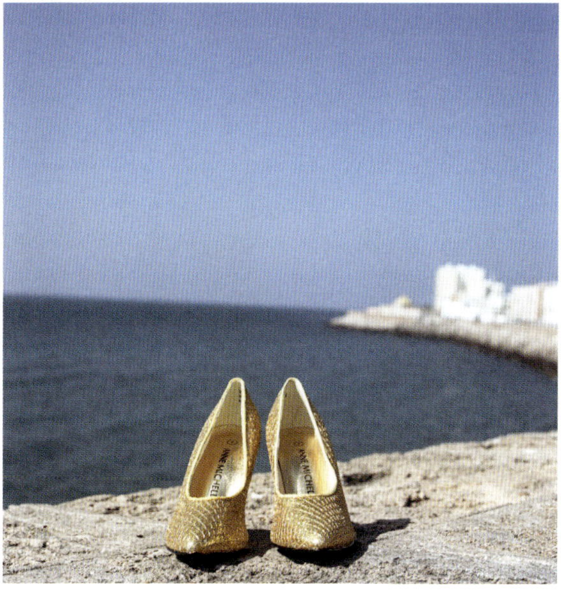

Cadiz

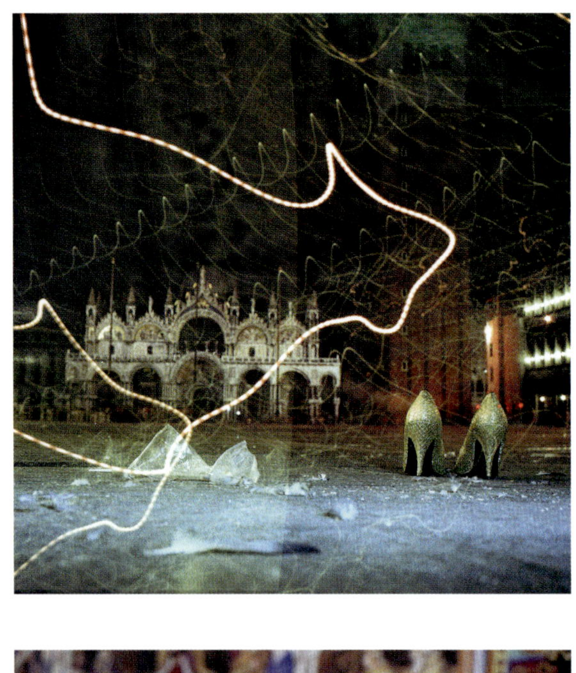

St. Mark's Square, Venice

Cristo Rei, Lisbon

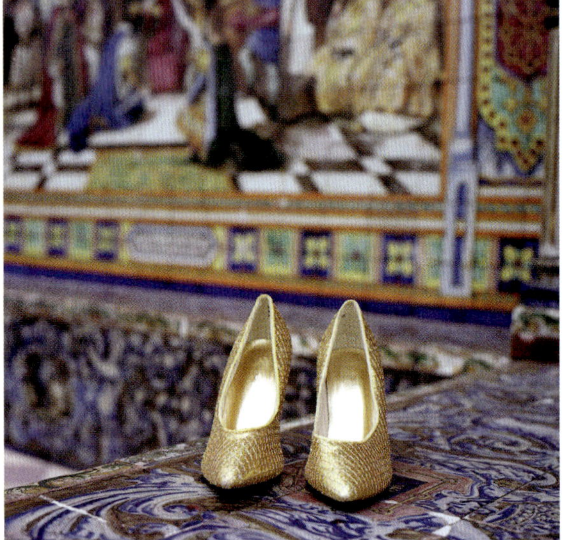

Plaza de Espana, Seville

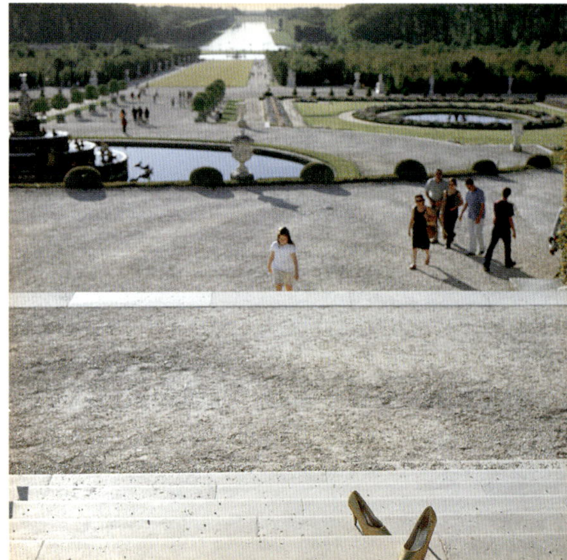

Gardens of Versailles

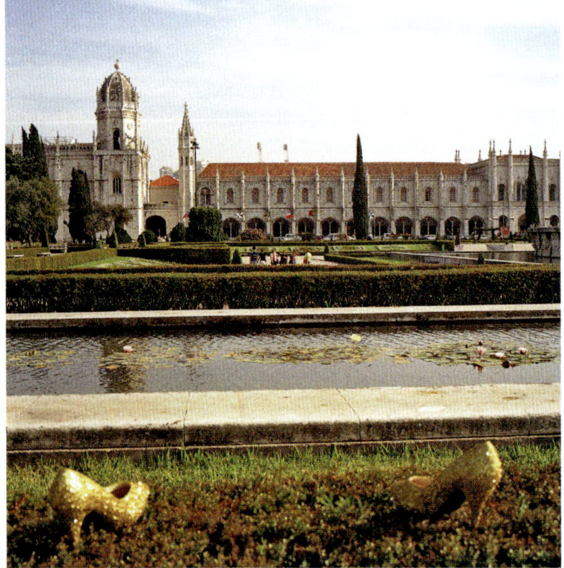

Mosteiro dos Jeronimos

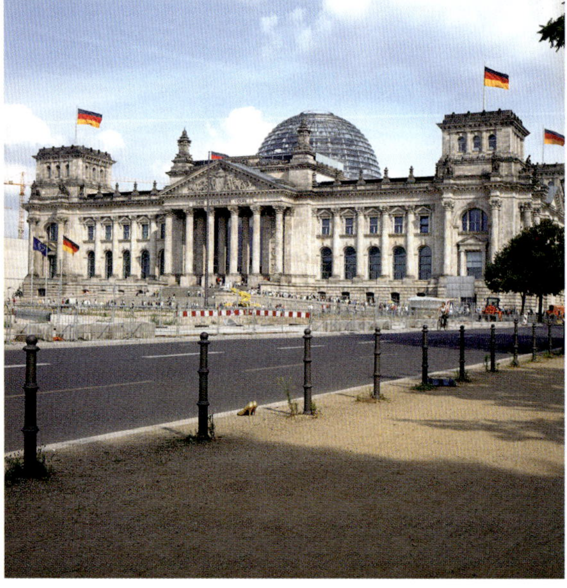

Reichstag, Berlin

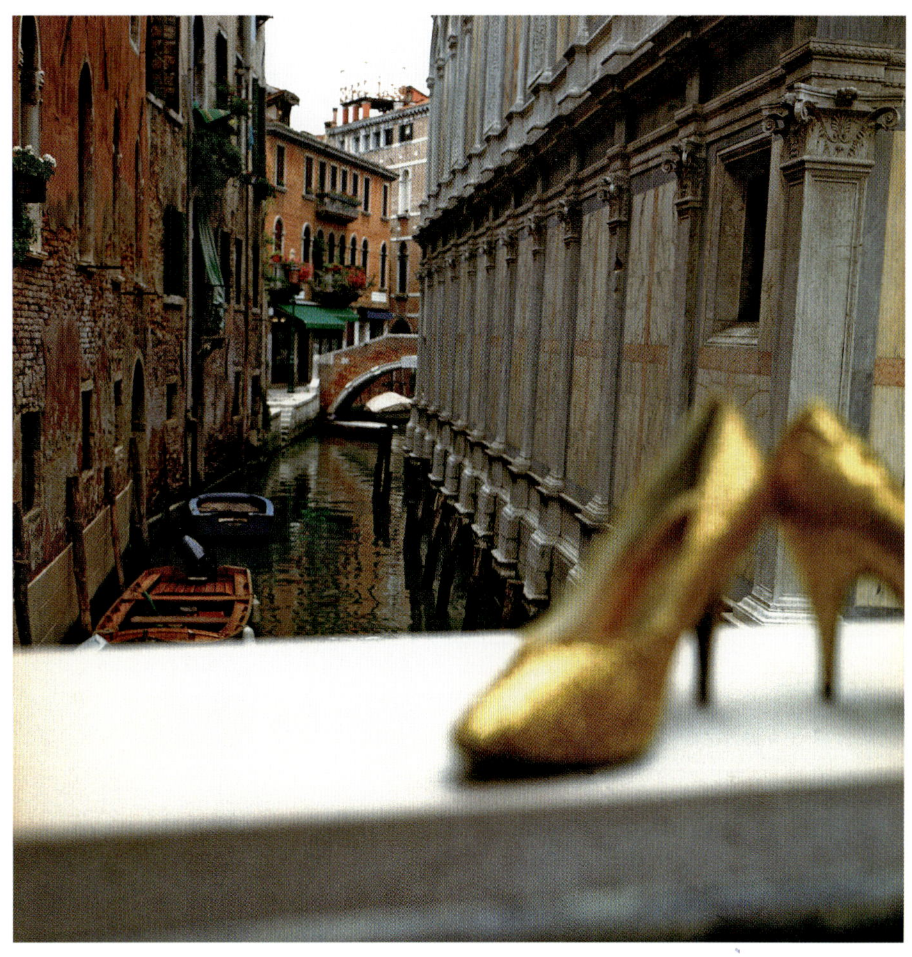

Bridge of Miracles, Venice

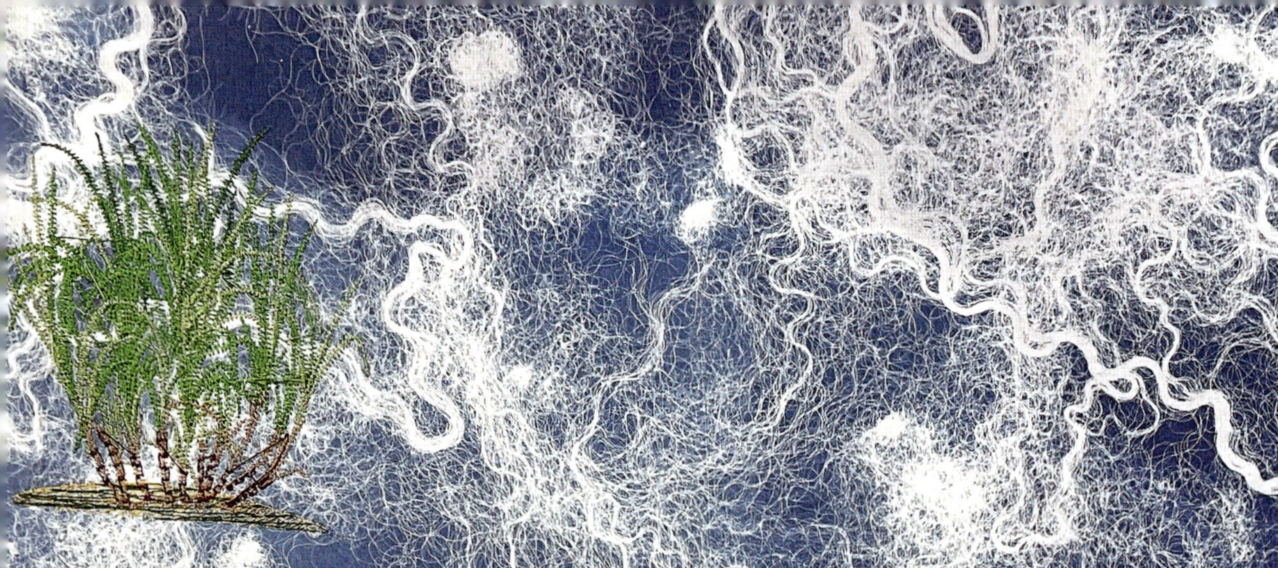

SHUTE HOUSE, AXMINSTER

Sir William Pole, 7th Baronet of Shute

OWNED

Golden Rock & Mills Estates, St Kitts

Enslaved 340

Compensation - £5296 16s 4d

Catherine Hall

Entangled Histories

Growing up in the very white, English town of Aylesbury in the 1960s, Joy Gregory spent much of her time wanting not to be seen. Her Jamaican parents had arrived in the UK in the late 1950s, her father from the rural parish of Clarendon, her mother from Kingston, though her birthplace was also Clarendon. Jamaica occupied a magical space for Gregory as a child, a place with relatives, different weather and a different landscape. Her parents returned to the island for funerals and her father held dear the memory of his homeland. She first visited with them in 1992, but it was not until later that she established her own relationship, through her work as an artist, with the entangled histories of England and Jamaica. Throughout the 1980s and early 90s, much of Gregory's work was focused on identity and self, mainly through photographic self-portraits. Her interest as a Black woman in seeing, being seen and not being seen has remained a central preoccupation.

Her own longer history as a woman of African-Caribbean descent was explored in *Memory and Skin* (1998). Her photographic practice was now combined with sound, objects and text to explore the complex fusion of cultures in the Caribbean, the layering of histories which have remained so central to her artistic vision. The sea, the forced migrations of Africans, the dislocations and re-makings of cultures are summoned up through the installation. Portraits of men and women, young people working or gathering together, were placed alongside landscapes featuring the lush beauty of the islands. Cabinets of curiosity, echoing one of the ways in which Caribbean objects first reached England, feature a poster of Liverpool, 'Capital of the Slave Trade', a bottle of liquor, probably the rum that displaced gin in popularity in the eighteenth century, shells, and fragments of leaves, recalling the natural history collections of Hans Sloane (1660–1753), now occupying pride of place in the British

The Sweetest Thing (detail)

Museum, the British Library and the Natural History Museum. A four-month visit to the Caribbean resulted in the series *Cinderella Tours Europe* (1998–2001), a fairytale of people transformed into golden shoes that fly, as if on magic carpets, on their own Grand Tour to European tourist sites. This was not the tour as undertaken by eighteenth-century gentlemen and aristocrats whose education required a knowledge of antiquities, sometimes transported back to Jamaica as in the case of James Dawkins who visited Palmyra and named one of the family sugar plantations in Clarendon in memory of his journey. This time it was the dream of the peoples whose ancestral histories had been fractured and whose imaginations were framed in part by a Grand Tour of Desire for Europe.

Gregory's special interest in Jamaican history surfaced in *Seeds of Empire* (2021), a series of exhibition projects with Gary Stewart and the composer Philip Miller, drawing on her research on the slave trade and colonialism. Her work, inspired and provoked by Hans Sloane's journey to Jamaica in 1688 to serve as the physician to the island's governor, combined moving image with photographs and soundscapes. Following in the traditions of Francis Bacon and John Locke, Sloane was already an enthusiastic collector and classifier, convinced of the importance of natural history, and with an 'unshakeable conviction that nature was a mechanical entity designed by God to be exploited for human profit'.[1] He enthusiastically recorded the weather across the Atlantic and on the island. As part of the project, *Observations: A Little Breeze* reproduces the testimony of this supposedly objective observer: the breeze, the tempest, the thunder and lightning, the earthquake, fair weather, heavy dew and mosquitoes. This is juxtaposed with stills of the enslaved woman Rose (the role of the historical figure enacted by Gregory herself) with her broom, her melancholy and her despair, sometimes shot in semi- or almost total darkness. An evocative soundtrack, a reworking of an African song that Sloane asked Mr Baptiste to notate for him, alongside the cello, accompanies the piece. The companion film *Observations: Rose* tells something of her story, as it was recorded in Sloane's *Voyage to the Islands Madera, Barbados, Nieves, S. Christophers, and Jamaica* (1701), one of 127 other case histories, the vast majority of these of white people. Rose suffered from severe depression, refused to eat and forgot her orders. If one 'put a broom in her hand to sweep the house, there she stood with it, looking on the ground very pensive and melancholy'.[2] Refusing to think about the cause of her melancholy, (was it resistance?), and believing that African claims to be sick were invariably associated with avoiding work, Sloane treated her with violent purges and emetics, had her cupt and scarified, forced concoctions down her throat, blistered her neck and maintained that 'diseases of the head' were understood

1 James Delbourgo, *Collecting the World: The Life and Curiosity of Hans Sloane* (London: Allen Lane 2017), 14.

2 Ibid, 51.

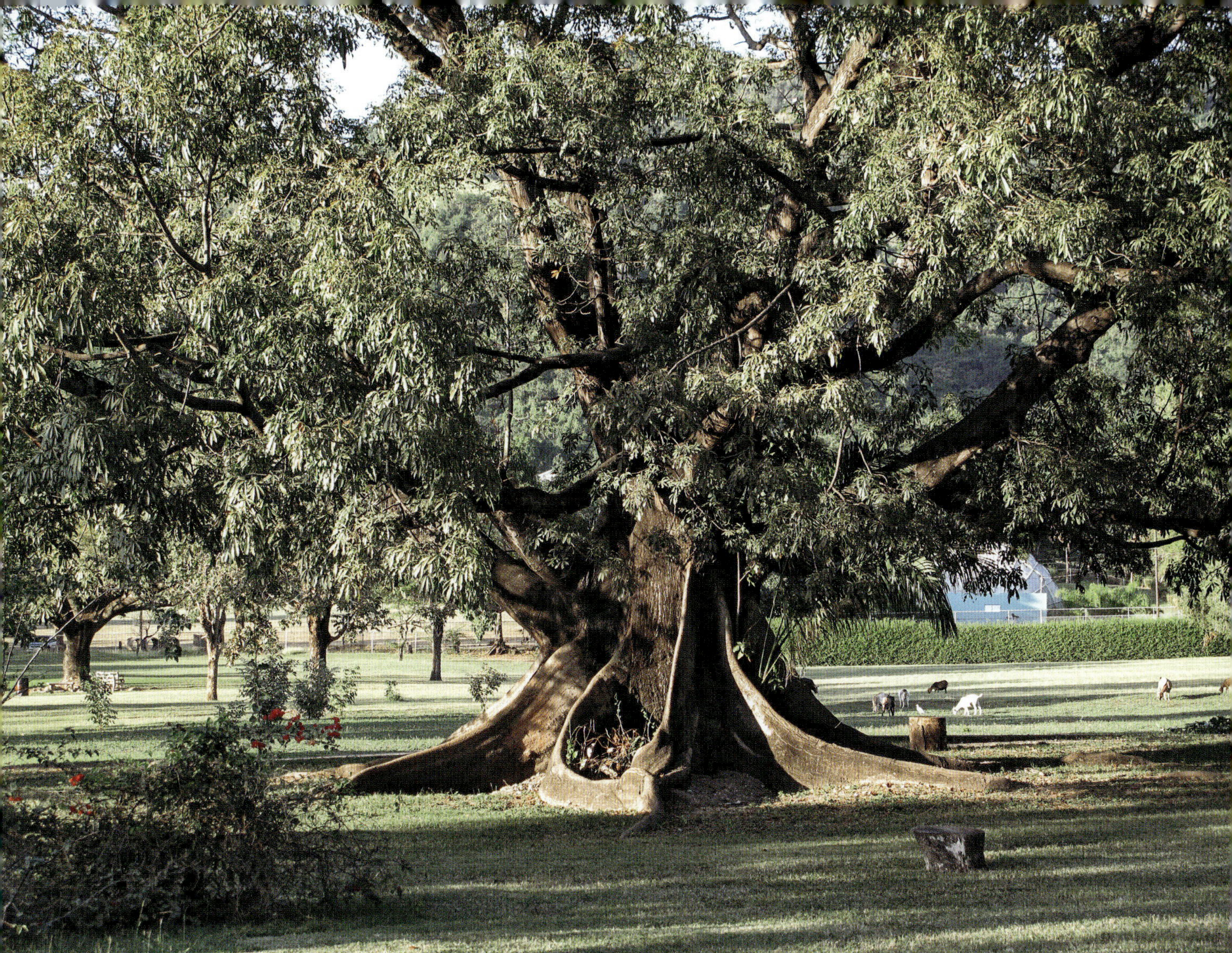

Cotton Tree, Hope Botanical Gardens, Saint Andrews, Jamaica

as witchcraft by simple-minded country people. He knew better. 'She came to herself, went about her business and was well'. Sloane had no problem with slavery, later marrying the widow of a leading Jamaican slaveholder and much enjoying the benefits of that inheritance. 'Negroes' were there to work, that, from his point of view, was the meaning of their presence in Jamaica. In the film *Observations: A Little Breeze*, Rose's story is interleaved with conversations that Gregory had with migrants about their own experience of the cold, smog, snow, rain and loneliness of England and their memories of the warmth and beauty of their homeland. The sadness of the sea with its dead harvest is contrasted with the marvels of the island's scenery and plants, including the wonders of Kingston's magnificent Botanical Gardens, created on a former plantation in the wake of the events at Morant Bay in 1865 as a form of repair at a moment of colonial guilt. The spectacular cotton tree was believed by the enslaved to have sacred properties.

Seeds of Empire also mirrors Sloane's preoccupation with the island's trees. Photographic engravings of the manchineel's poisonous leaves

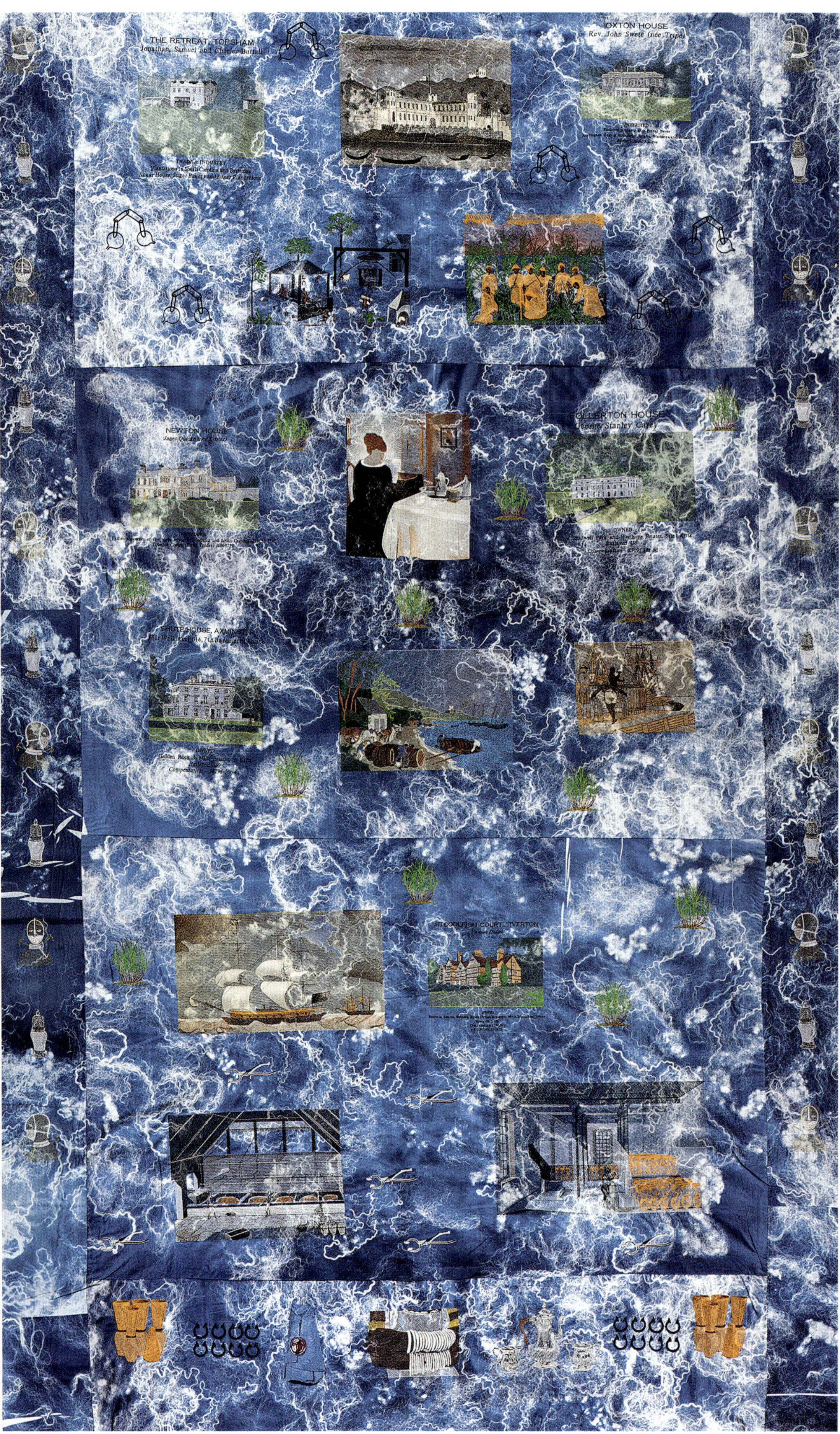
THE RETREAT, TOPSHAM
Jonathan, Samuel and Charles Buttall
OXTON HOUSE
Rev. John Swete (née Tripe)
STOODLEIGH COURT, TIVERTON

and fruits; the 'little apples of death' recall the story of Sally Basset who was alleged to have used the root as an act of resistance and was burned alive at the stake in revenge. Edward Long, whose *History of Jamaica* (1774) drew extensively on Sloane's text for his encyclopaedia of flora and fauna, was concerned to challenge the tales of the manchineel. But like Sloane he half believed in the mysteries of Indigenous knowledge while energetically denying any such wisdom. After extensive investigation and finding evidence that goats' taste for the fruits had no bad effects, he concluded that there was no basis for regarding either the bark, the juice or the fruit as dangerous. The puzzle as to what Africans *knew* remained a puzzle. Plants were commodities, not threads linking nature to healing and sustenance.

Gregory has always known that she loves to tell stories. Her work can transform things of ugliness to things of beauty, inviting curiosity, encouraging people to want to know more, feeding their imaginations visually, bringing histories together. 'Our generation sense that work dealing with serious issues', as she put it in a conversation with Hew Locke, 'needs to be aesthetically beautiful, so that people will listen.' This is the case with *The Sweetest Thing*, the embroidery that she created for a commission with Exeter's Royal Albert Memorial Museum and Art Gallery [RAMM] (2022). It tells the story of the slavery business for both Britain and the Caribbean: a painful and difficult history, but one that needs to be known and presented in such a way 'that people take responsibility and understand the relationship between themselves and history'. The Combesatchfield embroidery panel, created around 1750 and held by RAMM, inspired her. An elegant white lady, accompanied by a small Black child holding her parasol and seeming to be almost floating in the air, is positioned amongst a stylish couple, boats on the sea, flowers blooming, the child evoking the Black presence in Devon in the eighteenth century. What was Devon's history in relation to the slave trade and slavery? How did Black and white histories intersect in this peaceful predominantly rural county with its temperate climate and delightful villages and seaside towns? Her commission for RAMM, eventually comprising the embroidery, a film, *Sugar*, and a series of images of living descendants of the enslaved, was part of an exhibition – *In Plain Sight: Transatlantic Slavery and Devon* – exploring these questions. Local historians had been doing significant research on the area for decades, building connections with new work on Britain's forgotten history.

The *Sweetest Thing* begins with the slave trade and the forced migrations from Africa across the Middle Passage. The sea figures largely, its constant movement captured with Gregory's own hair, photographed so as to resemble streaming waters and white waves, providing the background to the embroidered images of people, places, ships and objects connected with sugar and slavery from the bundles of cane and shackles and head restraints associated with the plantation to the sugar cones of the grocers and the silver sugar shakers of polite society. Exeter received a royal charter in 1585 permitting it to trade with Africa. Topsham on the River Exe, dealing with cloth and sugar, became England's second largest port in the seventeenth century. Its sugar refinery processed the muscovado (semi-refined sugar) shipped from the Caribbean, while a factory produced manillas, currency for the slave trade. Ships were built, voyages embarked upon, factory workers and sailors all part of the labour force employed domestically while the enslaved peopled colonies. On the plantations, women dominated the field work, engaged in the heavy work of planting and growing cane. Men were the skilled workforce, in the boiling house and the distillery, for once the cane was ripe it had to be extracted immediately, requiring machinery. Plantations were 'factories in a field', slaveowners were farmers and industrialists, managing those they named 'chattels', ready to punish any signs of resistance. Once milled, the juice was tended through a series of processes, then packed in hogsheads and loaded onto small boats before storage on ships ready to cross the Atlantic. Absentee owners could reside in their splendid homes enjoying the fruits of this business. Stoodleigh Court, near Tiverton, features on the embroidery. Its owner, Thomas Daniel, was one of the wealthiest merchants and absentee owners in the region, dominating Bristol politics for decades with his antipathy to abolition and emancipation not to speak of parliamentary reform and religious toleration. His family had been in Barbados and Bristol across generations. He had interests in the importation and brokering of sugar, banking, iron importing, copper, coal and the Bristol Dock Company. Stoodleigh Court was his third establishment, alongside his Clifton town house and his country estate in Gloucestershire. He and his brother received compensation when slavery was abolished in 1834 for 4,300 men and women on 28 plantations across the West Indies. Also appearing on Gregory's embroidery is Shute House Axminster, the splendid property of Sir William Pole (see page 90). He received compensation for 340 enslaved men and women who had worked on his inherited estates in St Kitts. Between two properties of the wealthy and the privileged, sits a white woman, captured as she reads, with a silver coffee pot on a table by her side, enjoying the peace that others cannot have.

Reading features in the sequence of stills of the descendants, linking the past to the present. Each of them, the daughter, the mother, the father, the grandfather and the grandmother are reading. We, the watchers, observe the backs of their heads. Theirs is the opportunity, the time and the space, to think and dream. Their ancestors suffered the loss of their own histories but made one anew. Now, they can absorb the history, seeing it in a new way, in both its written and embroidered forms.

Joy Gregory's works invite us in, encourage us to reflect on shared histories and their connections to the persistent inequalities of today. Her hope is for change, for racial and social justice.

The Sweetest Thing (detail)

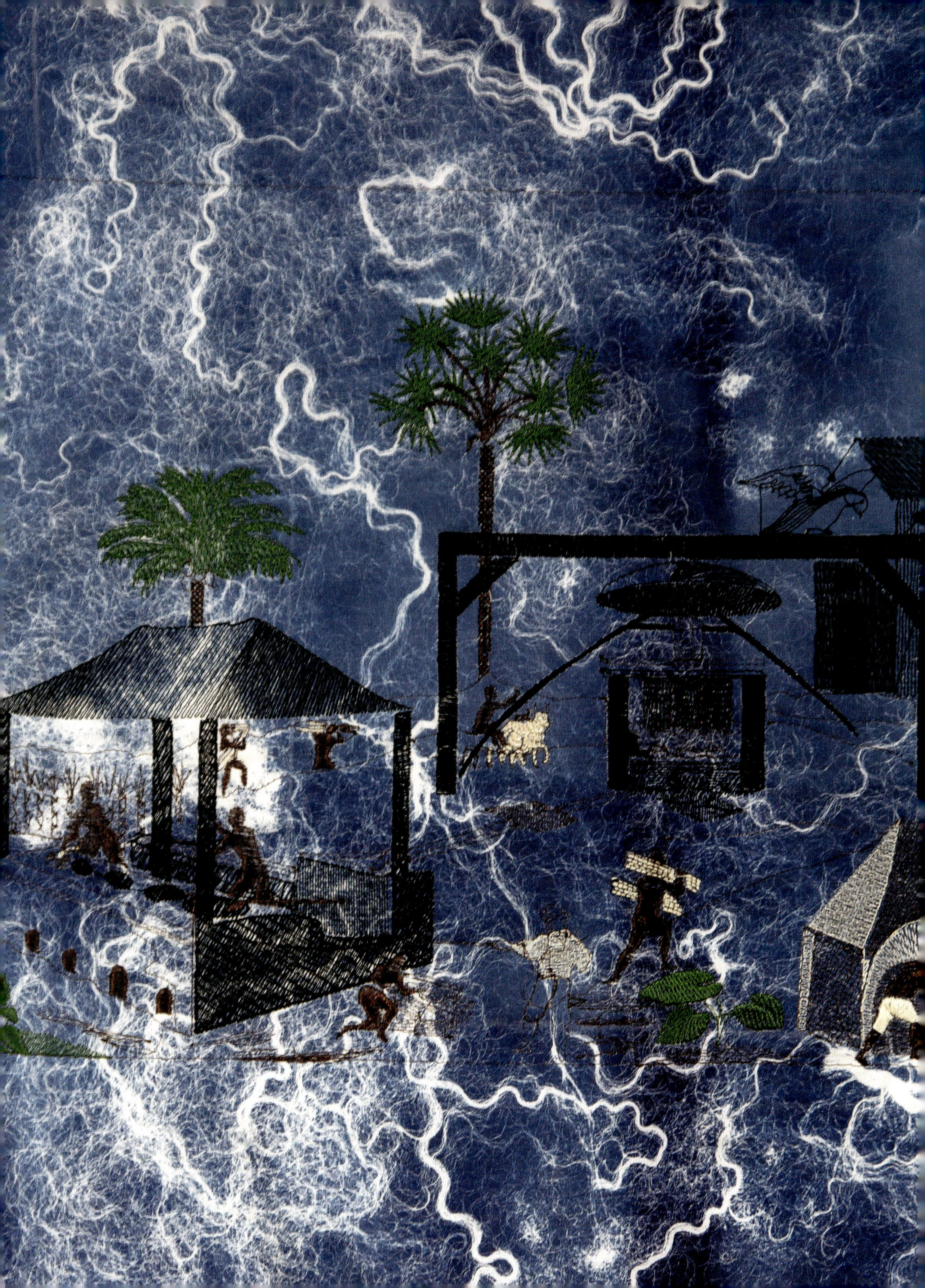

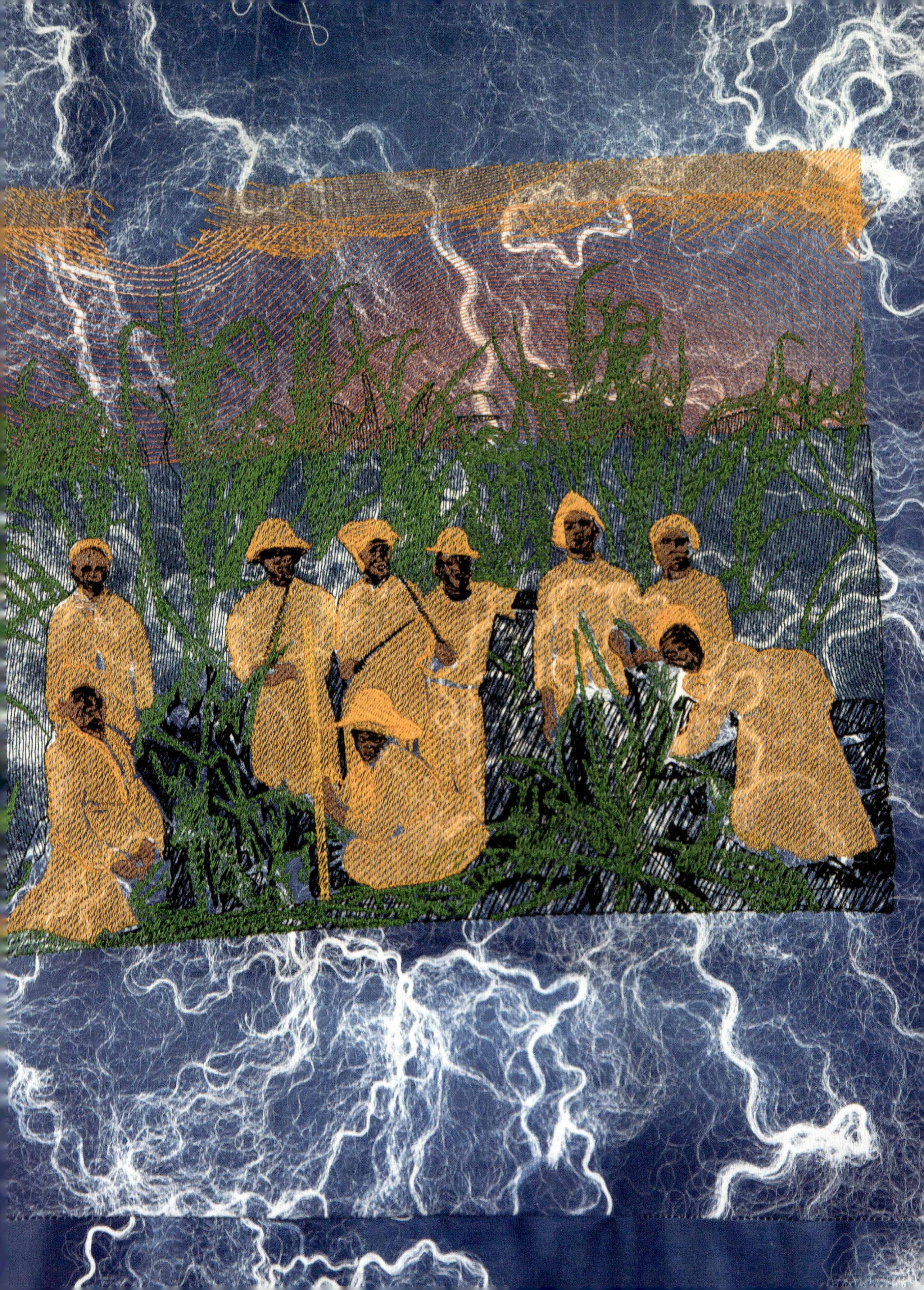

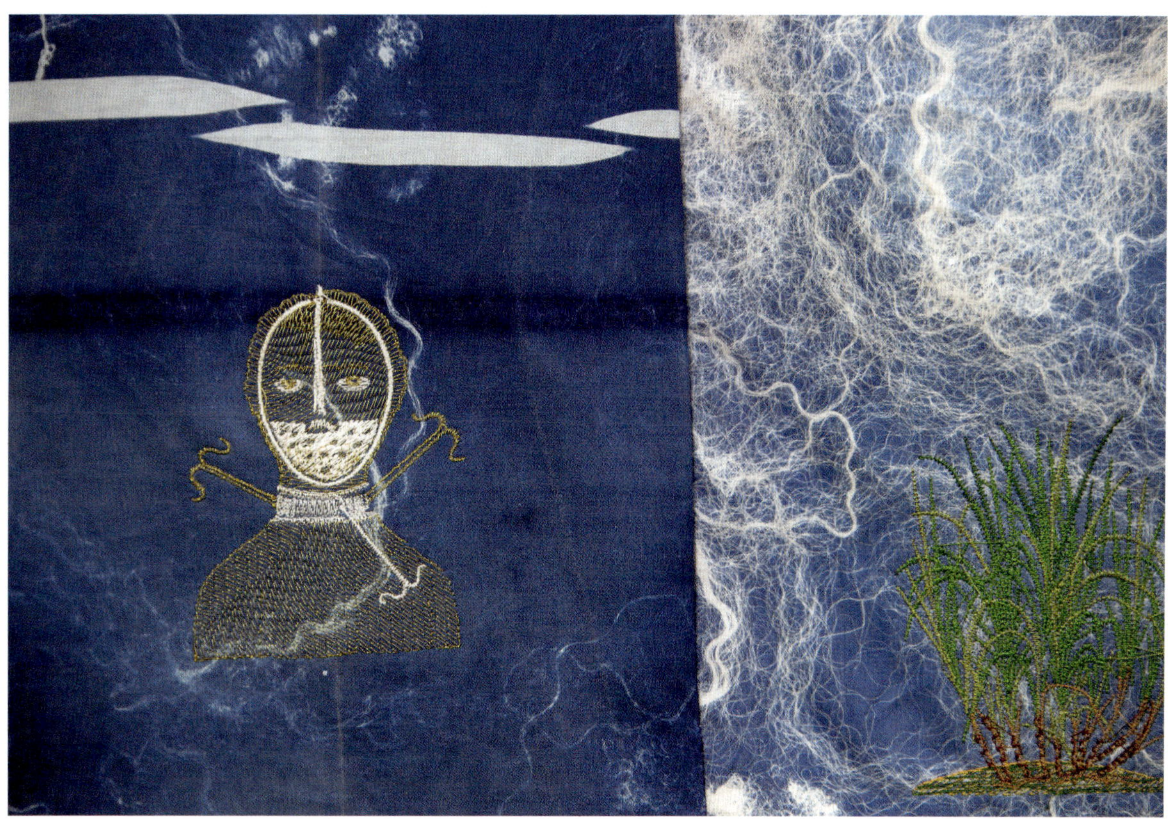

The Sweetest Thing (detail)

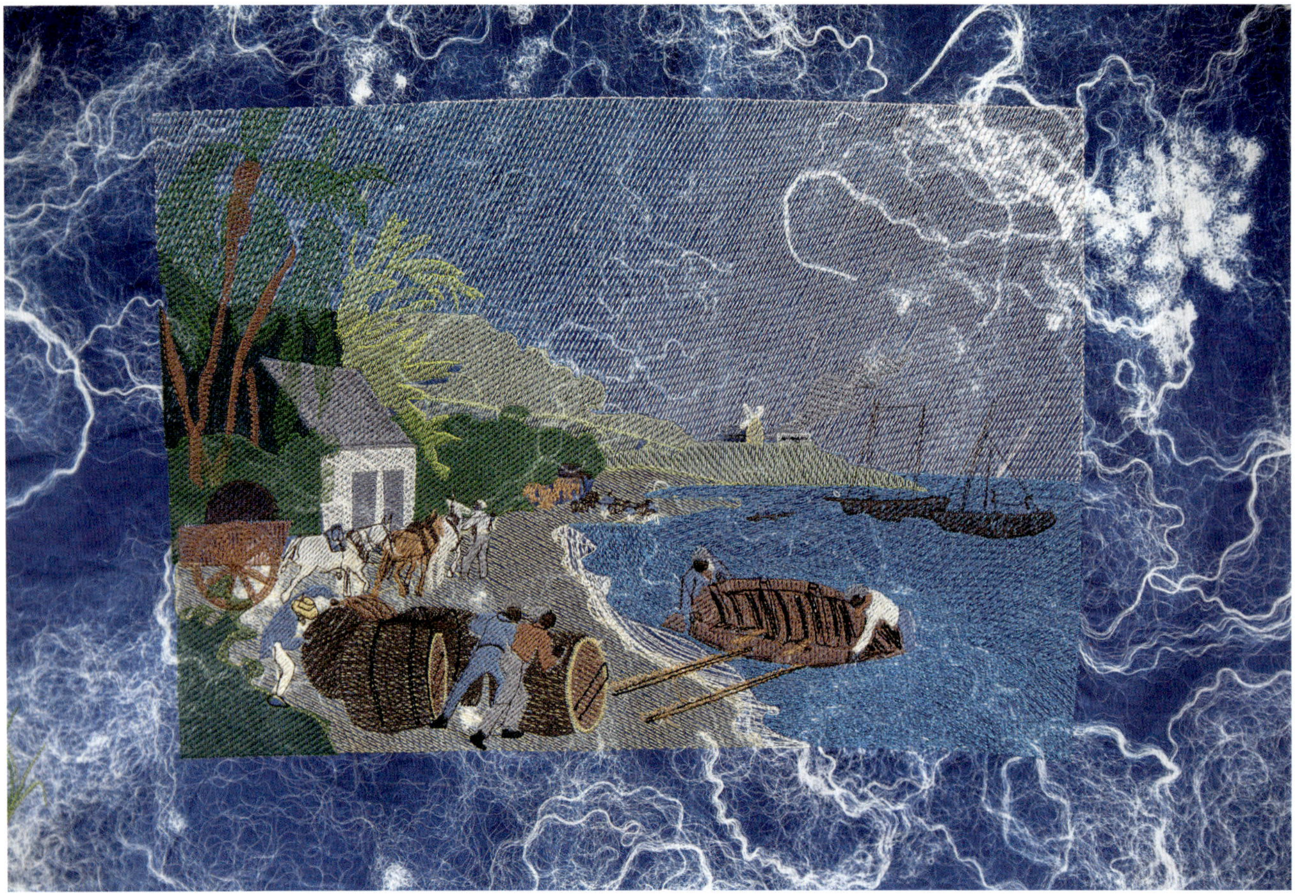

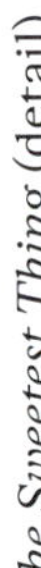
The Sweetest Thing (detail)

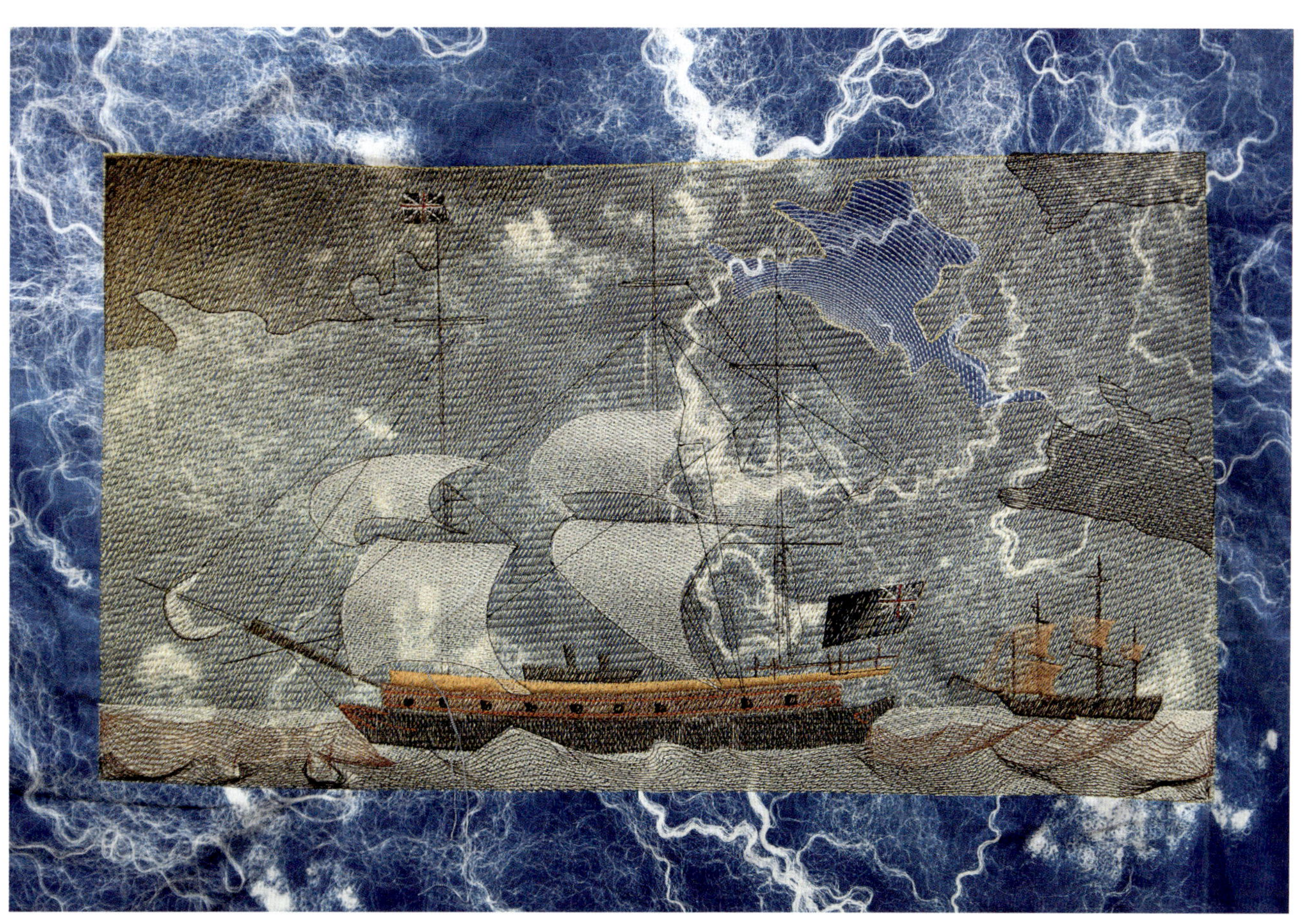

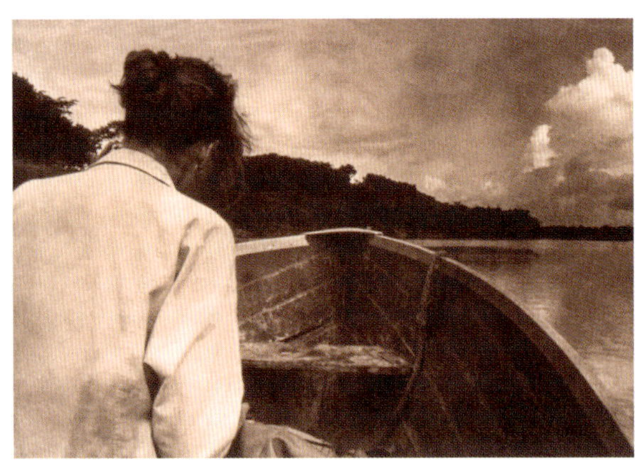

Viewed & Viewing (detail)

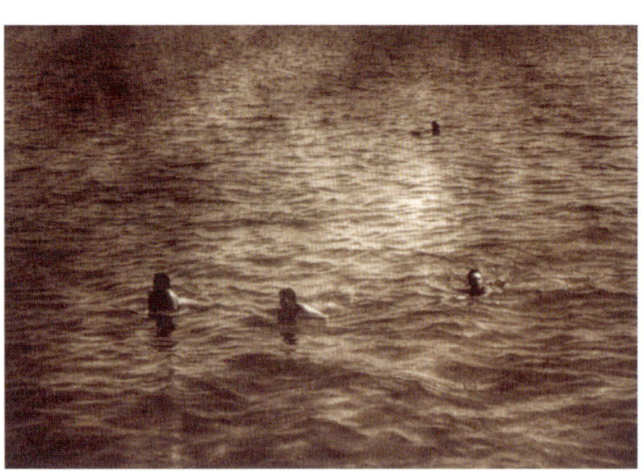

Memory Flickers (detail)

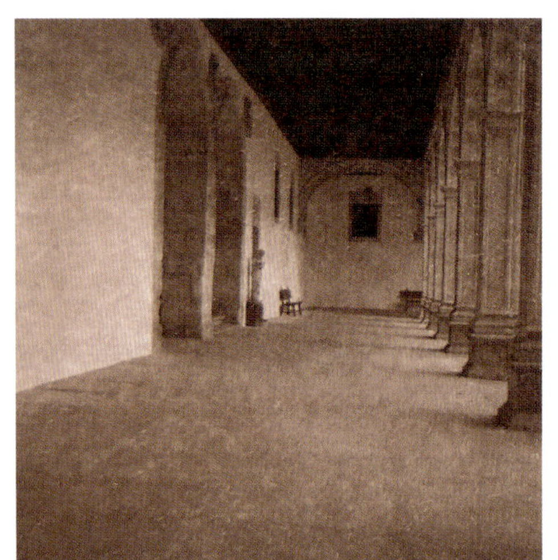

Breathing Out (detail)

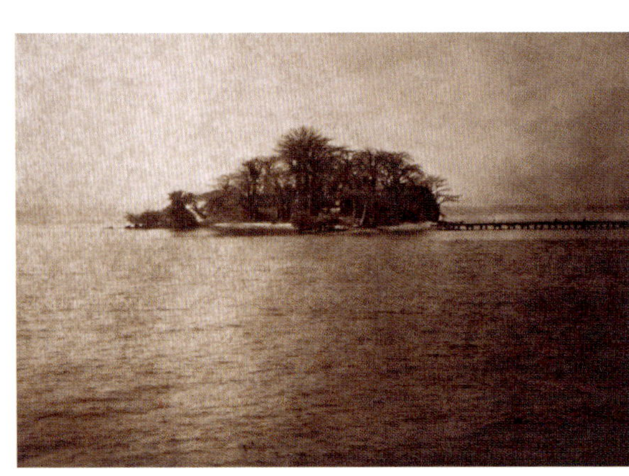

To survey from a distance (detail)

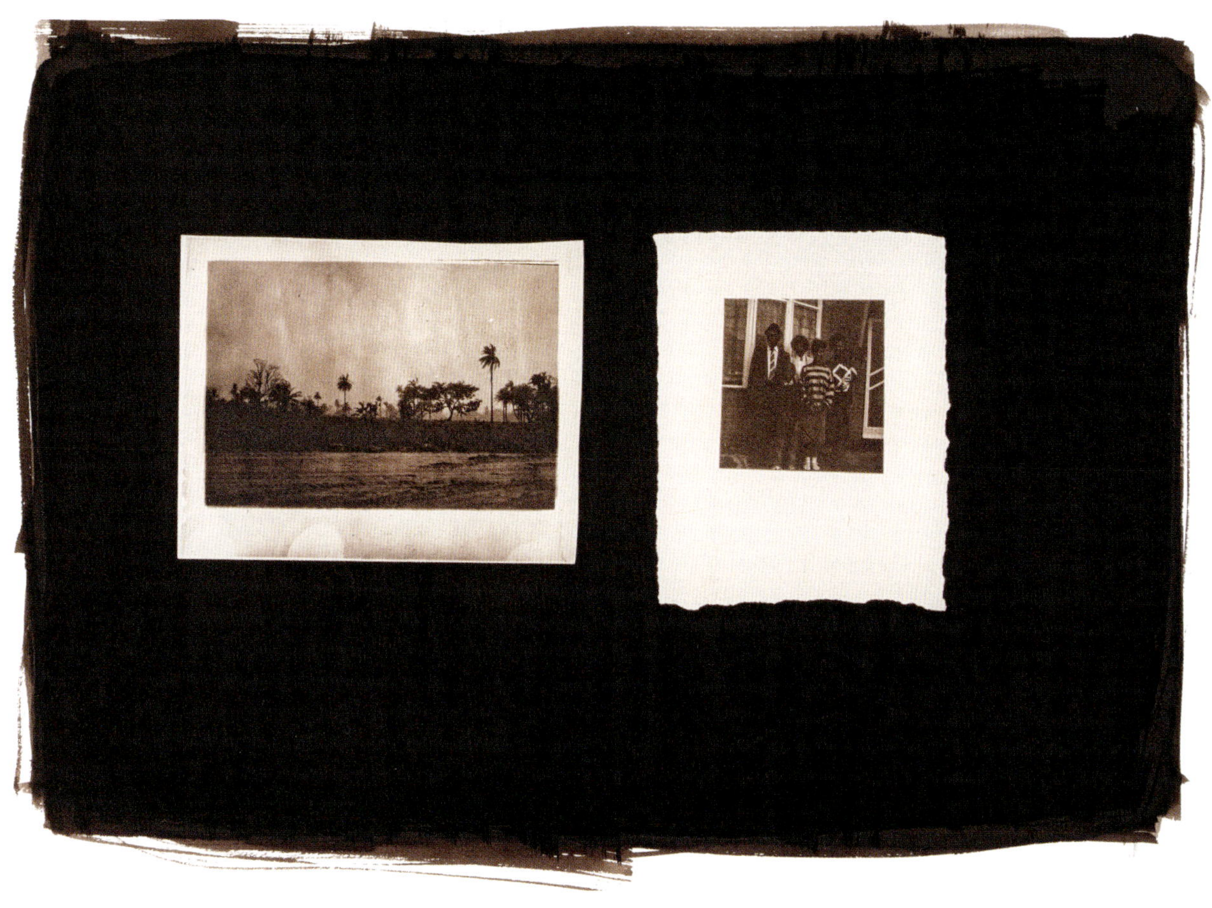

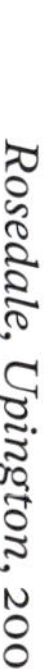

Rosedale, Upington, 2005

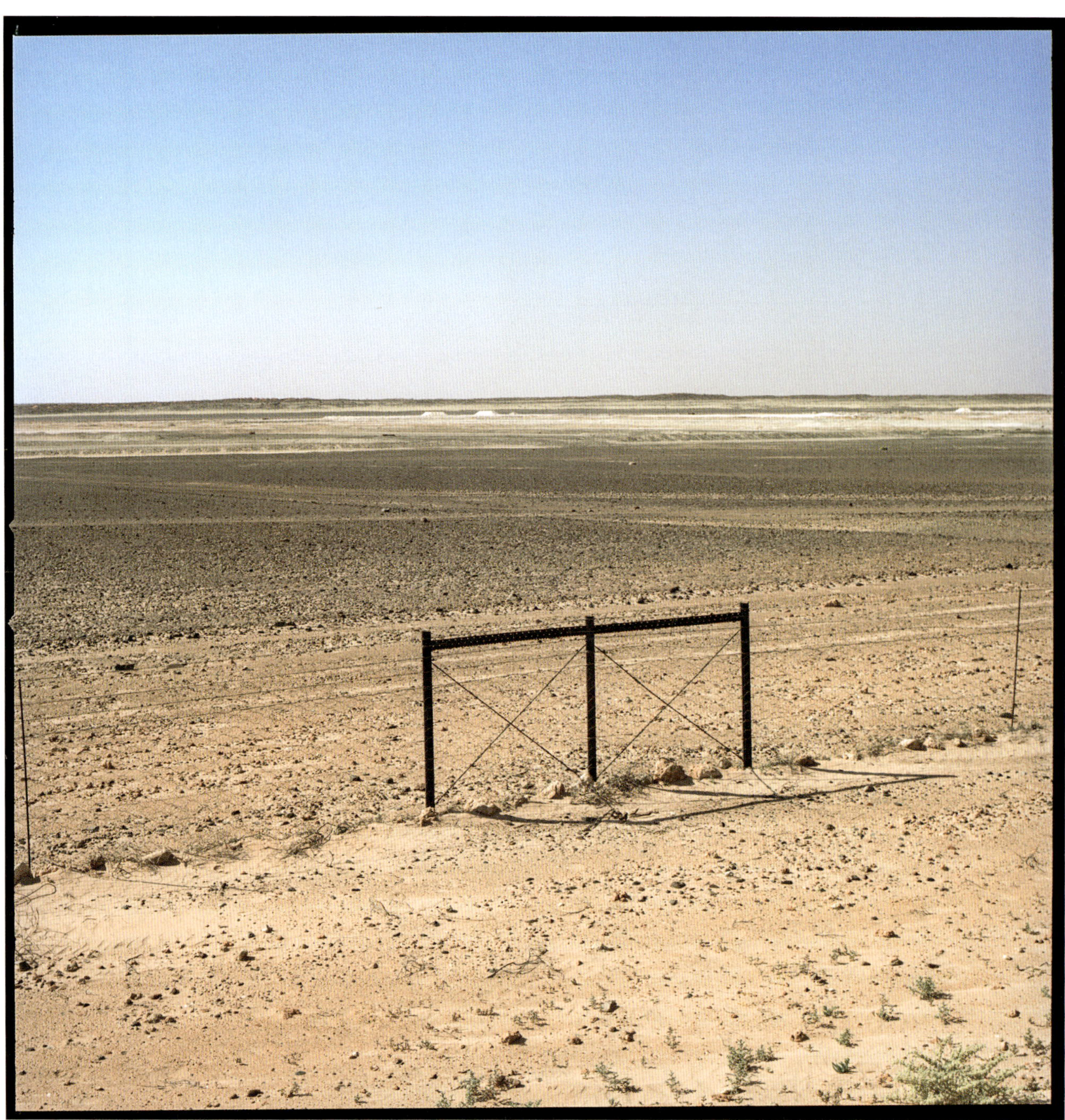

Salt Pan 2, 2005

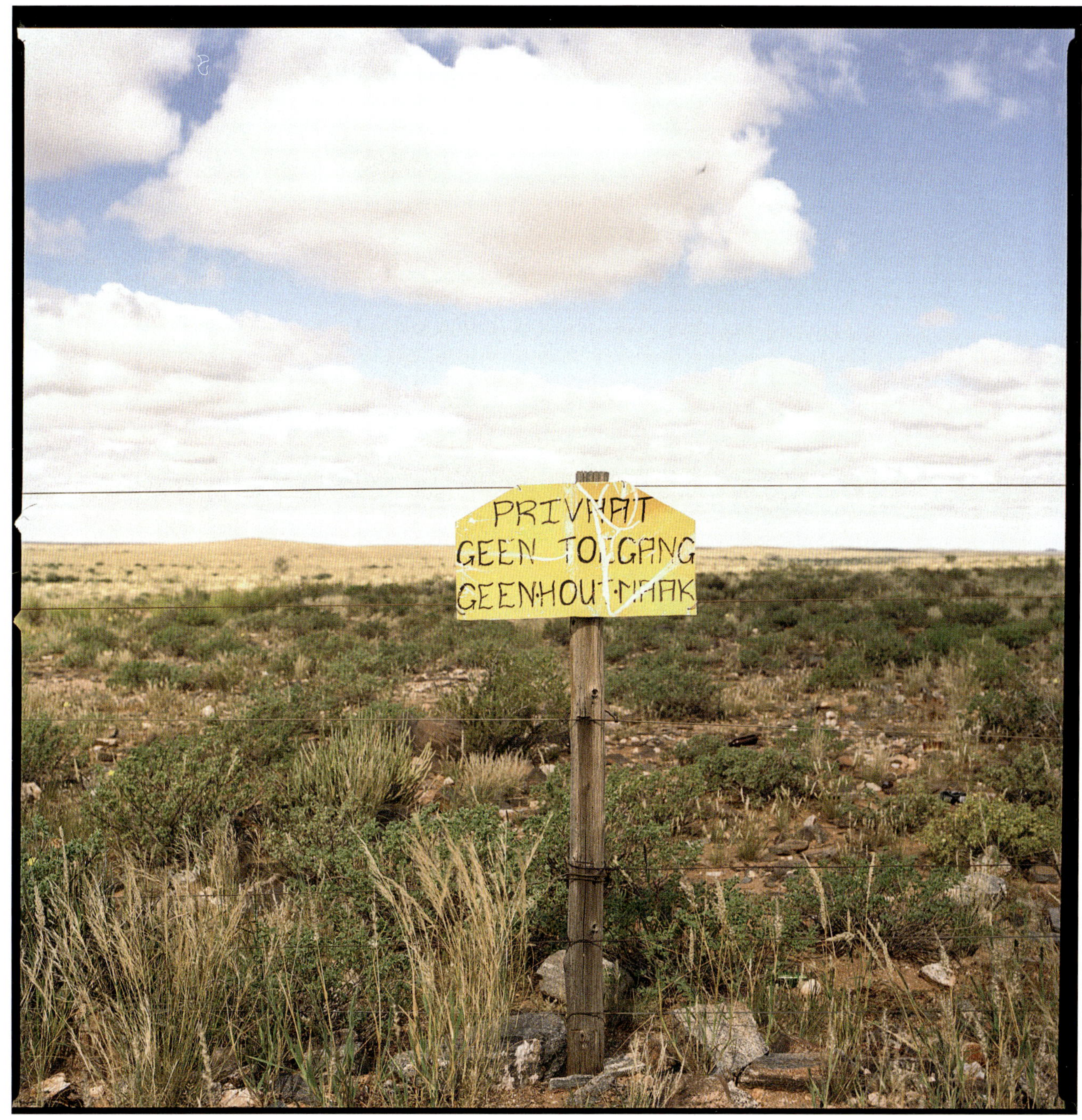

Sign, 2006

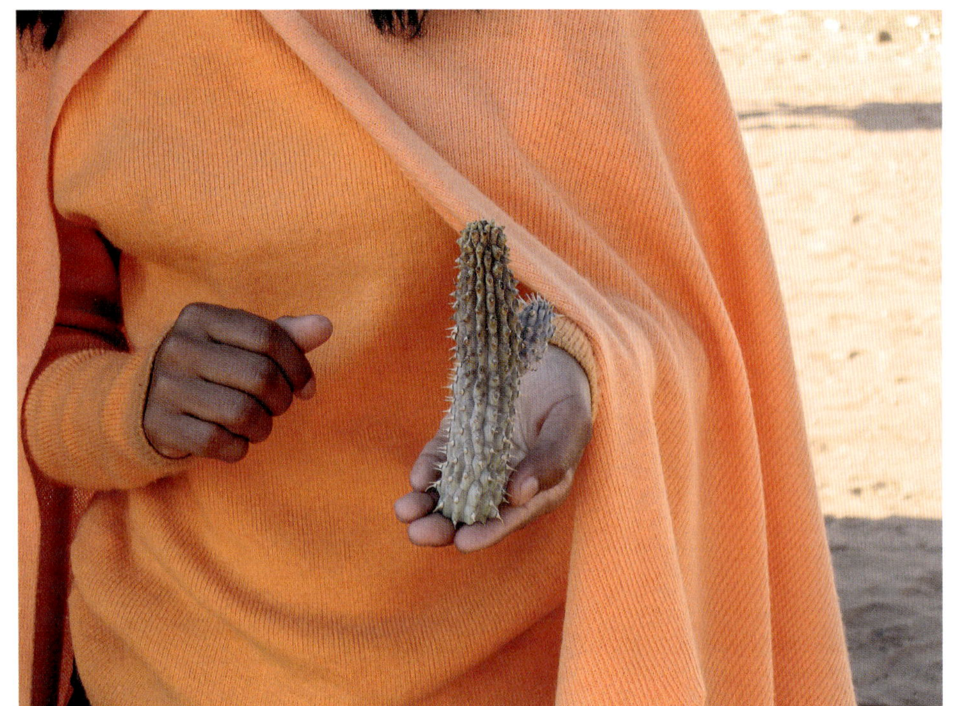

Sarah with Hoodia, 2006

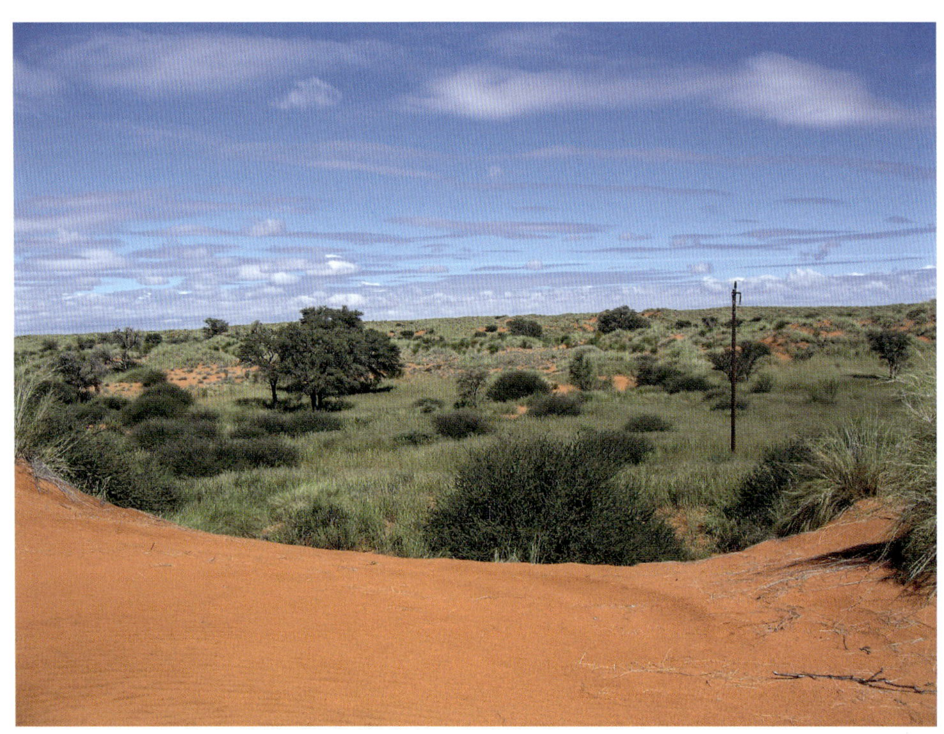

Red Dunes, 2016

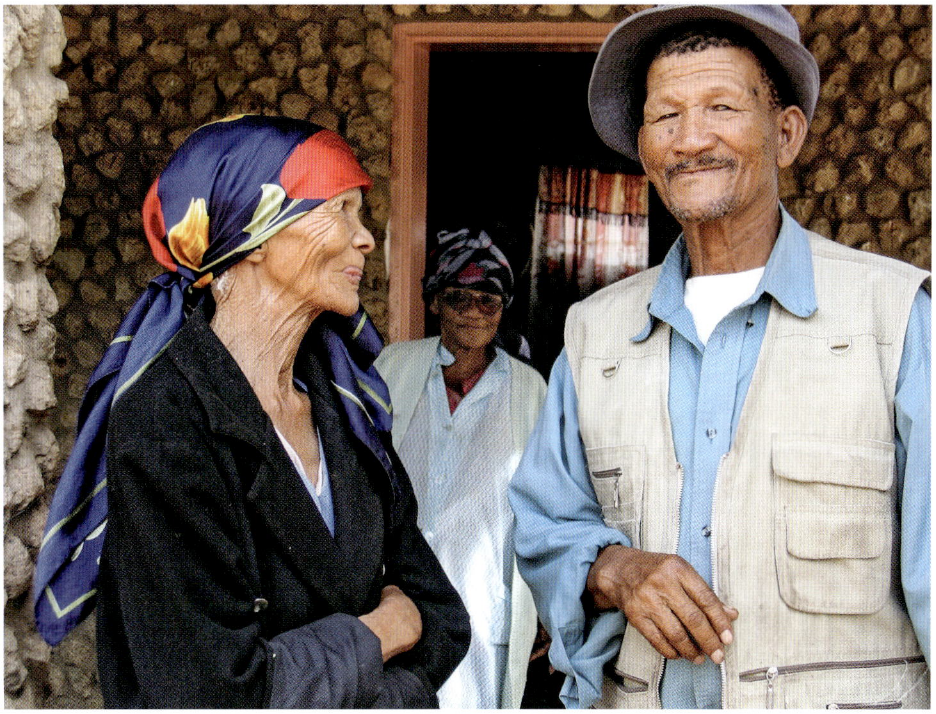

Ouma /una and Piet, 2006

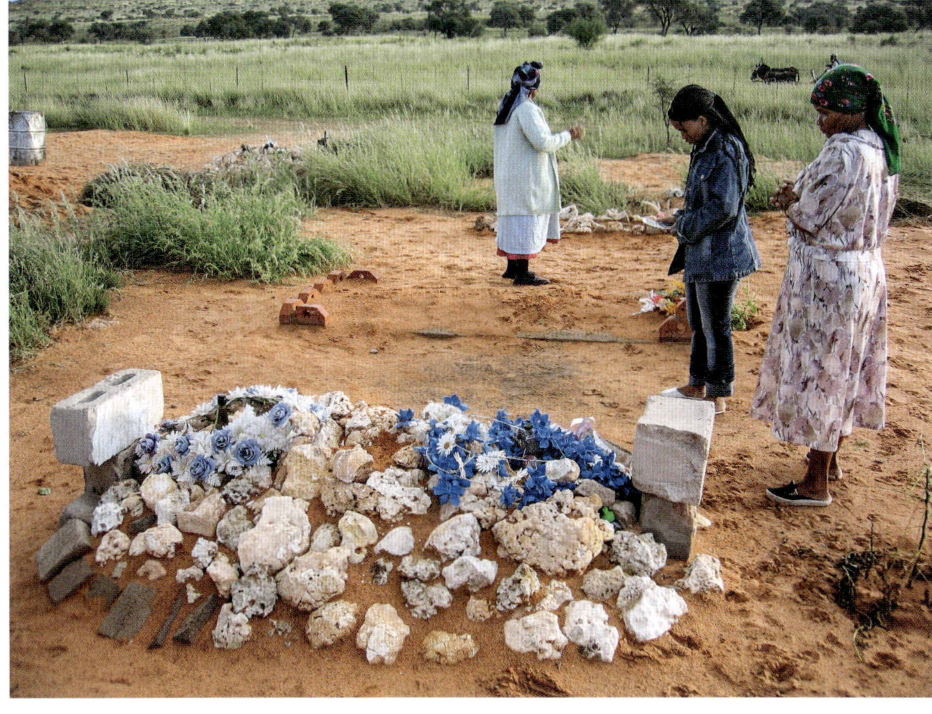

Visiting Ouma Kheis's Grave, 2006

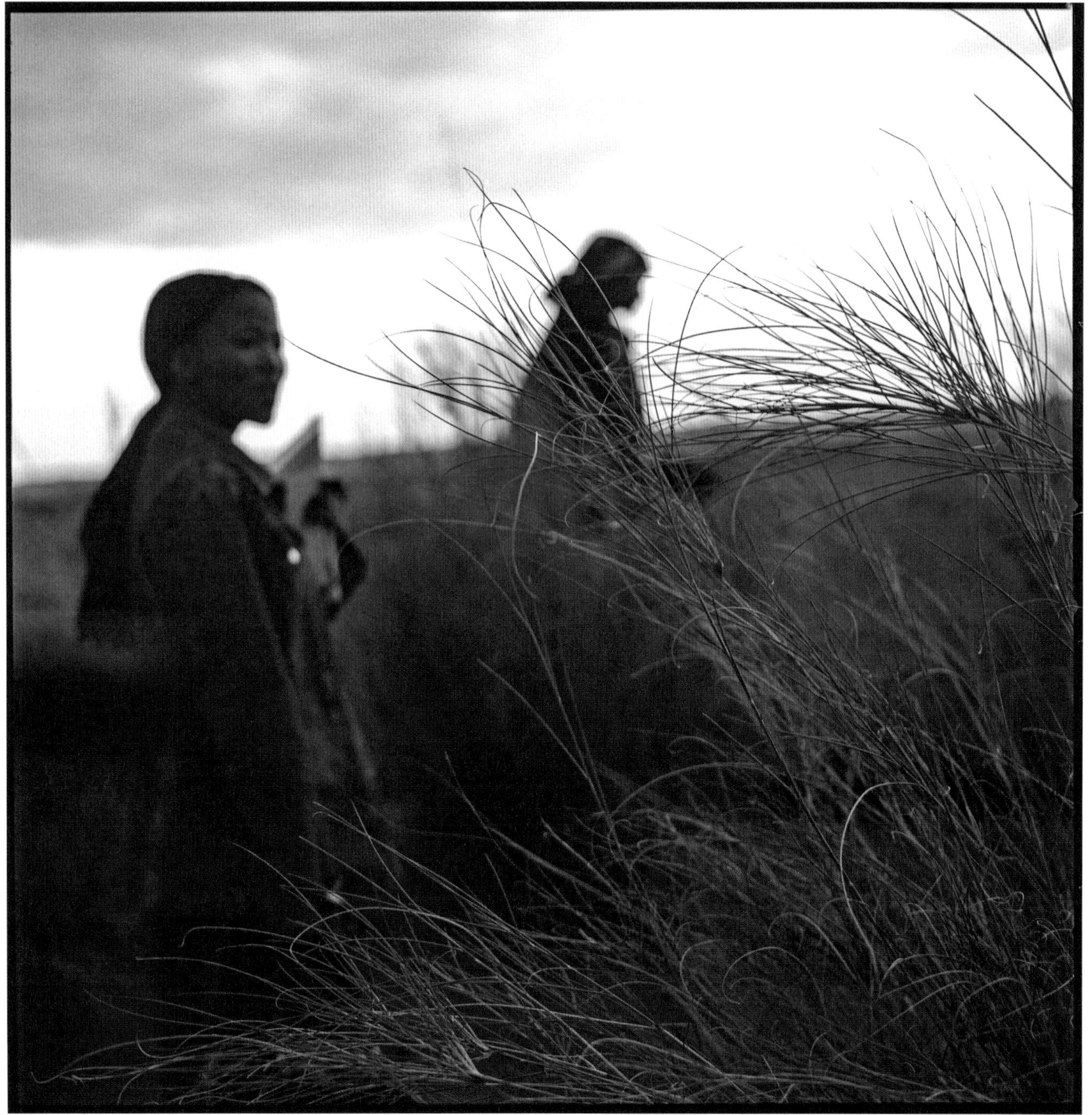

Sara and Ouma |una in the Park, 2006

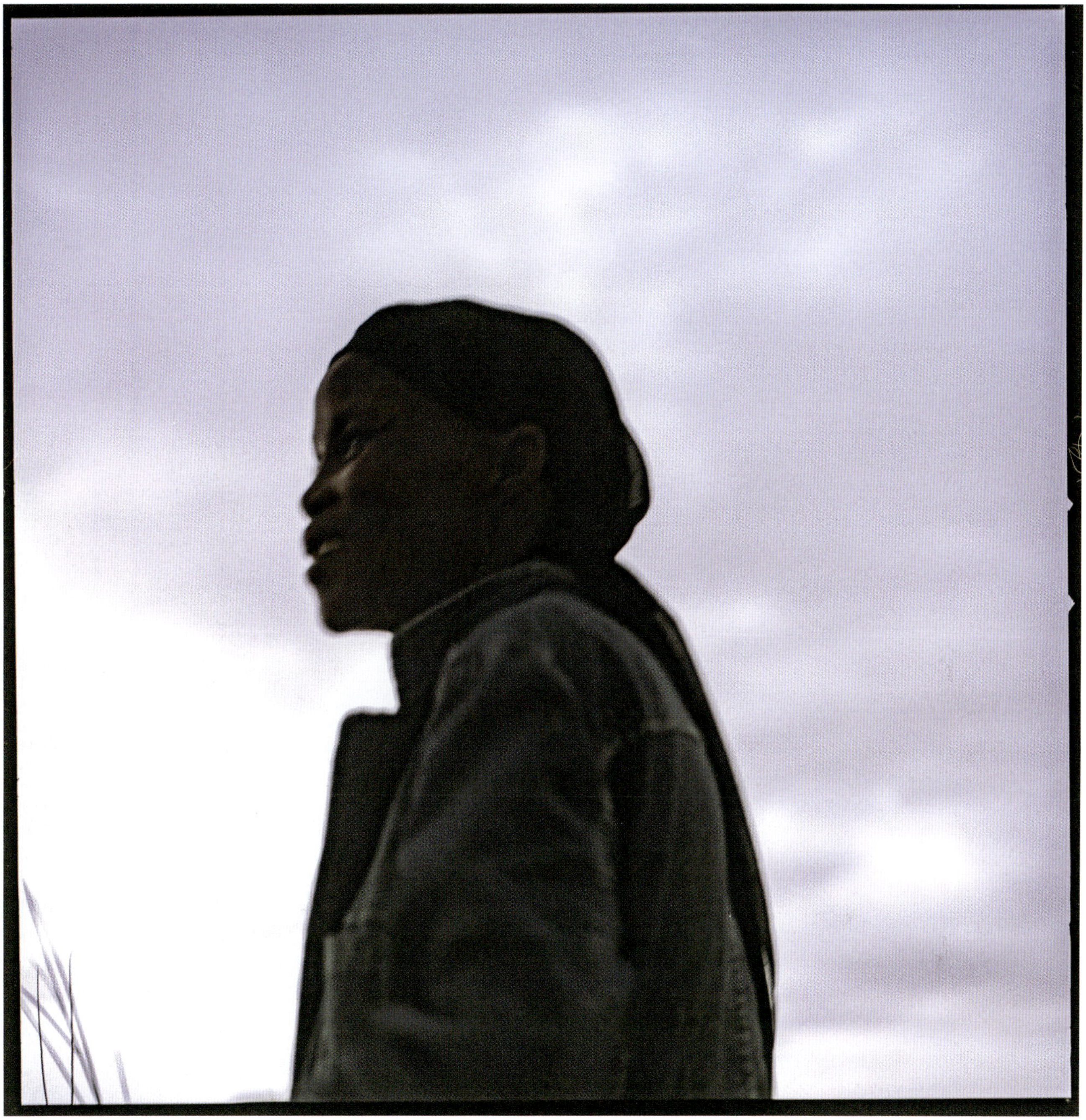

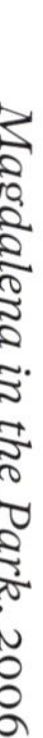

Magdalena in the Park, 2006

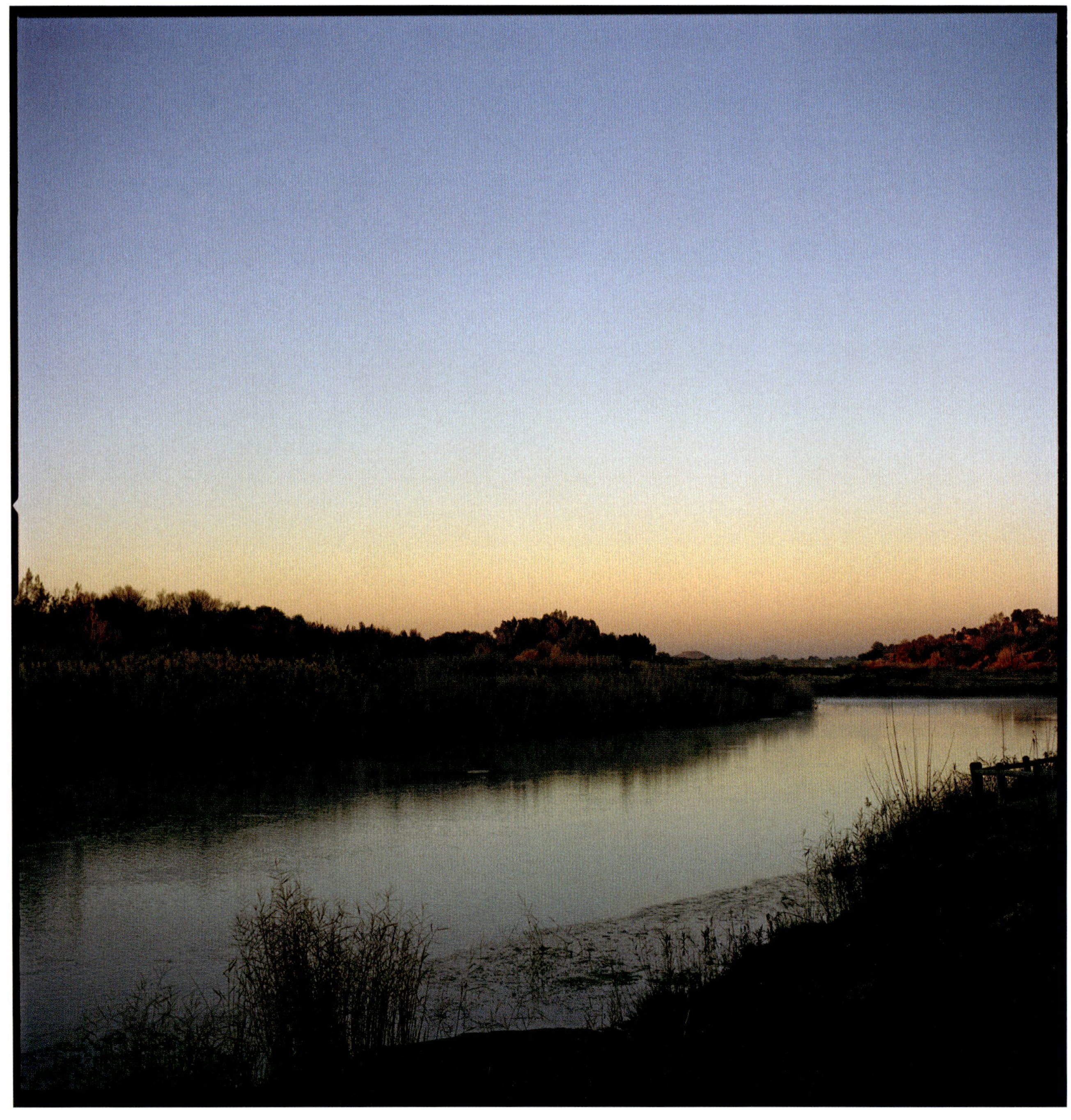

Orange River, Upington, 2005

Nigel, Magdalena and Magdeaena's House

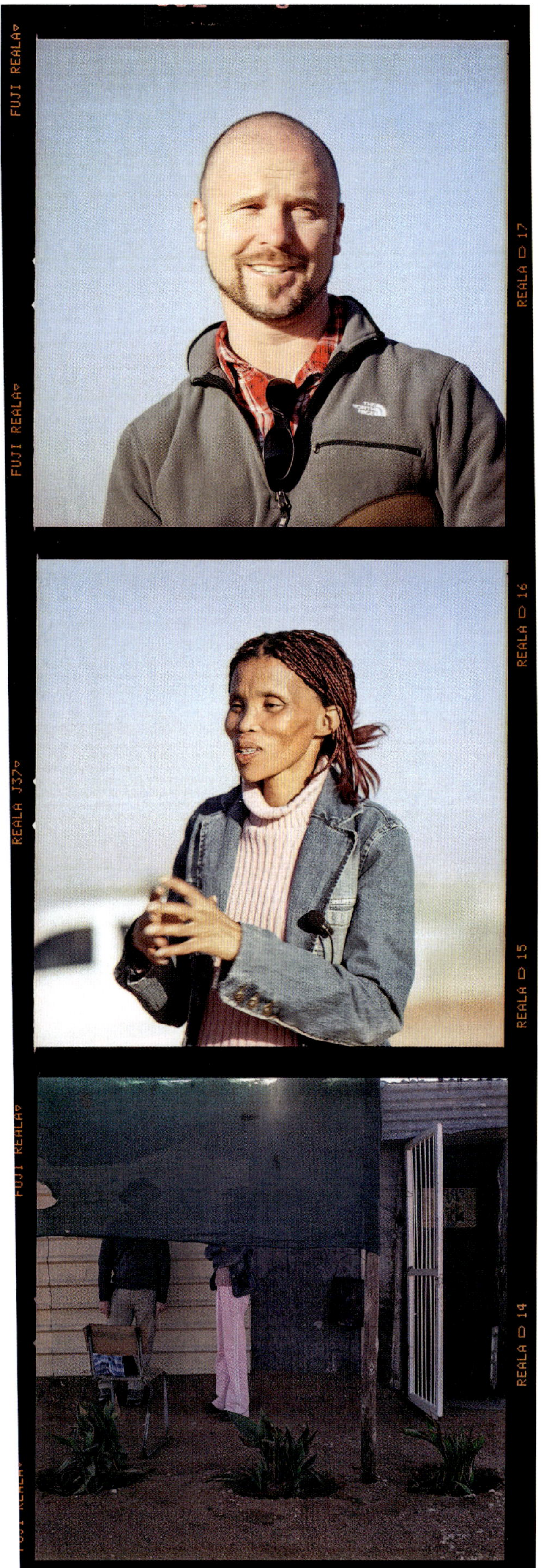

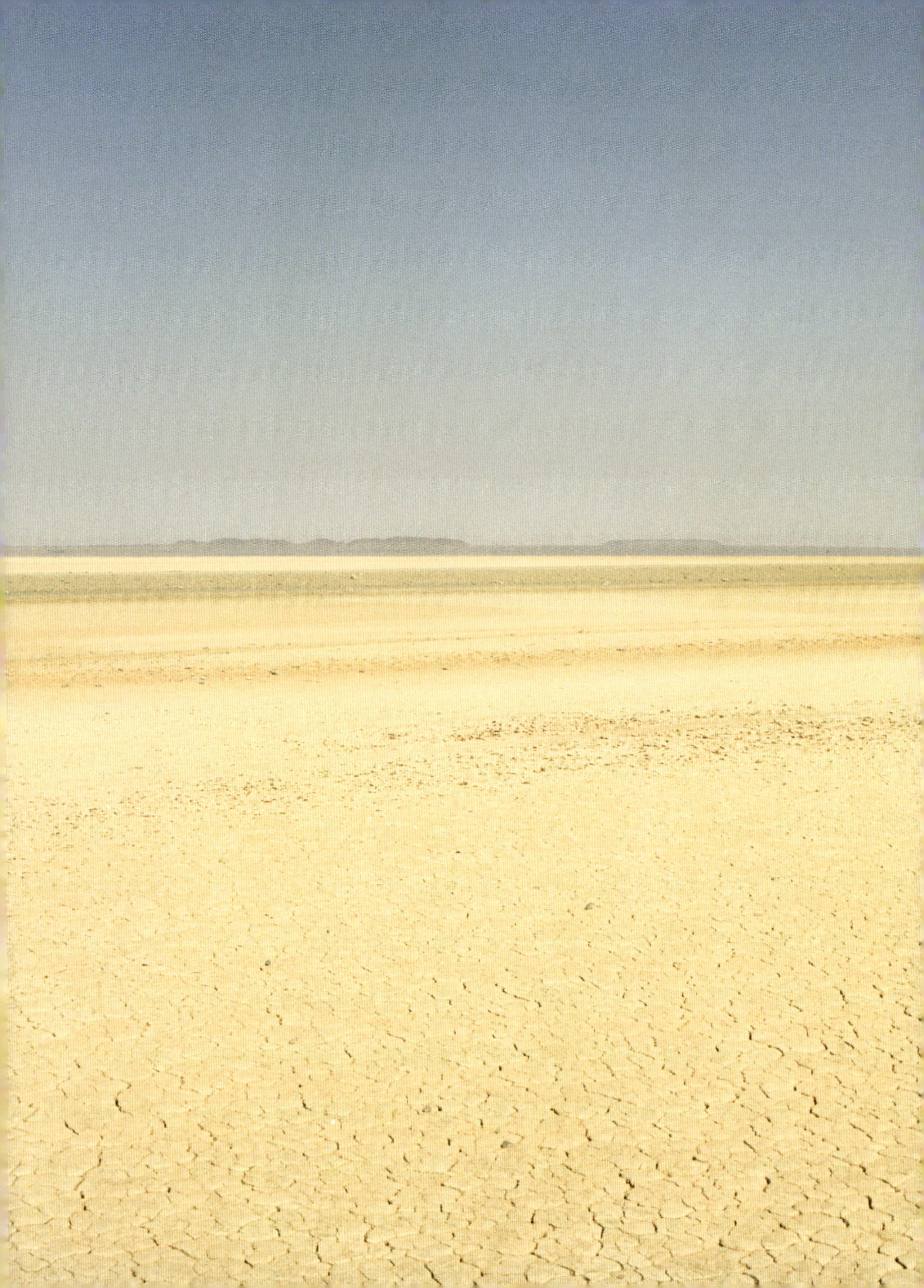

Penny Siopsis

Traces of Journey and Lived Experience

In 2004 Joy made her first of many journeys to the Kalahari, a desert area of South Africa's Northern Cape province. She was keen to engage with local San communities about N|uu dialect of the near extinct language N||ng. Her interest in language and identity had been sparked by a visit to Panama in 1997 after encountering an Afro-Panamanian community who spoke 'frozen' Victorian English. Whilst reflecting Caribbean roots, the language was distinct from that of other descendants of the slave trade, and of Jamaican migrants who came to work in colonial Panama. Joy's personal identity resonates here, but her process of engaging with N|uu was to become less about linguistics than the potential of lost language as an embodied form of communion with 'strange' people with whom she had little cultural affinity, yet as it turns out, a sense of intimate human connection.

'San' is a term for our ancestors who have lived for tens of thousands of years in the Kalahari, a region including Botswana and parts of Namibia.[1] Traditionally hunters and gatherers, their form of subsistence has been all but eroded by colonisation, war and other forms of dispossession; fences and farms now crisscross the land, their spiritual home. Languages are near extinct, and Afrikaans has become the means of communication.

The story of the San is politicised, with questions of representation and stereotyping persisting even amidst increasing recognition of how

1 Also described under the broad term Khomani-San. Other names have featured over time, and members often refer to themselves as Bushmen, although this term, with its colonial derivation, is generally regarded as derogatory.

Indigenous knowledge systems teach us the possibilities of communication and connection to land.

I ask Joy about the implications for her practice that has for years focused on the visual image to critique colonialism:

> *I wanted to see if aspects of language work could help shift my ways of looking at identity – to think about identity less centered on physical appearance, as is so often the case with work on race. Lost languages, being invisible, so to speak, came to resonate.*

Seeking critical engagement, Joy journeyed to Broome in Australia to attend a conference, 'Maintaining the Links: Language, Identity and the Land' hosted by the Foundation for Endangered Languages. There she met Nigel Crawhall of the South African San Institute (SASI) and Director of UNESCO's Secretariat for the Indigenous Peoples of Africa Coordinating Committee. She was intrigued by his discussion of Ouma Keis and Ouma |una, two San who had been 'displayed' on the Empire exhibition in Johannesburg in 1936 as children, and who were living in the Kalahari. Nigel accompanied Joy on her first visit to the community, introducing her to them.[2]

Joy's research came to embrace many forms, including listening to digitised copies of N|uu recordings made from wax cylinders by a scientific expedition to the Kalahari in 1936, coinciding with the Empire exhibition at Wits University.[3] Johannesburg had already impacted on Joy's creative life – in 1995 she represented Britain on the first Johannesburg Biennale.

Many threads come together in Joy's Kalahari project and take different forms of presentation – still and moving images, text and documentation. The different dimensions are not driven by aesthetic and conceptual

2 Nigel had spent years researching N|uu, for his PhD at the University of Cape Town looking at its social and linguistic history and the demise and identity of its speakers. Nigel had helped to locate one of the last remaining speakers of N|uu, Elsie Vaalbooi, who he had interviewed in support of a land claim by San descendants – Adriesvale, 1999. This was after Elsie's son, Petros Valbooi, first chairperson of Khomani Association and SASI, alerted Nigel to his mother's unique 'click' language. The claim was successful. Roger Chennells a human rights lawyer for SASI, was involved in the claim. Elsie's voice, her spoken N|uu, became the physical evidence of the community's rightful claim to the land. Petros was later to find another speaker, Anna Kassie, in Rosedale, where Joy met her daughter Magdelena.

3 A group of San were displayed ostensibly to raise awareness of the threat they faced regarding loss of land and traditions.

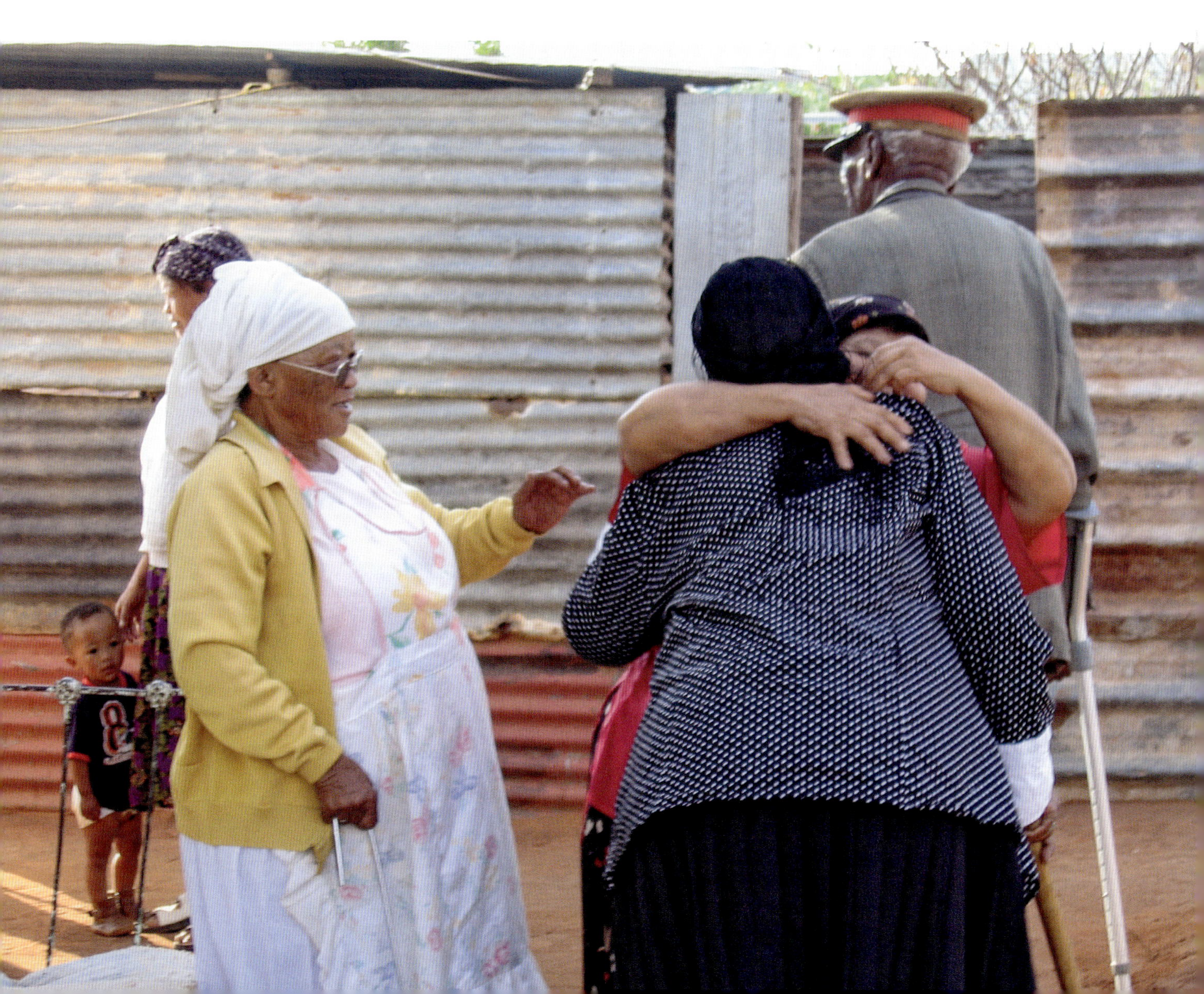

Oumas Anna & Johanna with Oupa Andries greeting family in Olifantshoek, 2005

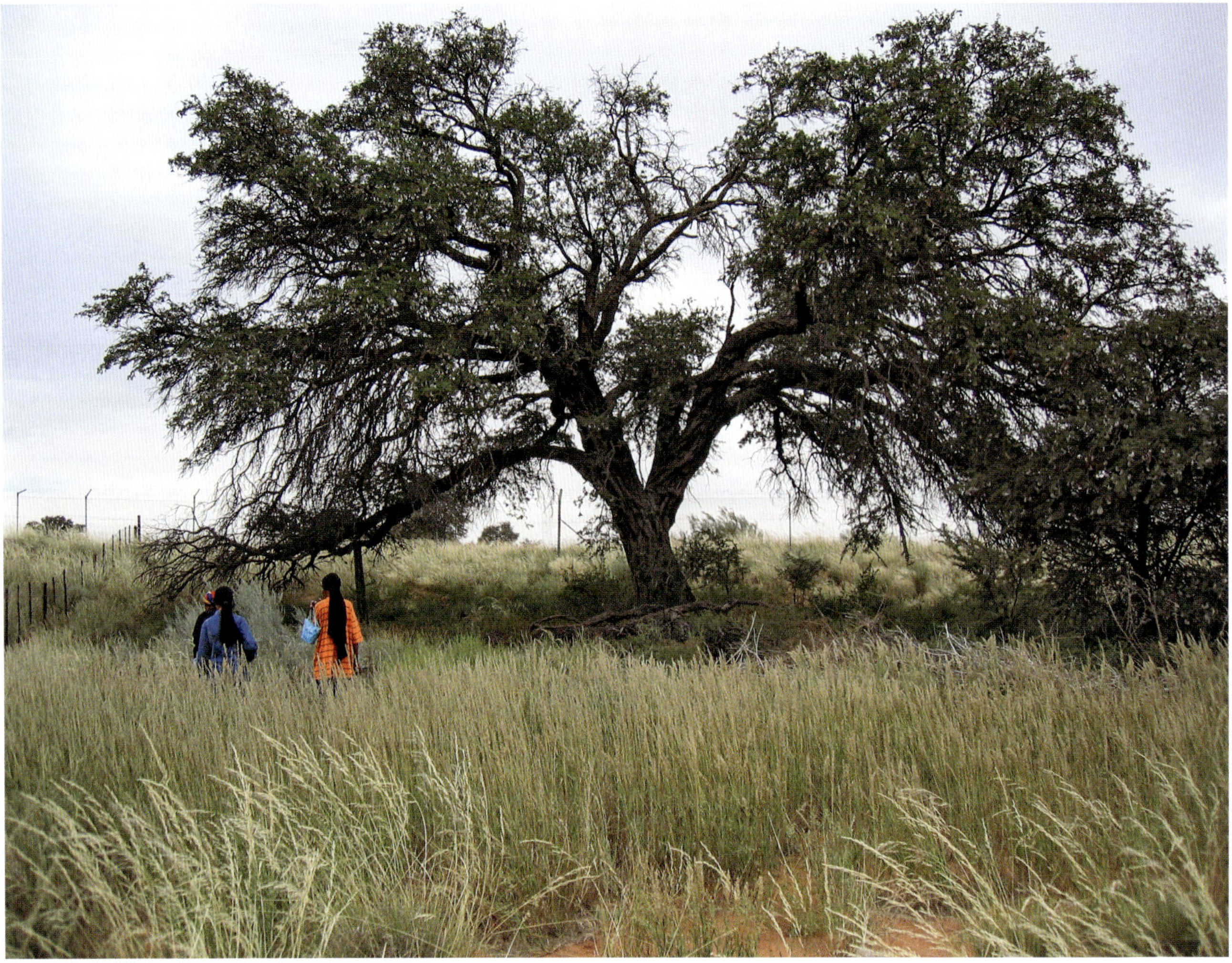

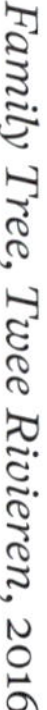

Family Tree, Twee Rivieren, 2016

choices alone, but by the traces of journey and lived experience that thrive in other forms characteristic of her very particular quality of human engagement.

Often this manifests in practical terms. Joy arrives in the region in a hired car. Some community members are intrigued that she comes alone. They are used to people travelling with support structures, researchers, assistants. And she doesn't speak Afrikaans!

'I come to a strange place,' she reflects.

> *I have a car. I'm with people who'd like to get around to see relatives in other remote townships. So, we hop into the vehicle and head for Adriesvale, the farm and land they won in the land claim. A third of the language community is in my car. We go from Rosedale to Raaswater, Swartkop near the Orange River, then it's Olifantshoek before driving across the desert to Askham, the settlement with a shop – a few things are needed after the journey. I'm with people who have no idea who I am, and I have no idea who they are … They sense though that I'm not there to analyse them and record their pictures … On the first trip I take Ouma Kheis to the hospital … On the second Ouma |una marches me with Magdelena and Sara across the desert dunes and across the border into Botswana. I'm worried I don't have a visa! Ouma |una shows me her birth tree. She reads the lion tracks there in the sand!*

In April 2025 Joy returns to the Kalahari, going from Cape Town in a regional bus. 'Aunty Joy' is welcomed with open arms by the community. They travel to Ouma |una's tree, now called 'the family tree'. They share photos of their ancestors. Joy names this segment of her project *Legacy*.

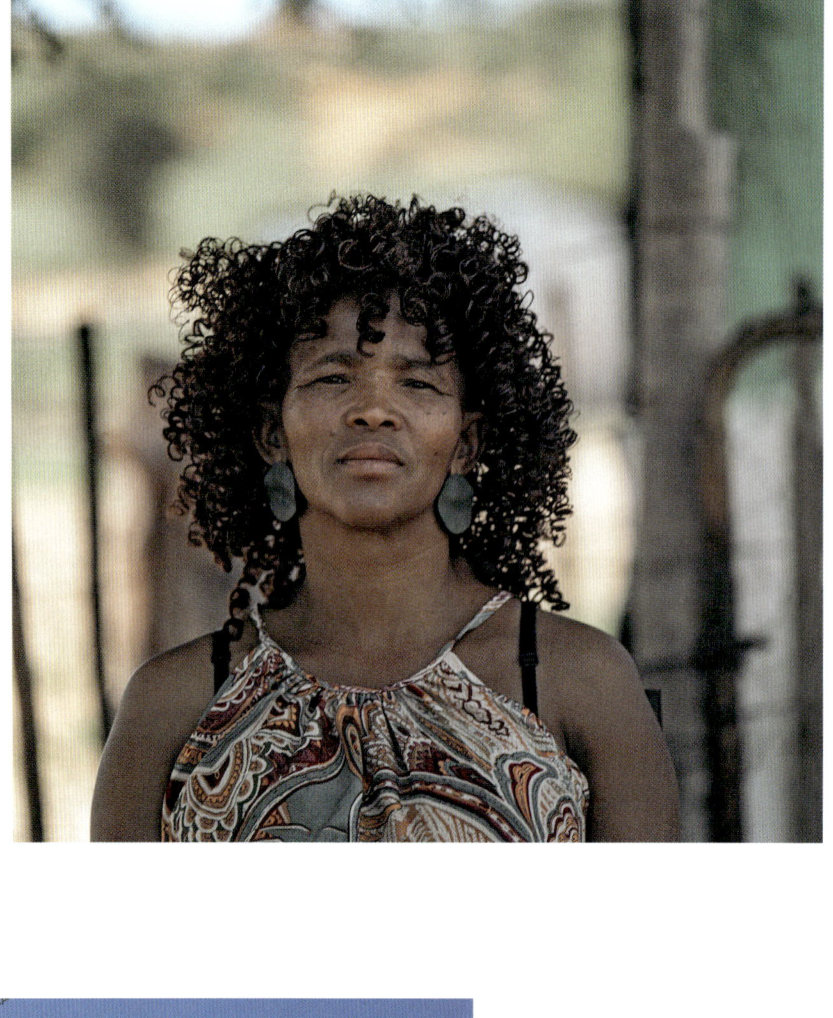

Sara Rooi

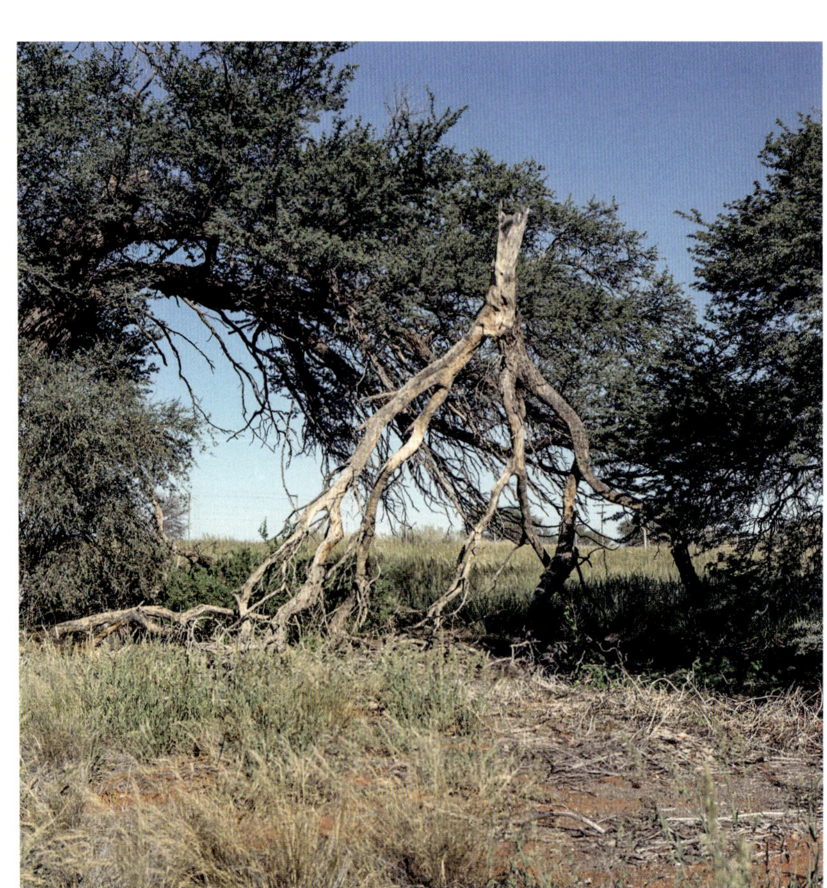

Broken Branch, (Family Tree)

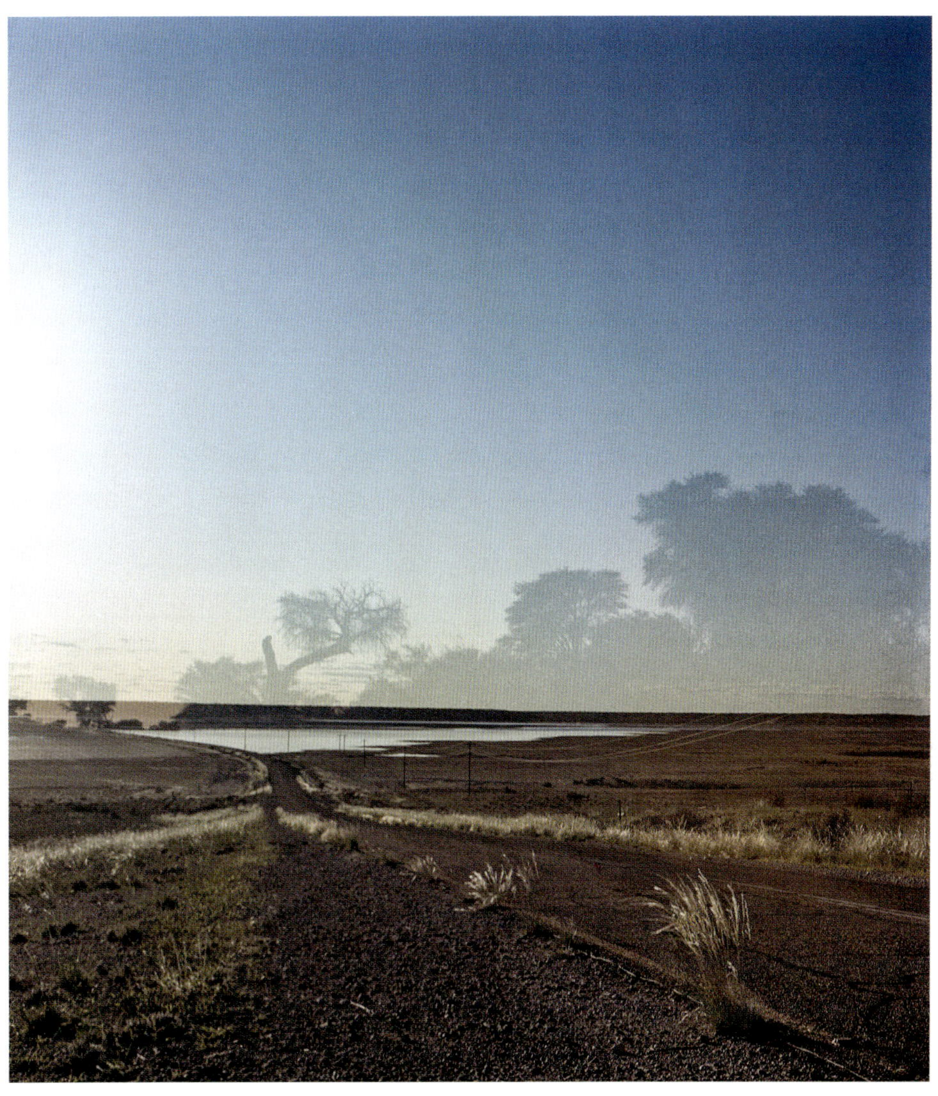

Koo Pan, Mier

Sussie Bock

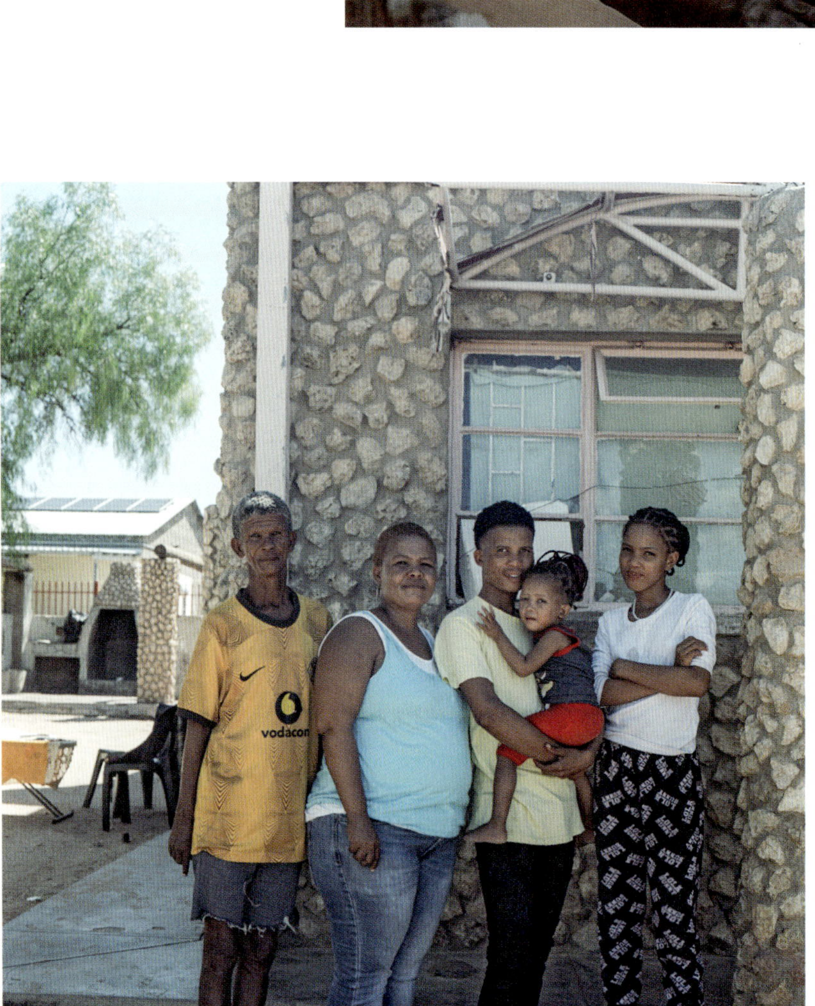

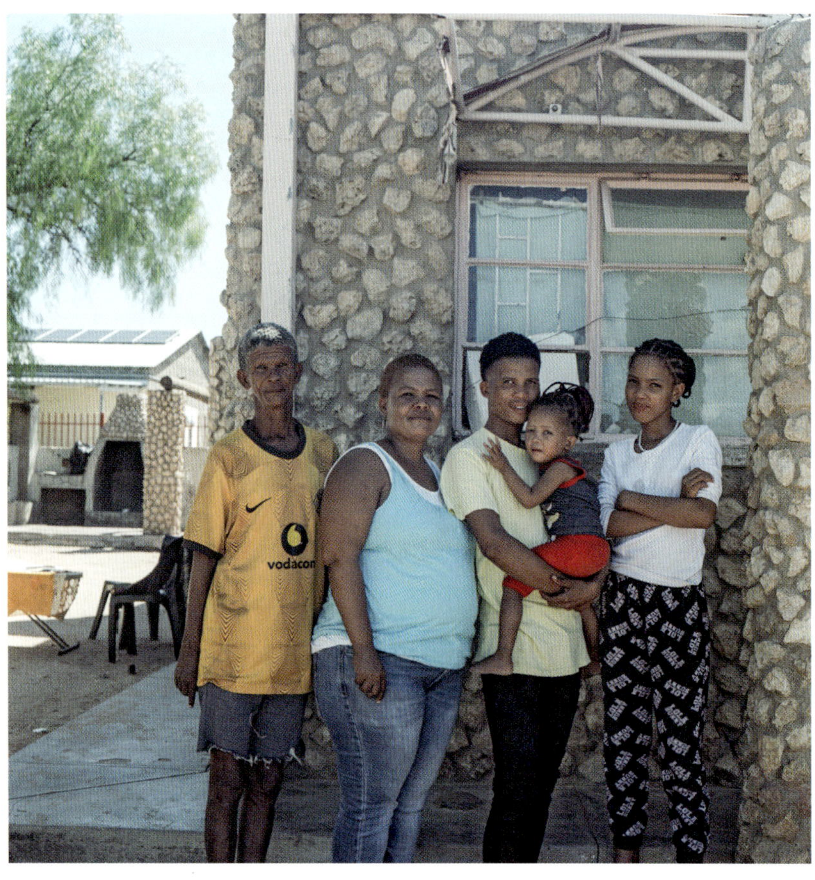

Juanita with her Family

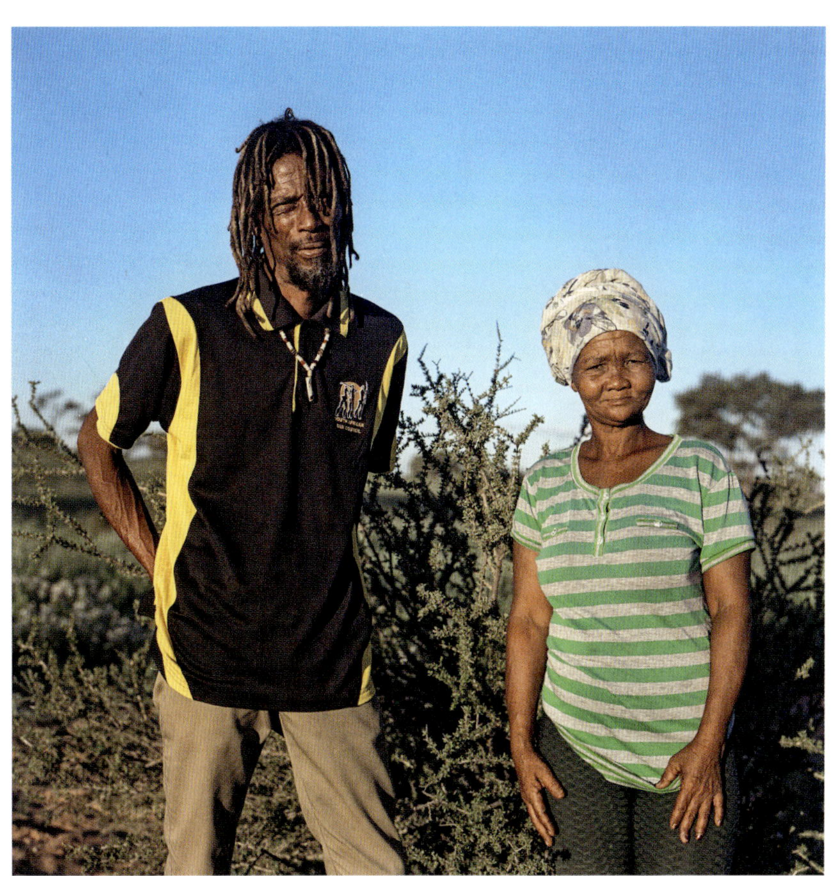

Oupa Jan & Oulet

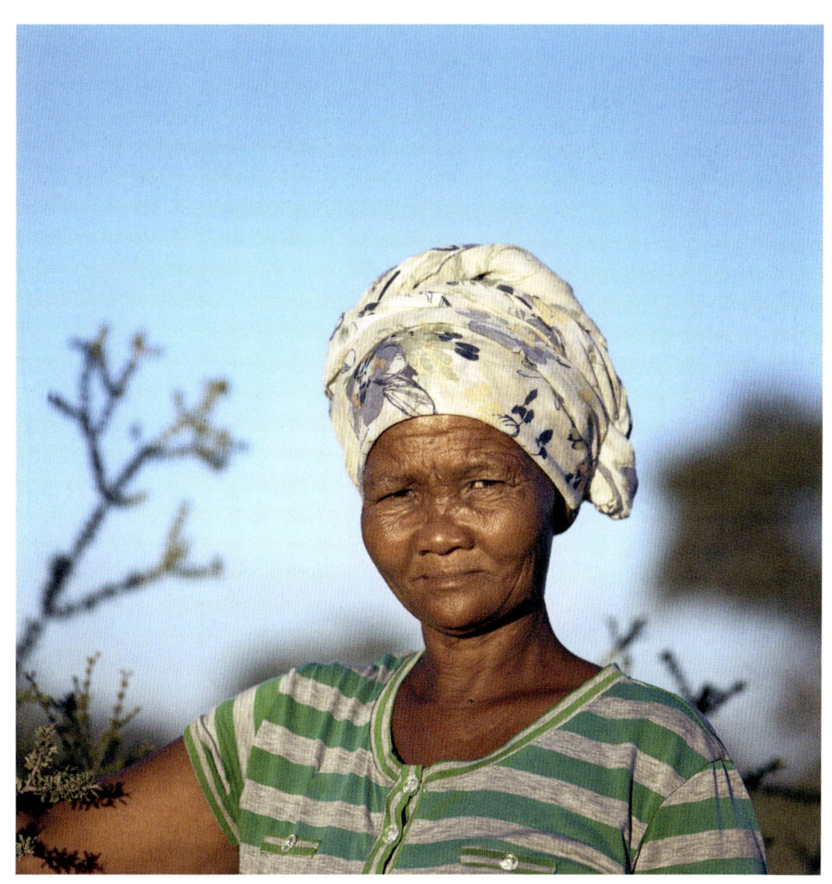

Oulet

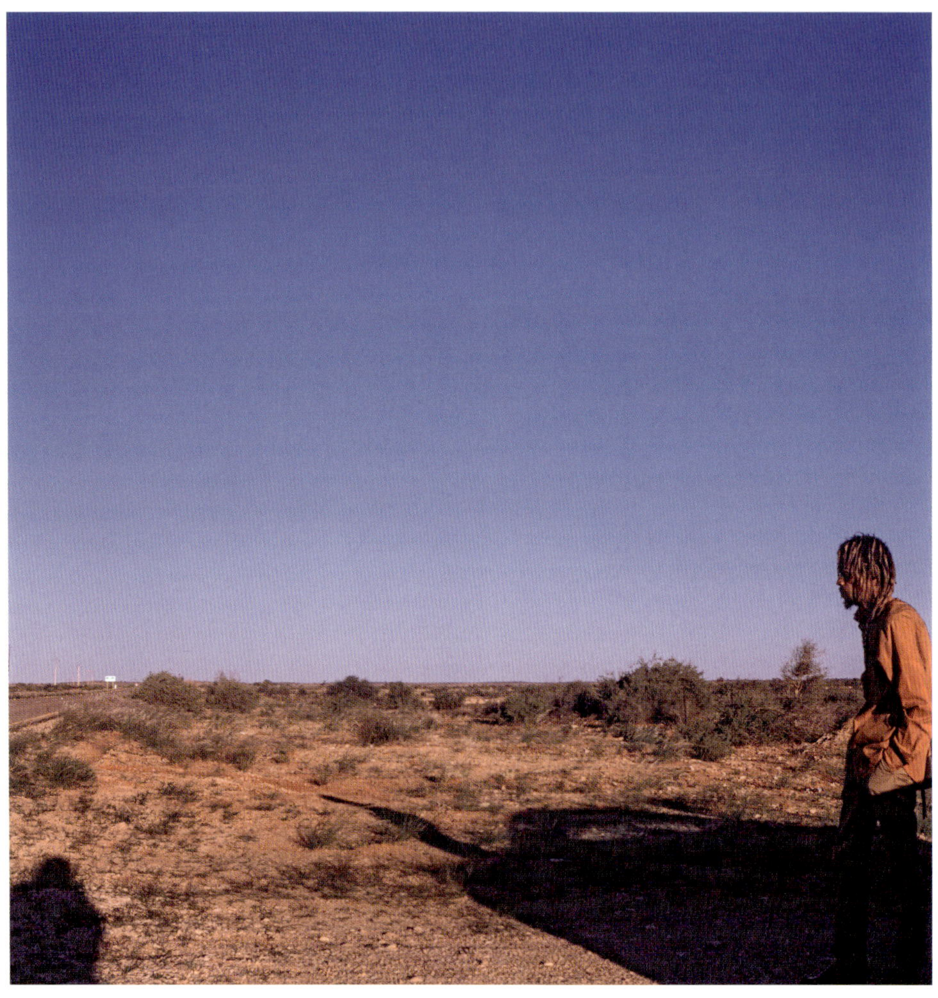

Oupa Jan at Koo Pan

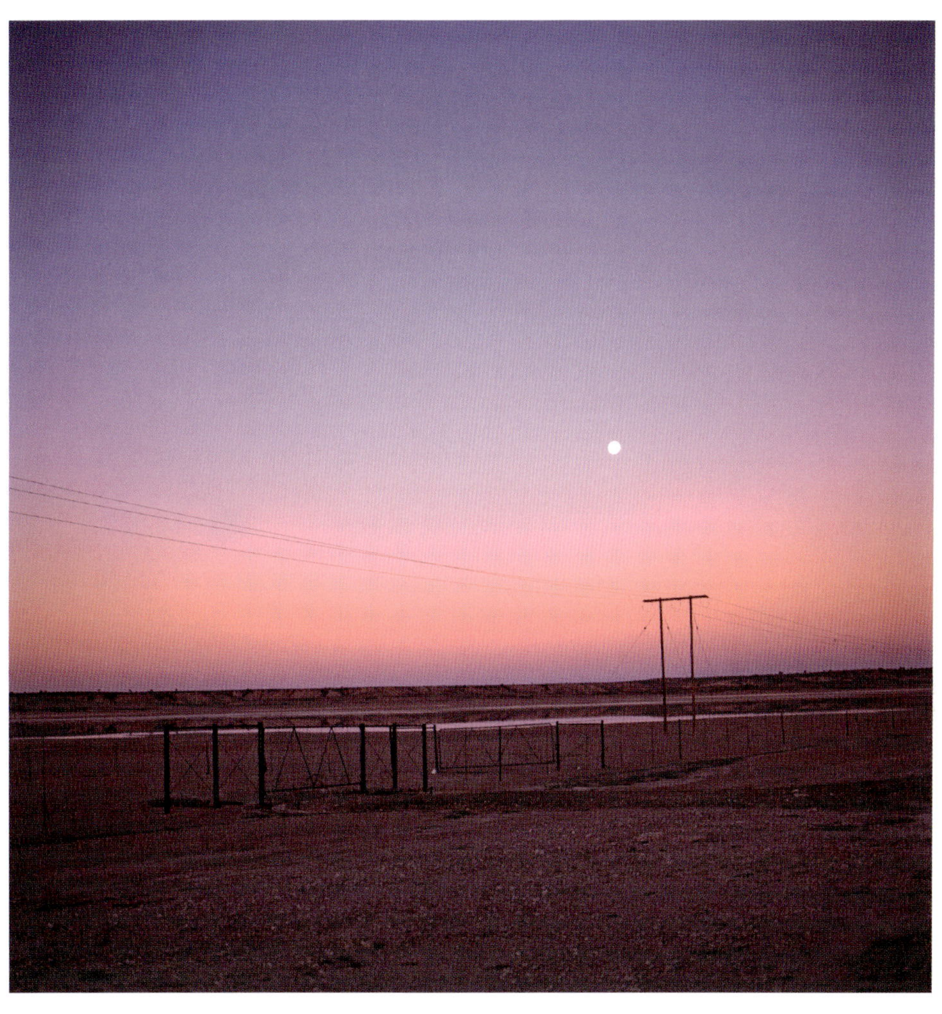

Koo Pan at Sunset

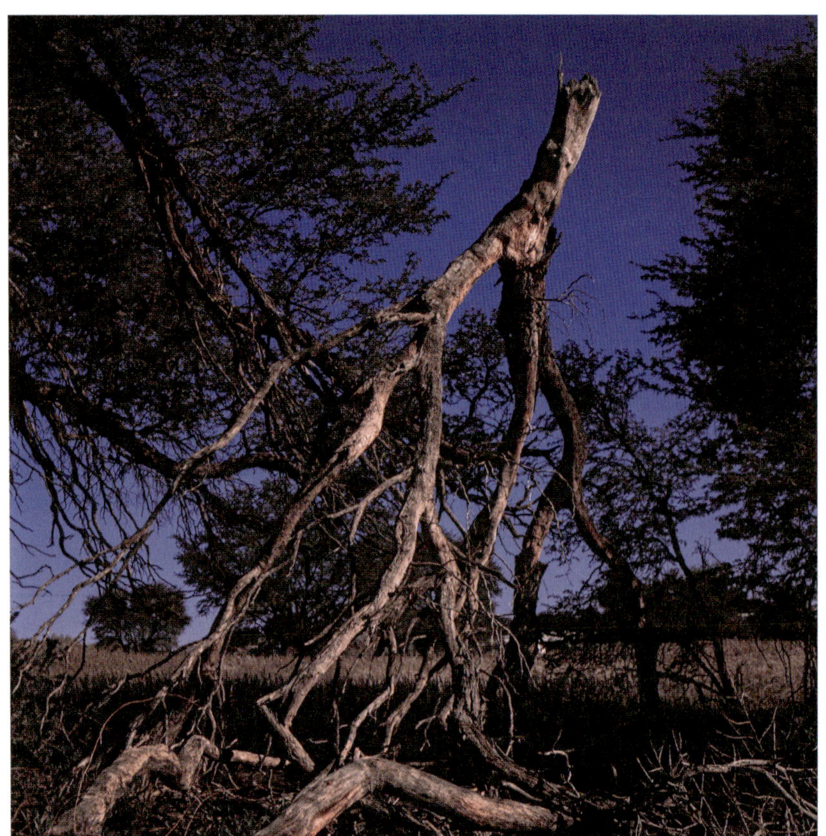

Family Tree, Broken branch

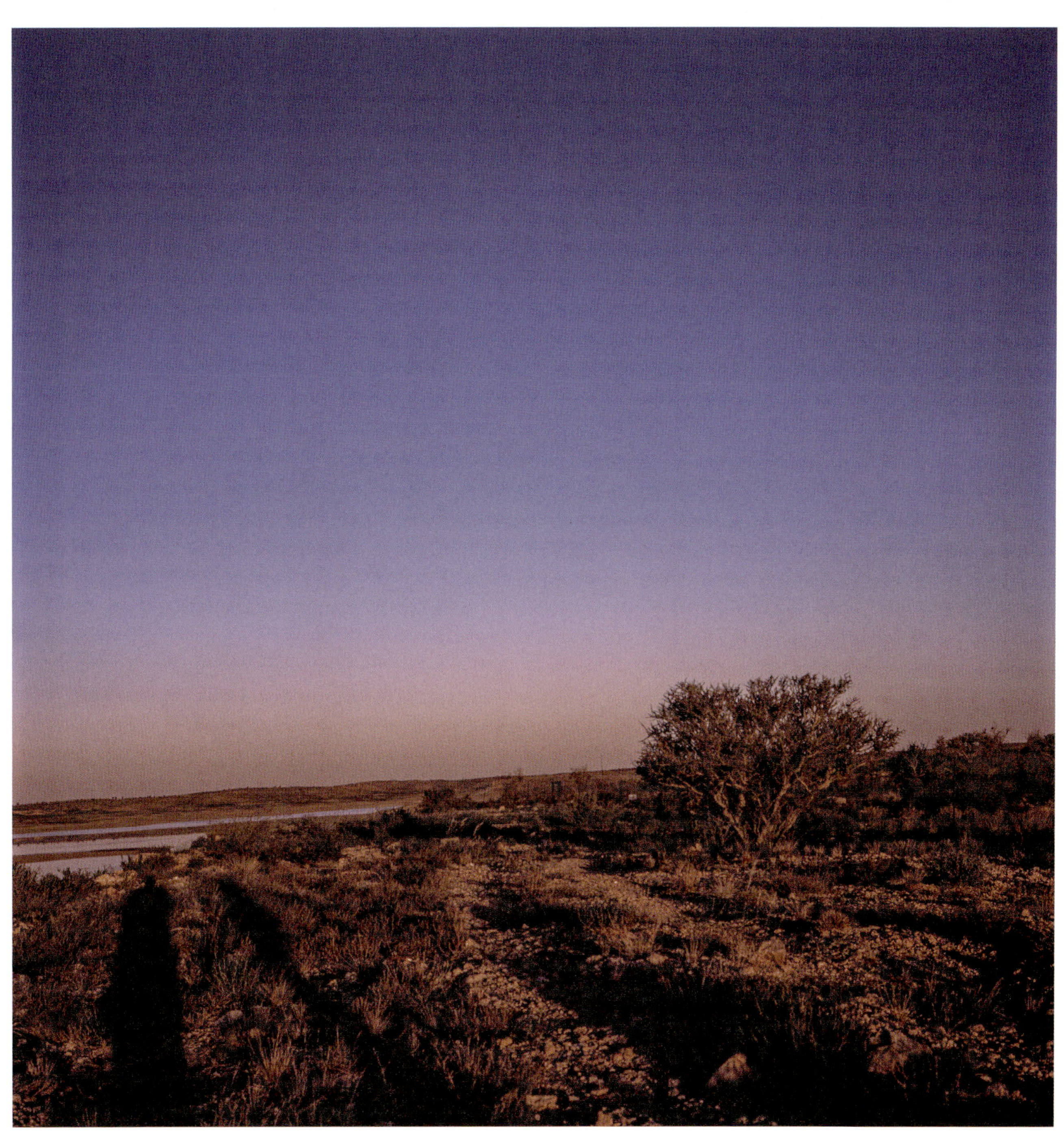

Dusk at Koo Pan

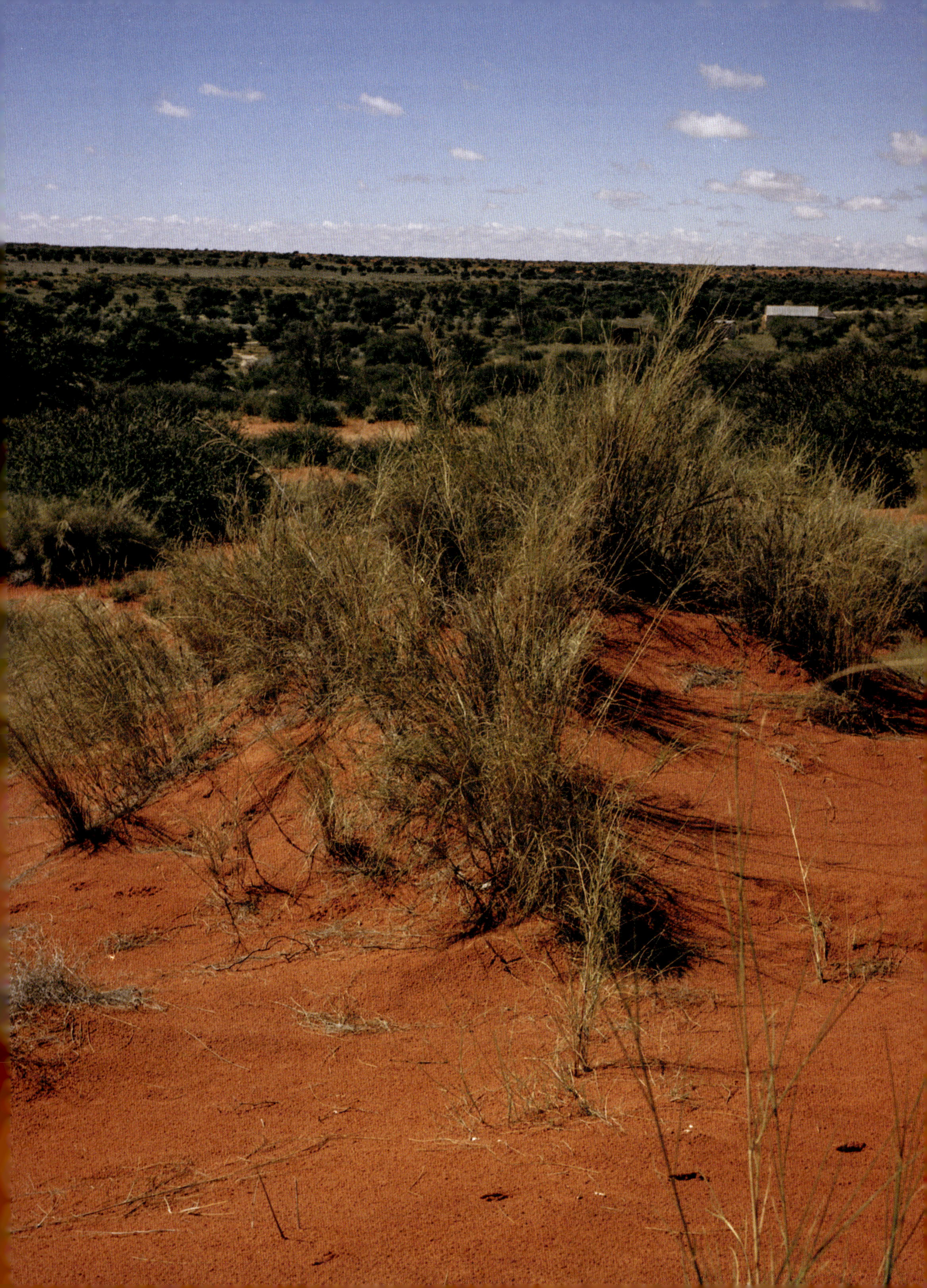

Journey,

Archives,

Voice and Power

Brook Garru Andrew I was just reflecting on when we first met at Gasworks in London. Can you remember what you were working on in that amazing studio you had?

Joy Gregory I think I had handbags in my studio on the walls from *The Handbag Project* (1998–present). I had just come back from South Africa and I was working on *Memory and Skin* (1998) around that time.

BGA What is *Memory and Skin* about?

JG It began with a journey around the Caribbean, and it was for me to try and understand who I was, because my parents had come from Jamaica. I'd only ever heard about Jamaica. I didn't realise it was part of a massive archipelago. It begins on the east coast of the Americas, from Miami down to Venezuela and all the way around until you start hitting Brazil. I travelled around that, trying to really understand where I'd supposedly come from. Of course, I came back more confused than ever because everybody from across the planet was there, you know, from Syrians to Chinese, to Japanese, to every European, and Indigenous people, and everybody's all mixed up.

Before I started this tour, I went with my parents to Jamaica because they wanted to come and show me where they'd come from and meet the family, and also the land, because land is very important.

BGA Do you have a sense of belonging to the land? I know that many Indigenous people or people of diaspora have a longing

Red Earth from The Kalahari, 2016

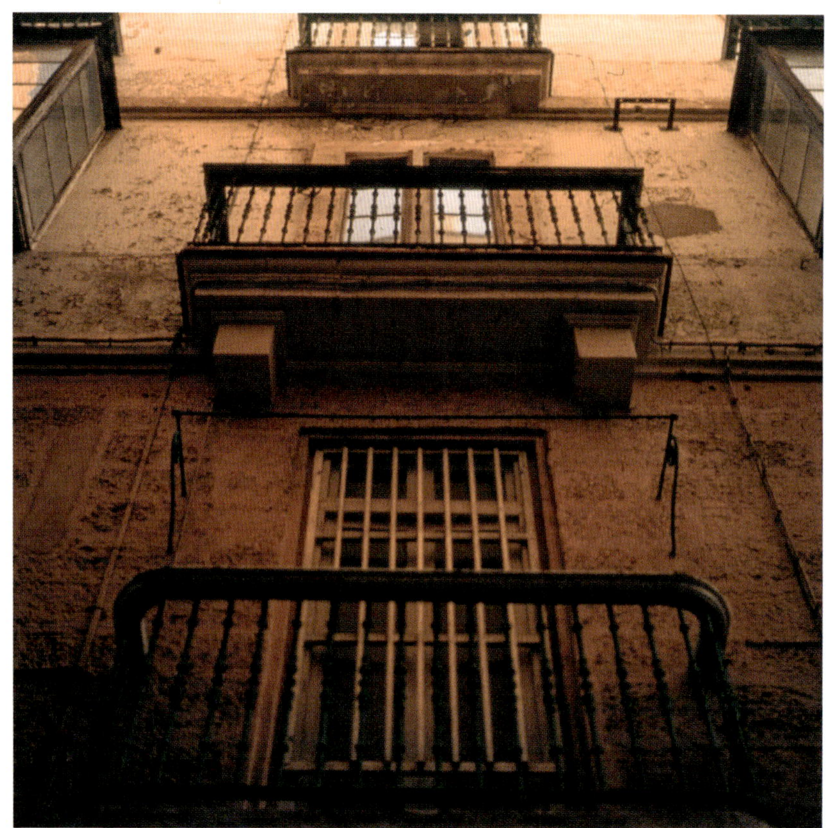

Watching Windows, Nantes

or tie to a land, which can be spiritual or about ancestry. Is there something that affects you still like a longing?

JG I don't feel as connected to it as, say, my brother, who was actually born there. My dad wanted to go home. He really wanted to go home and live out his last few years on the family land, do a bit of farming, eat mangos straight off the tree, and boil his own chocolate. My mother felt more tied to her children, so she didn't want to go, because the kids had no intention. But I do know that she did have that strong connection to her land, because every time she went there, she would go to the family land.

BGA These stories about connecting to land are really important. You said that you wanted to have a concept of where you came from, and going on this tour of the Caribbean led to creating the work *Memory and Skin*. What did this journey mean for you and how you came to know that place?

JG To go with my parents to Jamaica was one thing, and to understand their connection with the place. For me to be curious was to go beyond that connection and spread out to other places. I started off in Cuba. Then went to Jamaica, came back, then I went to Panama, to Trinidad and then across to Guyana and Suriname. I just went with a camera and a rucksack, a few bits of clothing and a sound recorder. Every day or every few days, I would move on to another town or another country. Every person I met I would ask them about five questions. I came to understand that the Caribbean, in some ways, is a completely manufactured place. It's a new world. It was an Indigenous space, but most of the Indigenous people had been killed out by disease, or by enslaving them.

BGA Like when Australia was colonised, the British brought smallpox. What shifted for you after this journey, and how you came to make *Memory and Skin*?

JG I was asking people how they saw Europe, because I wanted to understand the cultural connection between Europe and the Caribbean. That was my thesis for doing this journey. And whether everybody in the Caribbean felt a connection to each other. If there was some sort of, not a national, but a spiritual aspect that bound them all together because all the histories of migration became interlaced. People coming from different places and ending up there several generations along and then creating a people out of many peoples. But there are, of course, lots of complexities around class but also race and colourism.

BGA I want to come back to *Memory and Skin*, the work you made from this journey. It is a form of archive, including a sound archive, right?

JG Yes, I recorded everybody I spoke to.

BGA What does that mean for you in regard to archives? As we both know, with the places we come from, it was so often the colonists or the enslavers who did the archiving of our ancestors, bodies and voices through film, drawing, photography or other means. They come to hold sway over our representation. But what you're doing is creating your own archive about your own journey, of looking back to Europe. What is the significance of creating an archive like this on your own terms?

JG I didn't even think about it as making an archive. I was thinking about making recordings so I could make a piece of work at the end of it. I was working in photography, so I was taking loads and loads of pictures. I have thousands of pictures from that journey.

BGA What do you think about that now? It seems to me that you want to represent the world from the perspective of your experience, and not through a dominant gaze.

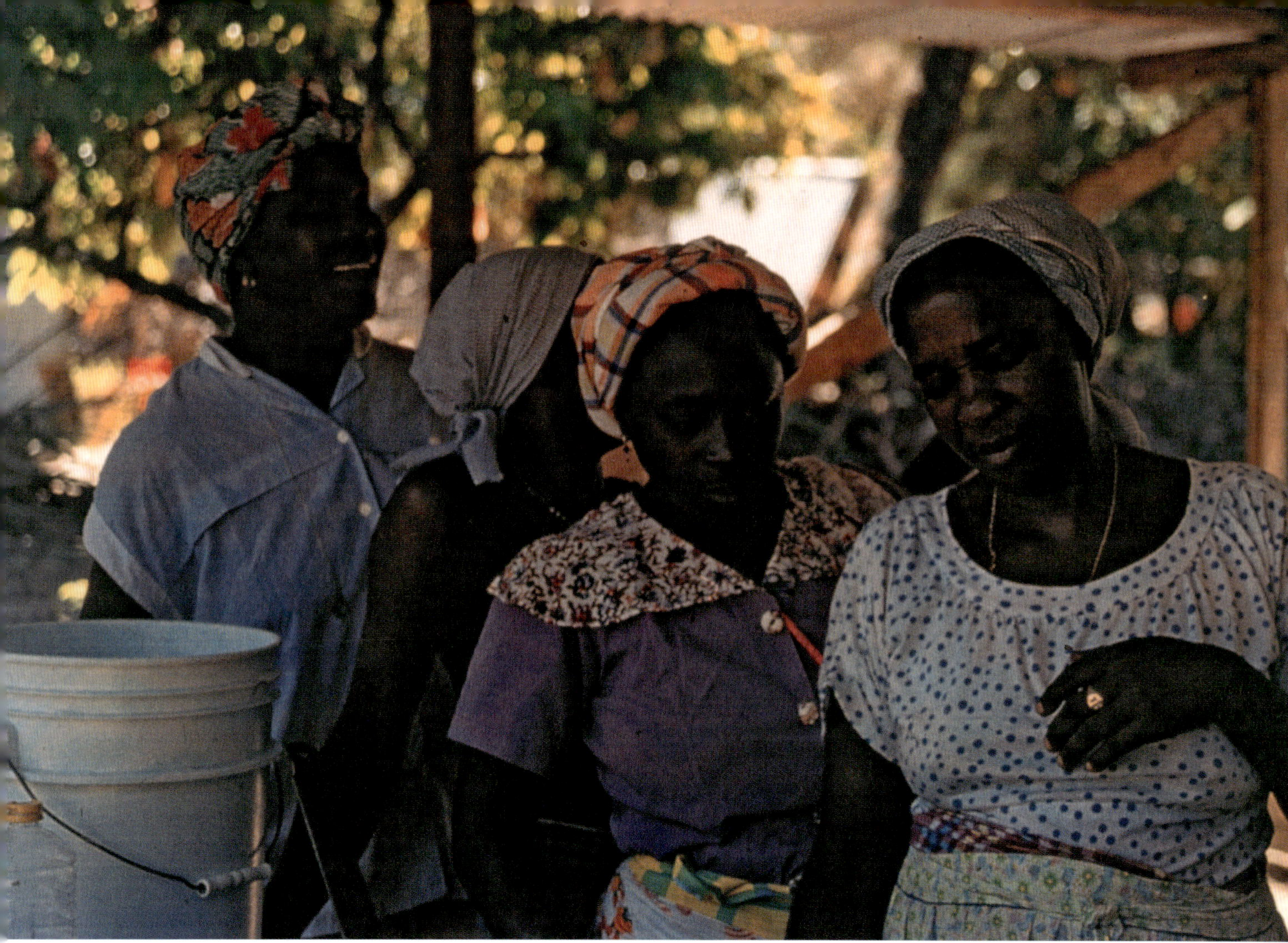

JG *Memory and Skin* actually started off in the official archives here in the UK. I went up to Liverpool to see what was there in the archives. There wasn't the slavery museum at the time. I went to the Royal Geographic Archives. I looked at everything that was around, and then I did the same in Spain, the Netherlands and France.

I was mainly looking at imagery, to see how people were represented. The representation that was in these archives, in the libraries and the museums. I wanted to see if that meshed with the way in which people [of Caribbean descent] saw themselves, and how they saw people from the other side of the Atlantic, from both perspectives. How they viewed the Caribbean as a place that was so far away but that had so much to do with the construction of their identities because they wouldn't be here if there hadn't been for the whole imperial project from Europe.

I also wanted to see how Europeans saw the Caribbean. Invariably it's sort of like a place of paradise, beautiful islands and drinking cocktails.

BGA Not slavery.

JG Not slavery, but also not the poverty that exists there now. When I came to interview people on my journey, I also asked them about how they were presented in the archives, or currently in newspapers.

In the UK, at that time, there were lots of news stories about young women in the UK from the Caribbean, mainly from Jamaica, single mothers having children, with lots of different husbands or boyfriends or whatever. Part of my project involved seeking out what was seen as an issue in the country that was opposite. So, when I was in Jamaica, I went to meet with some very young mothers aged between 11 and 15, and to talk to them about their dreams, the future, and what they hoped. I was interested in hearing how they saw the world. It doesn't matter how the rest of the world sees it.

BGA It's almost taboo right? These kinds of issues are very shocking for me, because when they do happen in Australia they're very rare, or they're kind of hidden, because it's about sexual abuse. It's about rape. I find your approach to the archives is more than political, about who can represent who. You come from a very intimate, obviously gentle space and trying to understand.

JG I use that example of thirty young girls because each of them had a vision of the world, and all had a vision of the future, no matter what had happened to them before. They were incredibly resilient about what was going to happen to them in the future, and I think for me that was quite empowering to hear those voices.

BGA When you visited these young girls in Jamaica did you also do photographic workshops with them?

JG I spent a lot of time with them, and we made portraits. They each got a portrait. I think it was really important for them to be photographed in the way they wanted it. Where would you like to be? How would you like to be photographed? It was also a time when people didn't have access to photography like they do now. They didn't have photographs of themselves, so it was special to have a photograph and to also have someone spend time with you, to take that photograph. I had enormous respect for every single person that I worked with when I was on that journey. It was a journey that taught me about what it is to be in the world.

BGA Would you agree that it is about visibility? About the voices of the people themselves.

JG With my work in the Kalahari in South Africa [since 2005 Joy has been visiting the Kalahari] and with the Caribbean, it is really important to have the voices of the people I record. As you were saying if you go and look at the official archives, it is about how somebody from outside sees them. I'm really interested in how the people on the inside see themselves, and how they see the world outside.

BGA I want to ask you about the word 'power'.

JG Power is having your voice and people hearing it. I think that's power for me. I want to hear people's power. In the Kalahari, the women, on the one hand are quite powerful and they have so much of the knowledge. But then they're also subjugated by male power within the community, which tends to be very destructive in some cases mainly because they feel without power within the structure of society. There's also racism, especially because they are an Indigenous community, and the community is quite small and very isolated.

BGA I know the Kalahari project's been a very long passion for you, and it's complicated because it's about linguicide. I would love to hear you talk about the complexities of this.

JG The way in which they were represented in the nineteenth and twentieth centuries was basically as animals. I've been working with Bushmen, who take pride in calling themselves Bushmen – although this is seen as a derogatory term. They've taken this derogatory term. It's a bit like Queer: 'It belongs to us. So therefore, I'm going to own it'.

Bushmen were not seen as people. Under Apartheid their identity was changed to 'coloured', and many people then decided that they'd rather be 'coloured', so they didn't tell their children that they were Bushmen, that they were Indigenous, because to be 'coloured' was better than to be Black. That's why the language wasn't passed on. They were told to speak Afrikaans.

BGA So much about your practice is about these journeys of self-discovery.

JG It's about voice. The Kalahari project is about an endangered language but also my work with the Caribbean is about voice. I wanted to hear the voice of the people who've had so much in terms of other voices painted on them from the other side of the Atlantic. I wanted to hear what they had to say about their lives, and who they were, and how they viewed the world.

BGA So how has that helped your voice? What has that done for you to find your voice? Because I know when you started off and the journey through the Caribbean you said you wanted to understand yourself.

JG When I'm talking to people, I'm actually very quiet. I barely say anything at all. I might ask one or two questions. I'm trying to understand what my voice is within that. I think, as a child as a baby, the only way you find your voice is by listening to other people speak and I suppose that's what I've been doing. I probably still don't know what my voice is, but I feel like this has been a discovery for me. It's been really important to listen to other people and to learn from what they have to say, and then to see myself; because I felt these people have a language that belongs to them. I don't have a language that belongs to me, and I don't have a land that belongs to me. And then, of course, I'm lots of different people mixed up into one person. Taking ownership of all those bits of me, is realising that the world is incredibly layered and complex.

BGA What does this show mean for you? Are you going to show archives?

JG Yes, we are going to show some archives. I was going through my stuff from the Kalahari from when I first started going [in 2005], I realised I have got a whole archive of stuff from there. I asked people about their life, what it was like as children. They were very happy to talk about their journey to Johannesburg in the big truck which took them down to the Empire Exhibition [in 1936] to put them in a human zoo. The site of this exhibition is a university now and they have a medical school. When I visited in 2007, I could access their archives. They had body casts and face casts of the people who'd been in the Empire Exhibition. I had a look at the material that was in the archives which they [Bushmen / San] didn't really have access to; there are countless of photos of the Bushmen community, and they're also depicted in books the British Museum Library.

BGA It's interesting how these government sanctioned colonial archives are about shame as well. Depending on the extent of the violence or the trauma within the photos, or the kind of repercussions back on the history of those people, affects what's visible and what's not visible? What can we find? What can't we find? And we just seem to be on these journeys of evidence. You seem to be creating your own evidence by meeting these people, and they're telling their own stories.

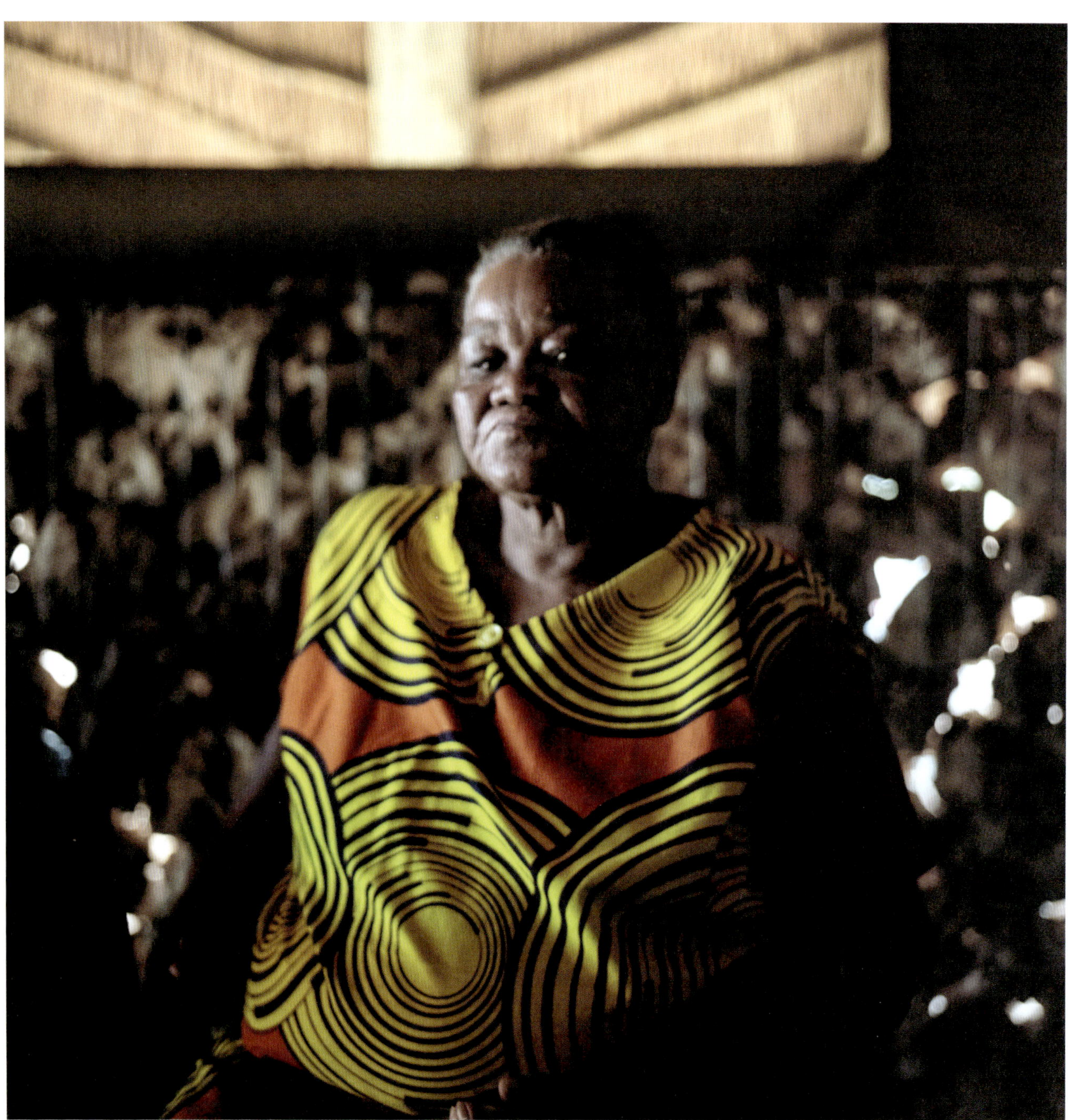

Caroline Brou Setswalo

JG Yes. I think that's important that they tell their own stories because too many stories have been told about them that they have no control over. Worse than that, they don't even hear the stories. They don't have the access to it, they can't go into the archives. They can't go into the medical school at Wits [the University of the Witwatersrand, Johannesburg]. They can't do any of that. They barely have money to cross the road.

BGA Exactly. It's about power.

JG It's about power at the end of the day, and I suppose, in a way, what I'm trying to do is to put cracks in those official stories.

Edited conversation between
Joy Gregory and Brook Garru Andrew
5 March 2025

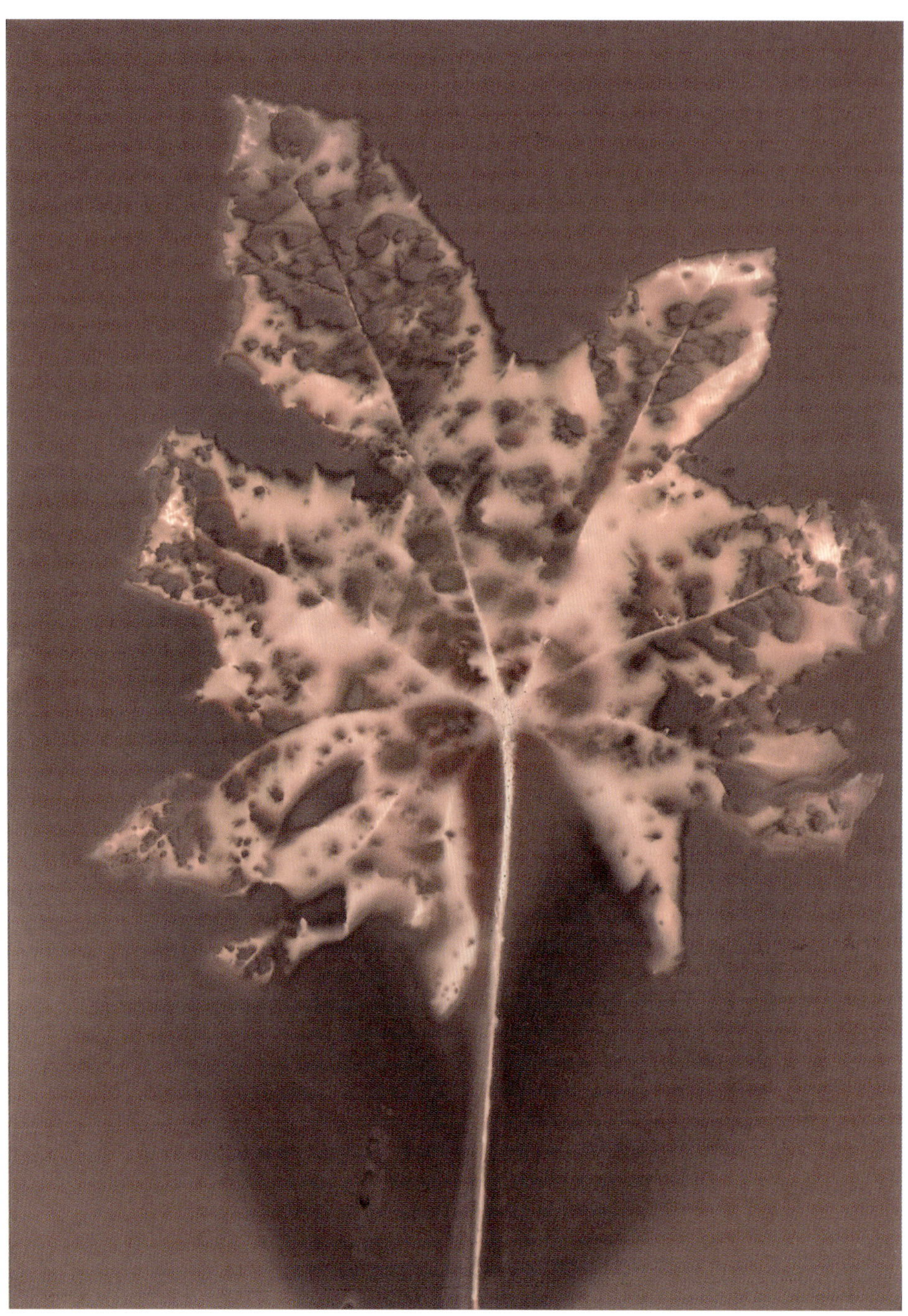

Horse Chestnut

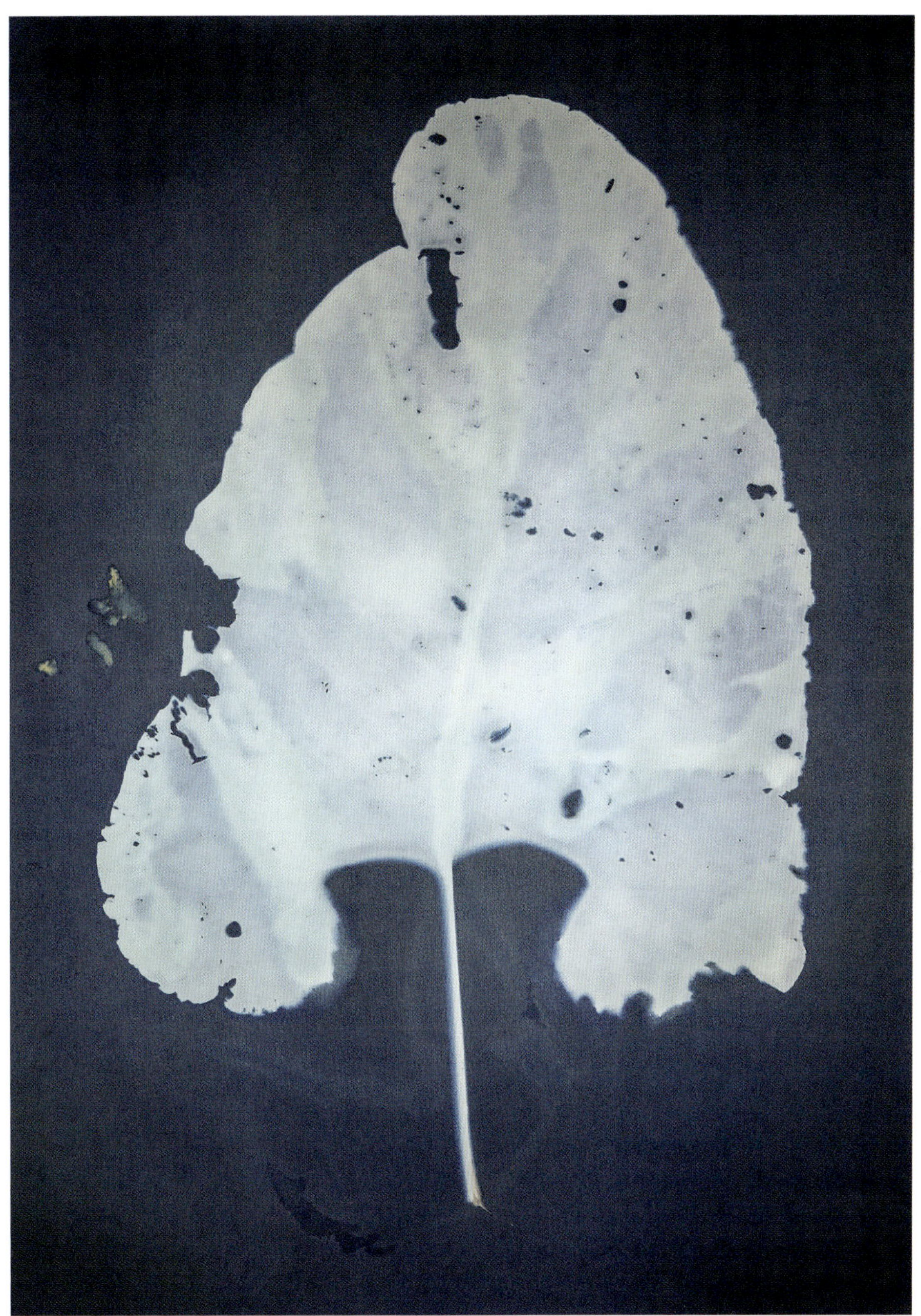

Rumex obtusifolius (Bitter Dock)

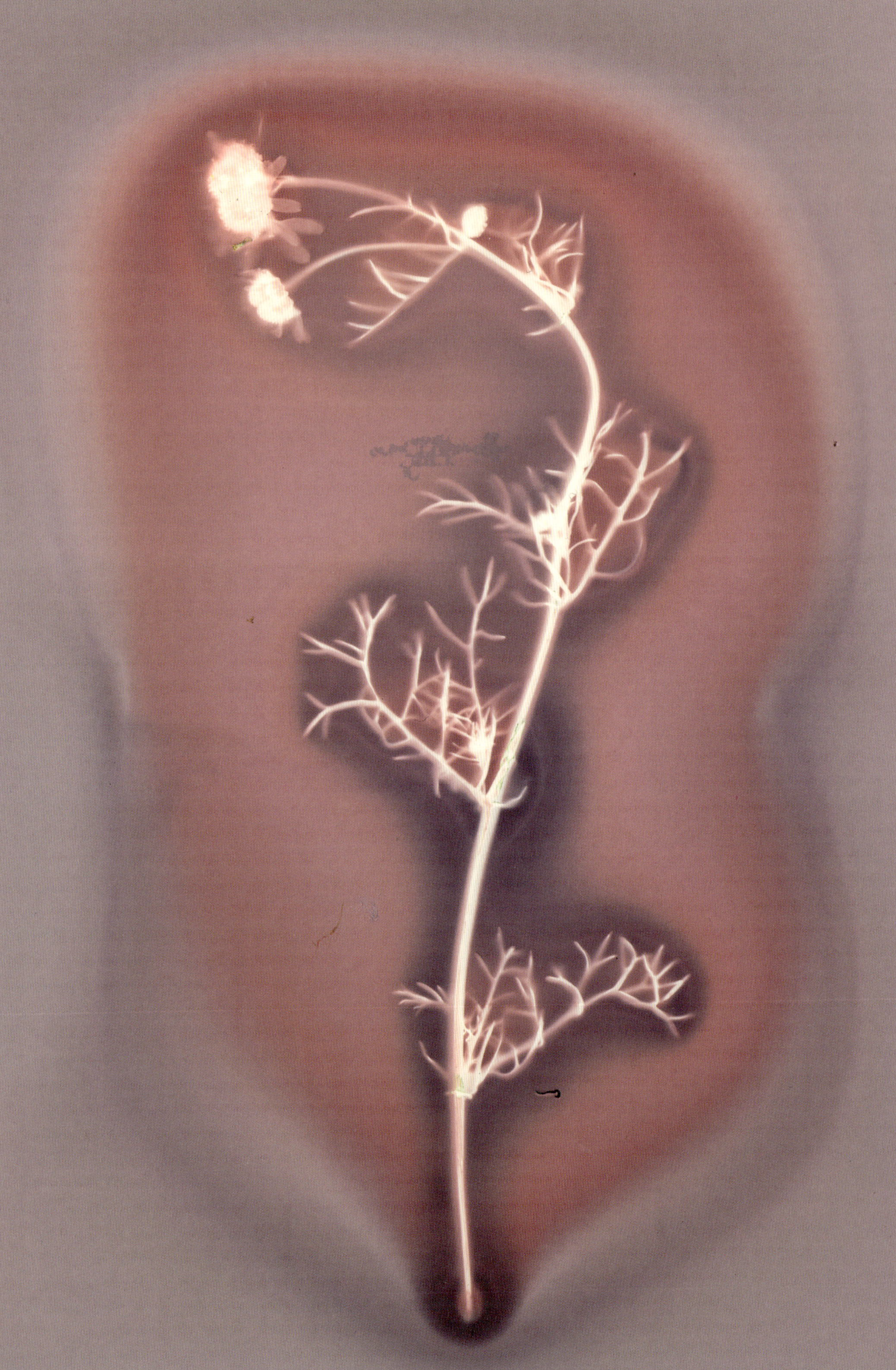

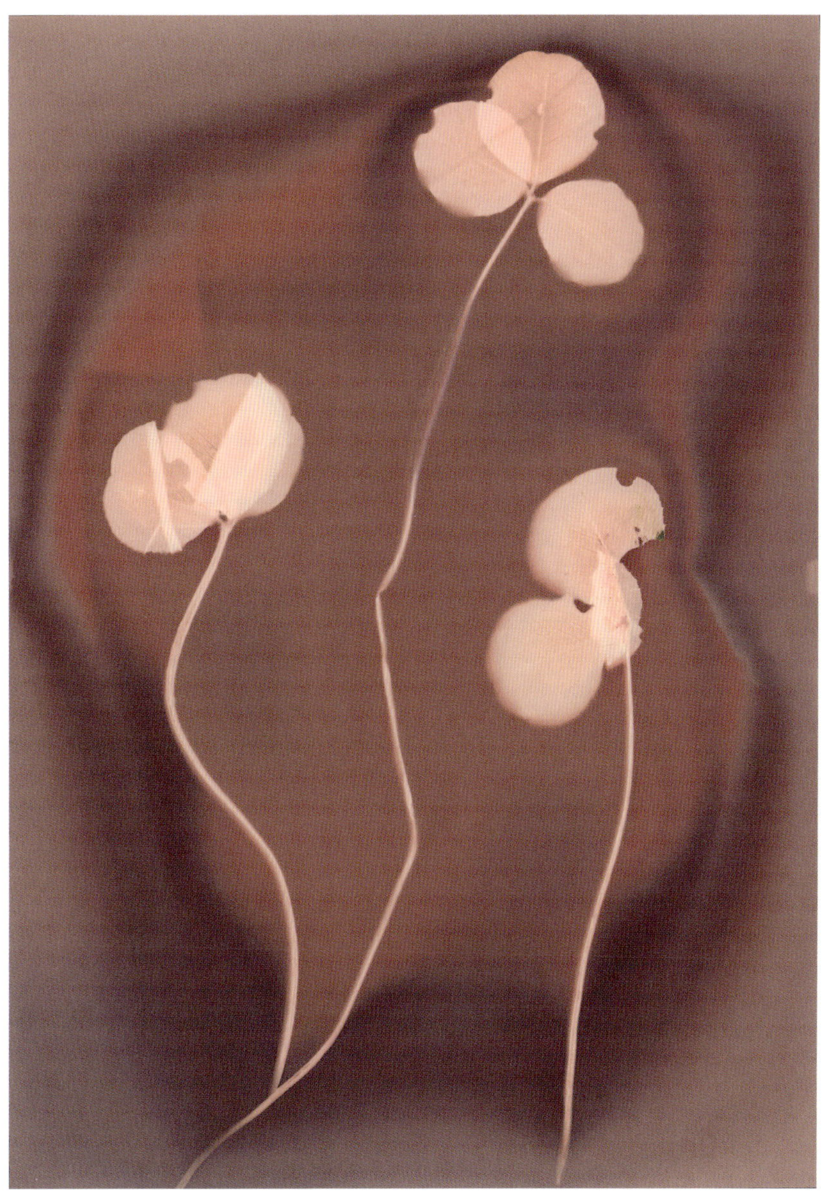

Clover

Chamomile

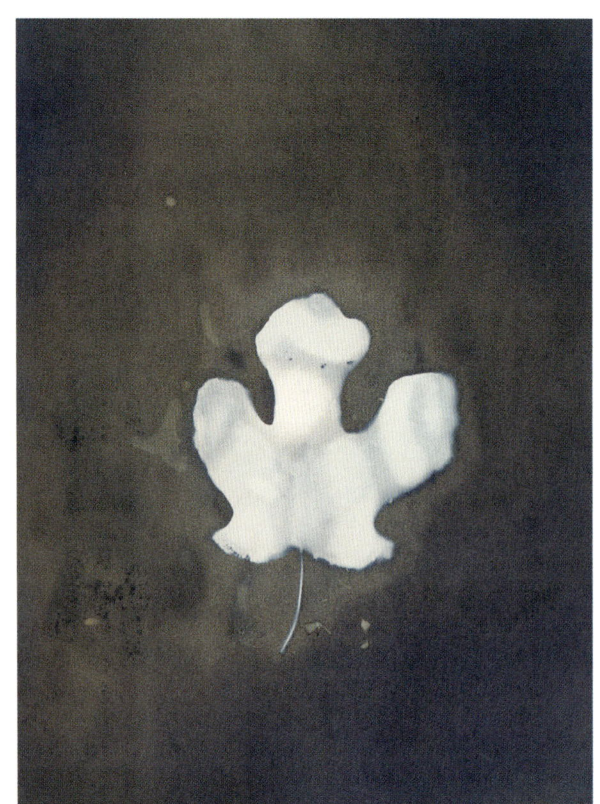

Ficus Carica (Fig)

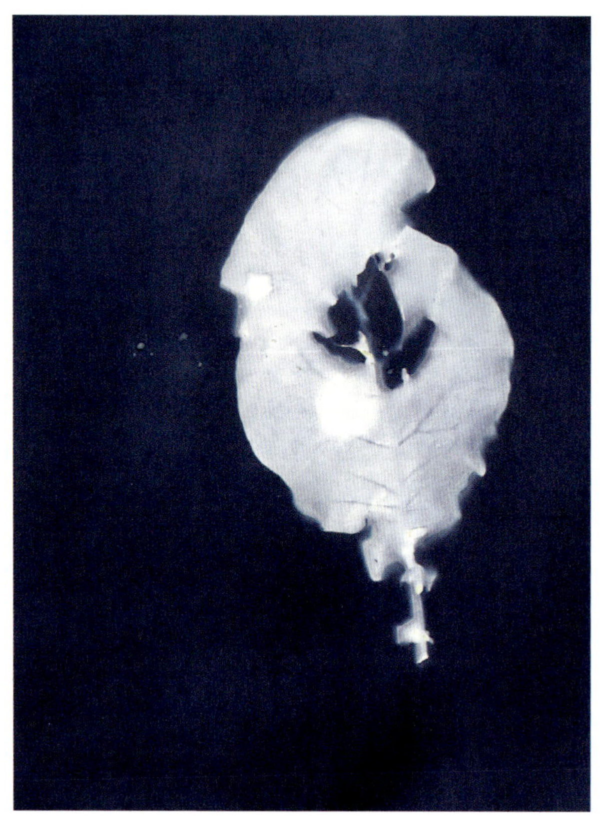

Brassica Oleracea (Broccoli)

Invisible Life Force of Plants 2020

Daucus Carota (Carrot)

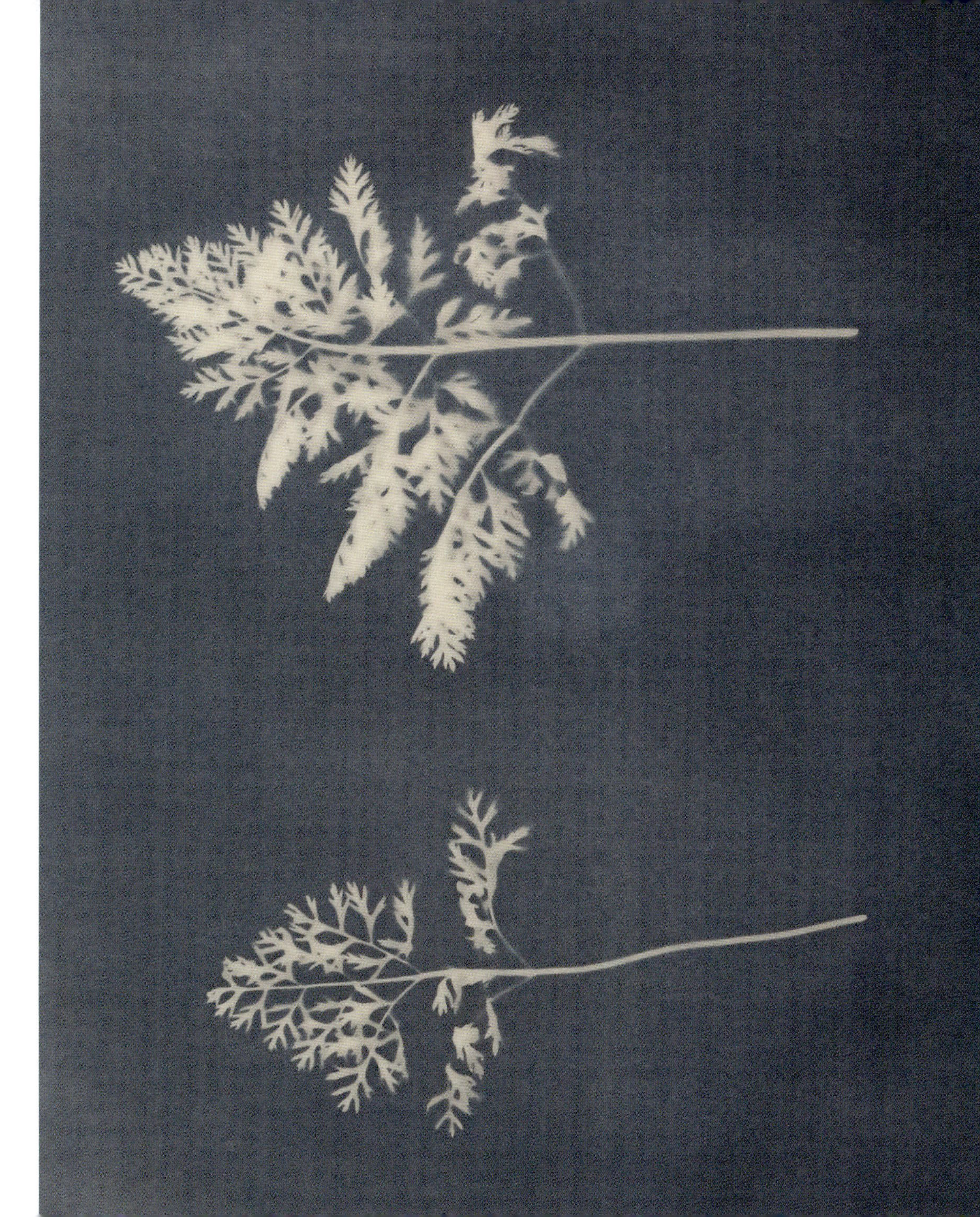

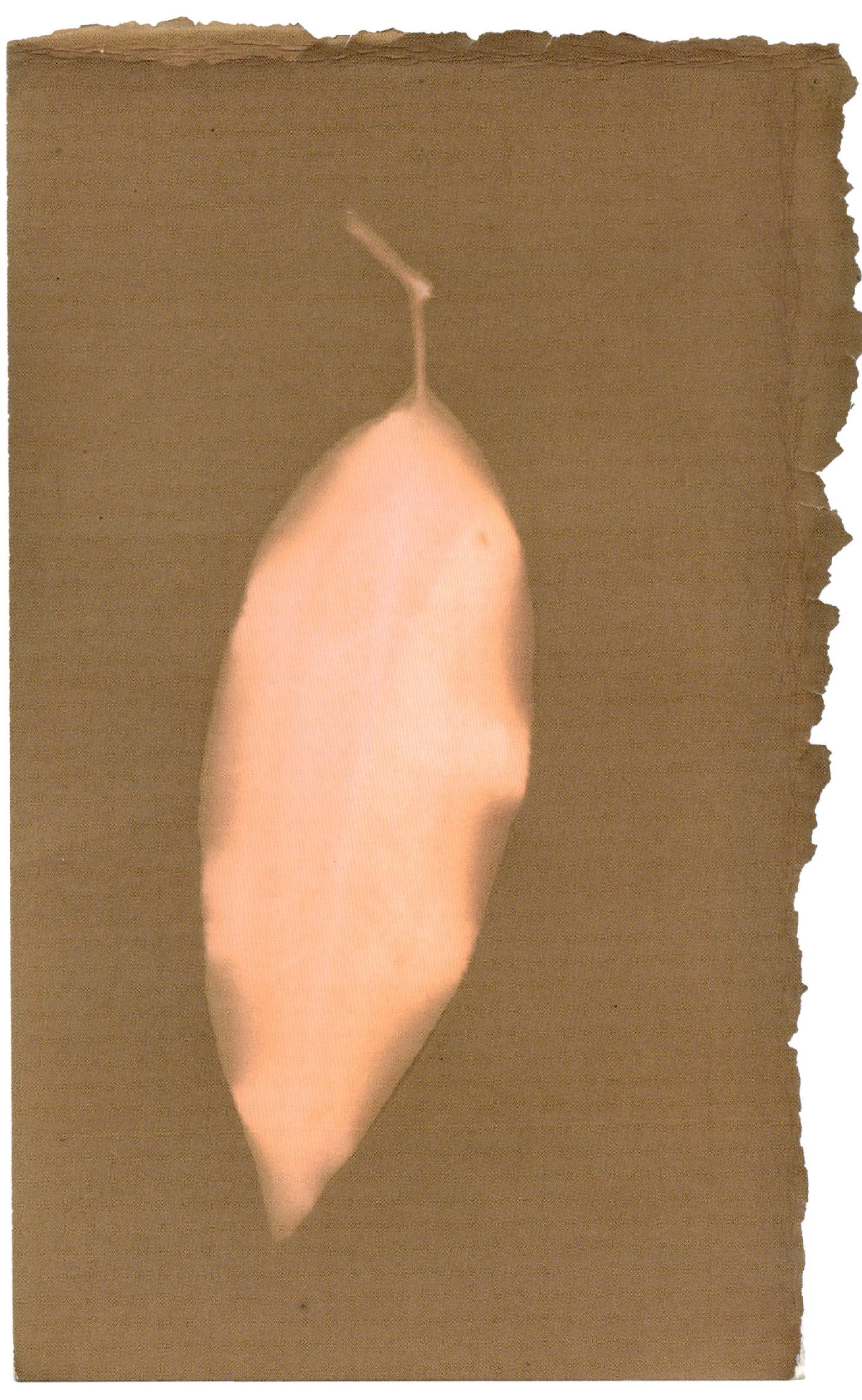

Leaf 2

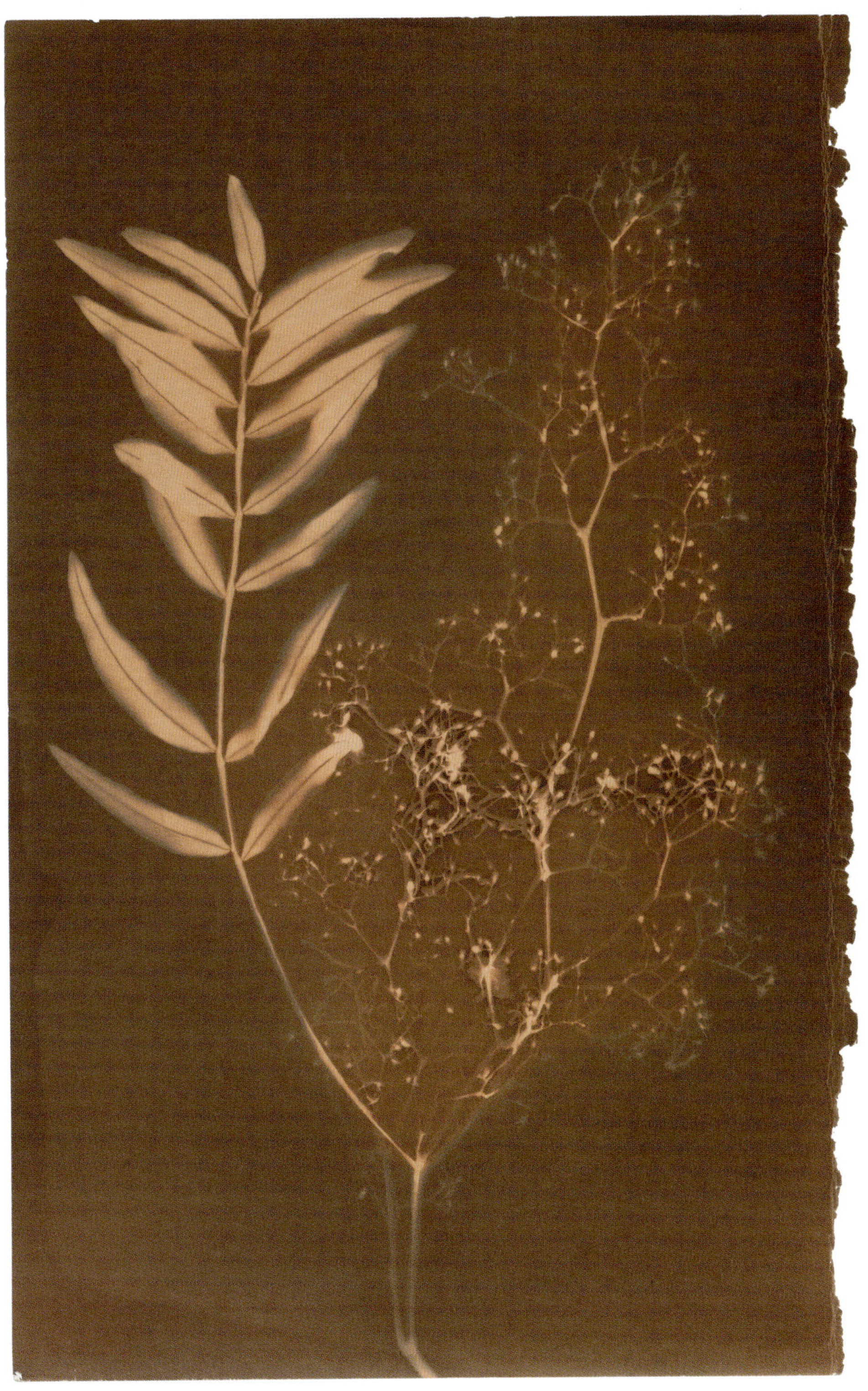

Stripped Gypsophila and garden leaves

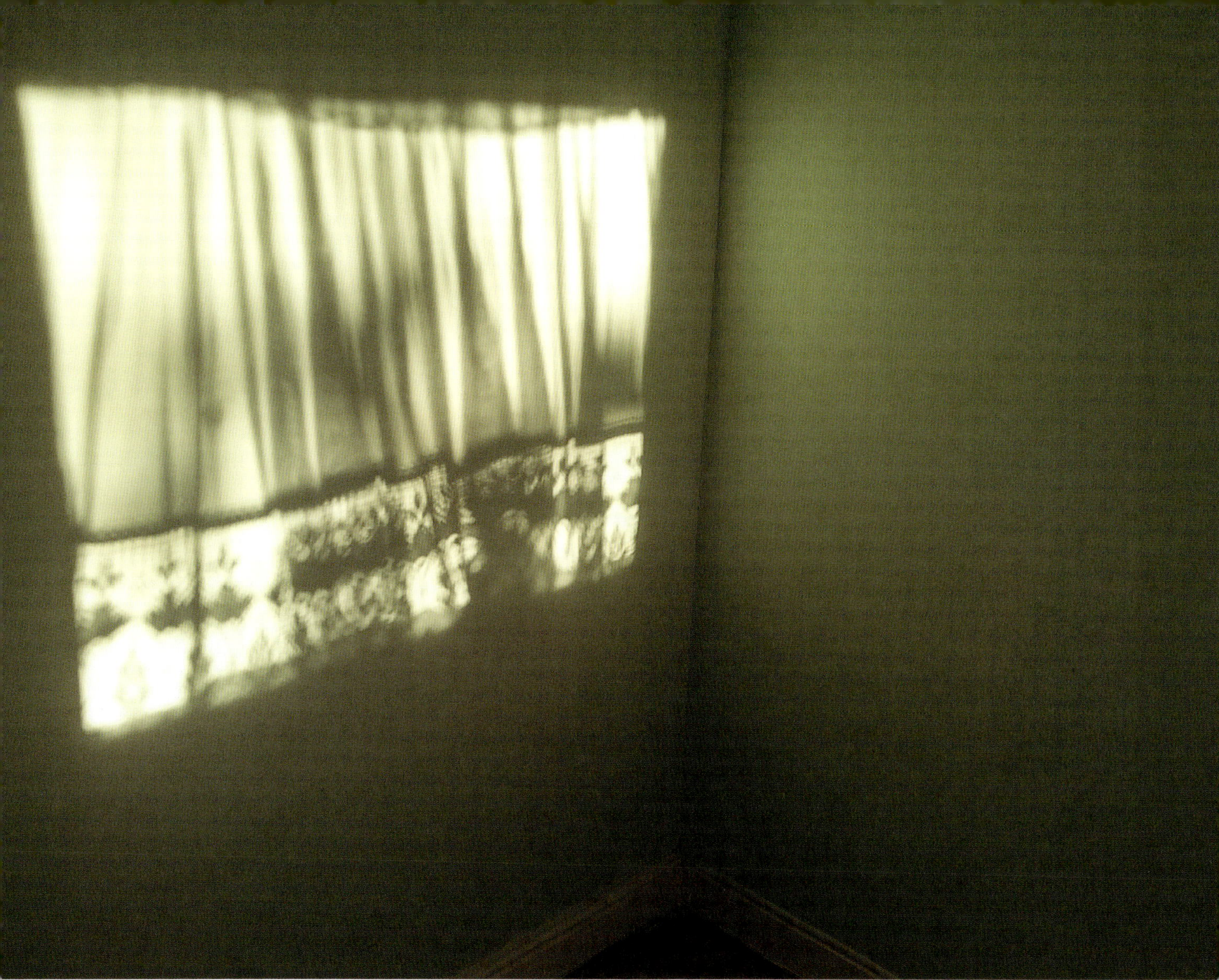

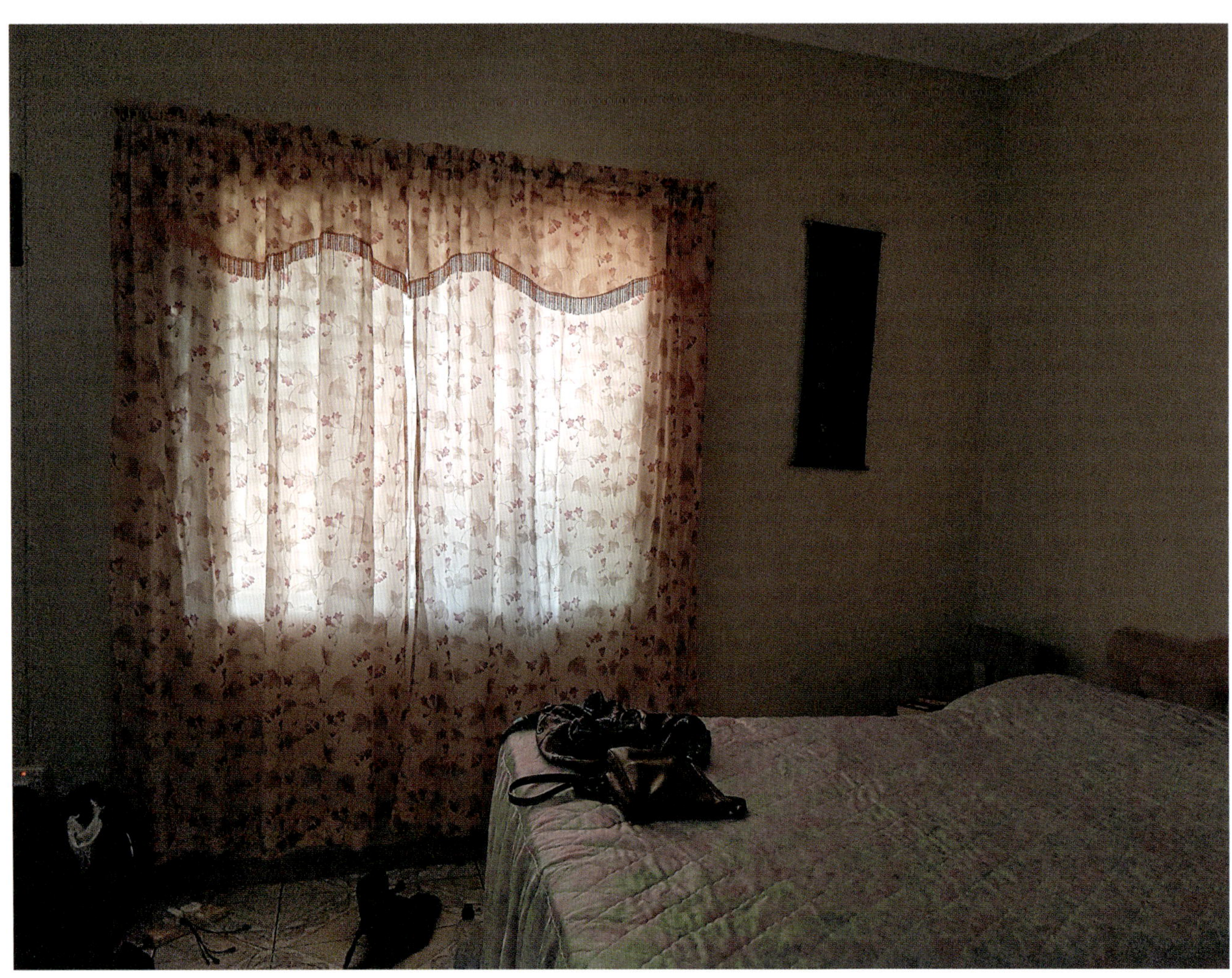

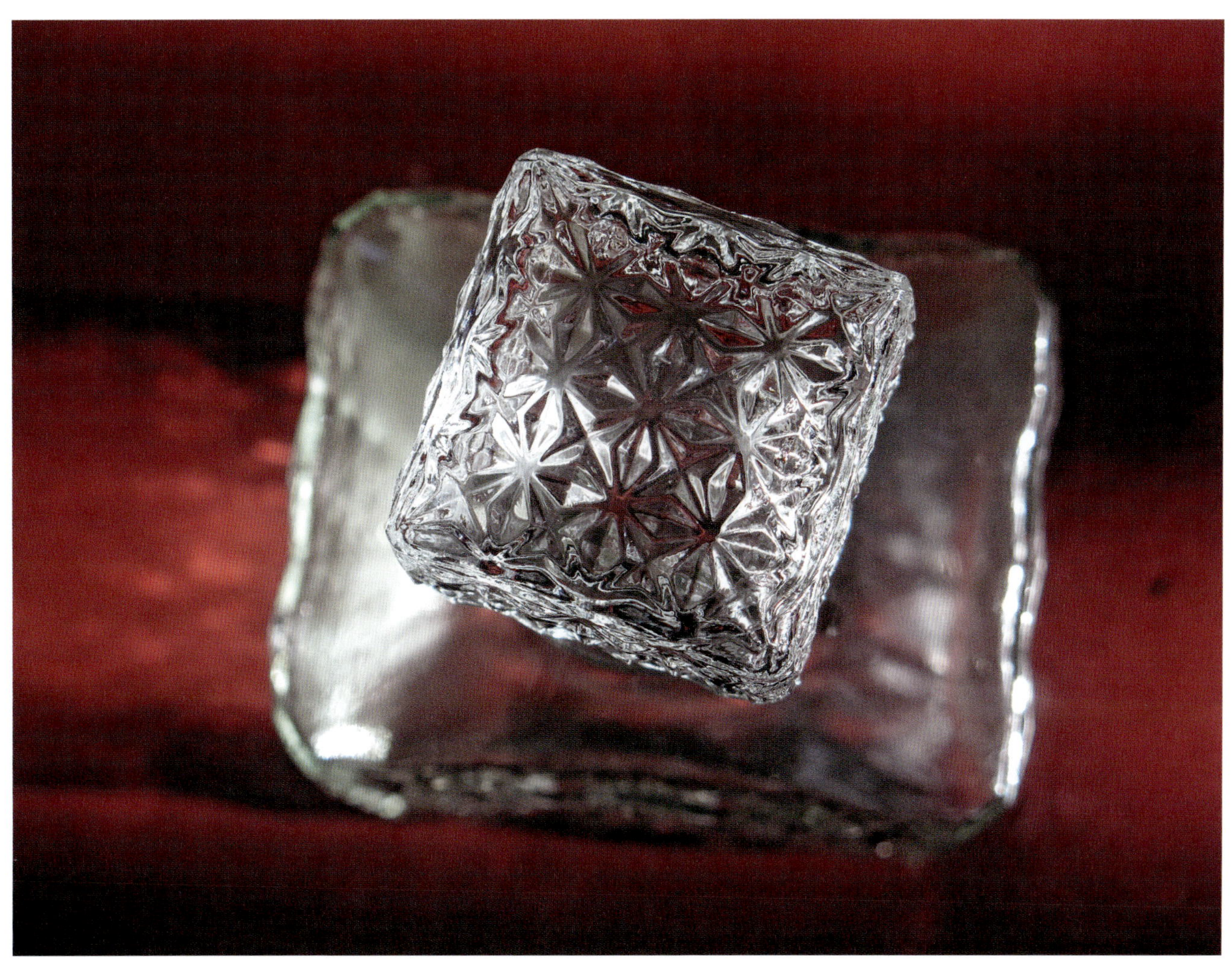

Crystal Decanter

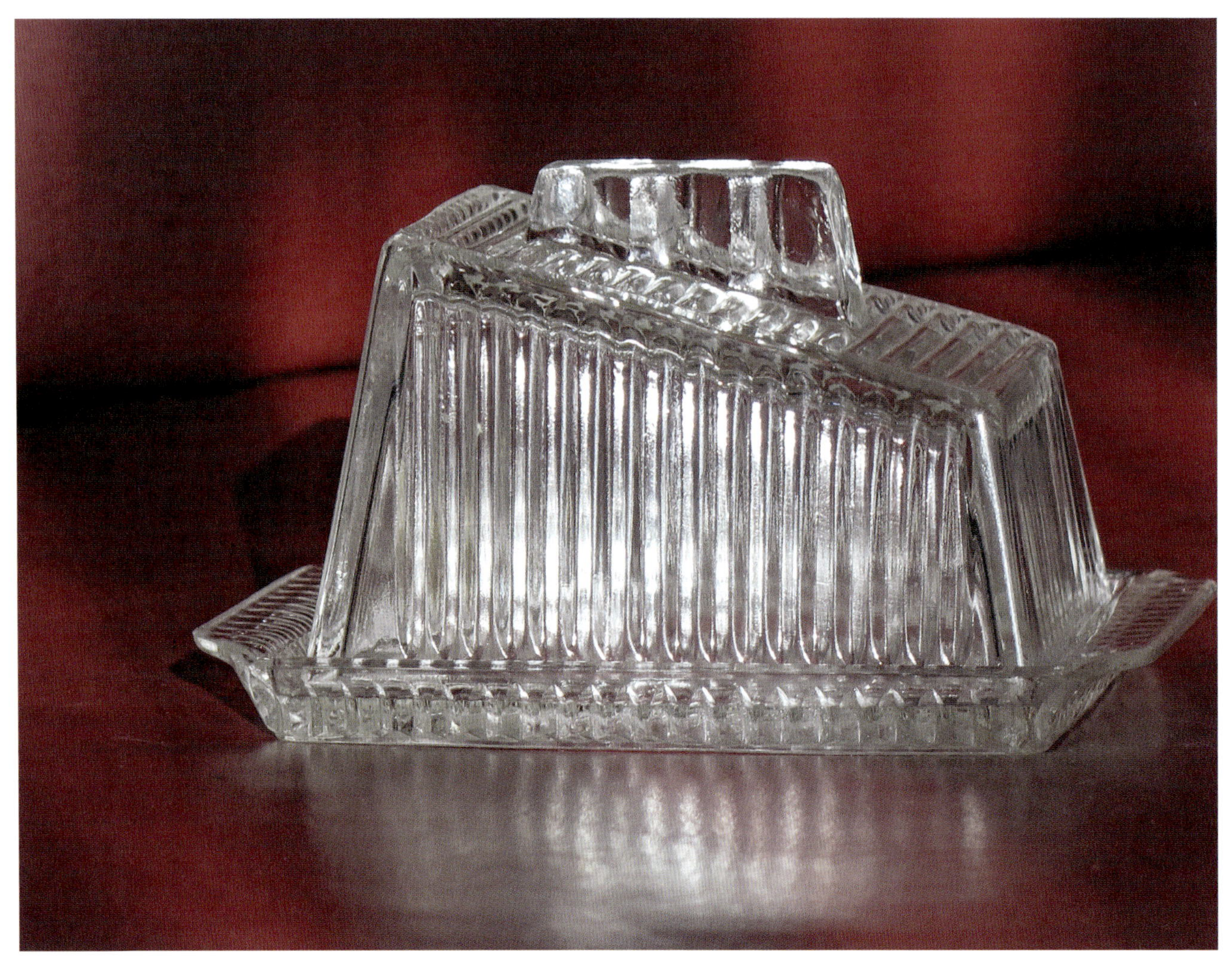

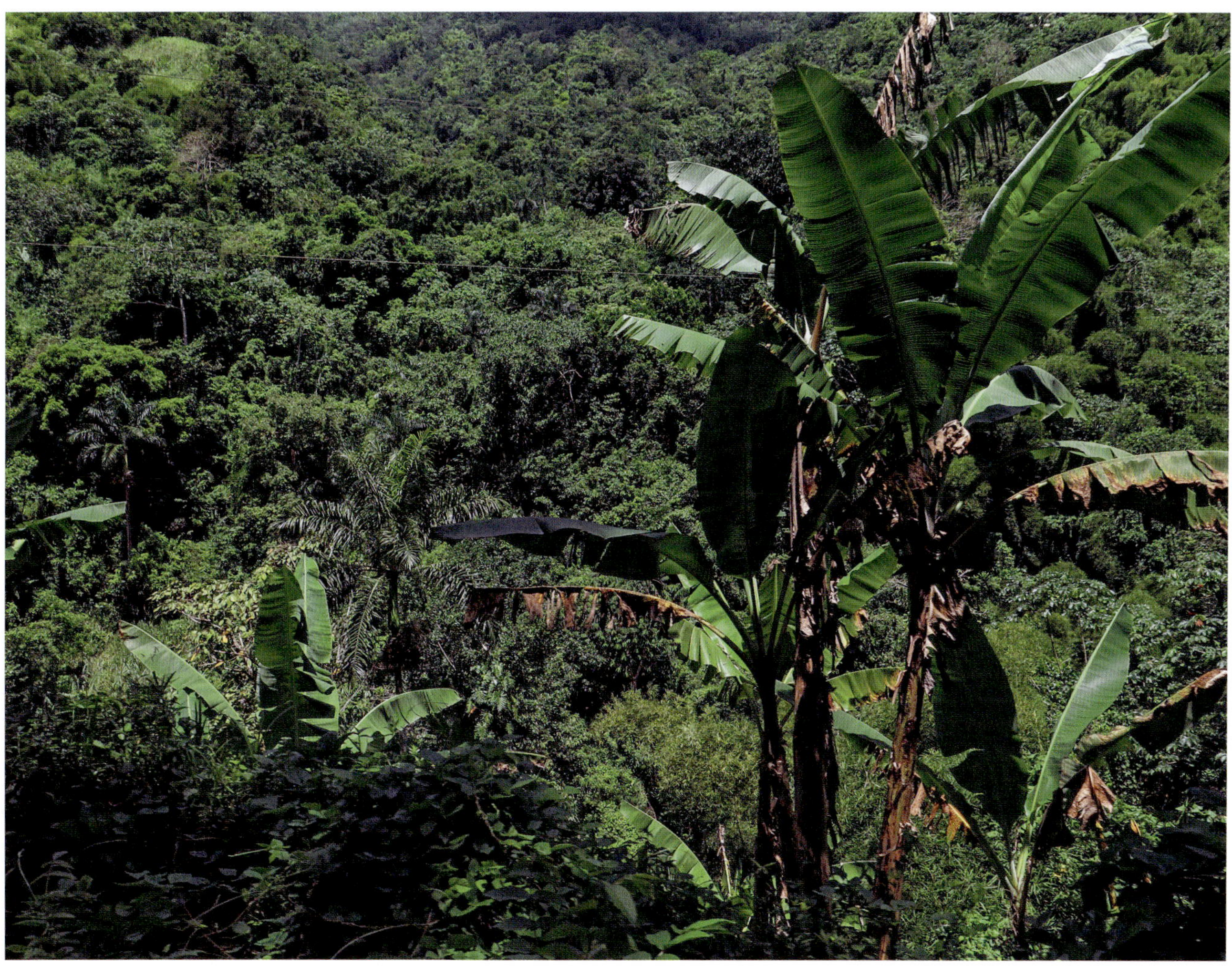

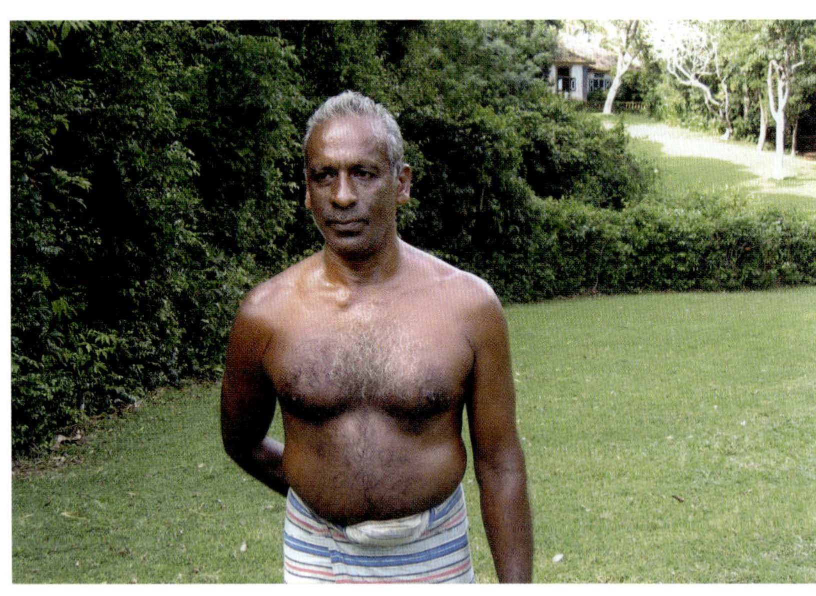

Chandrapala by Joy

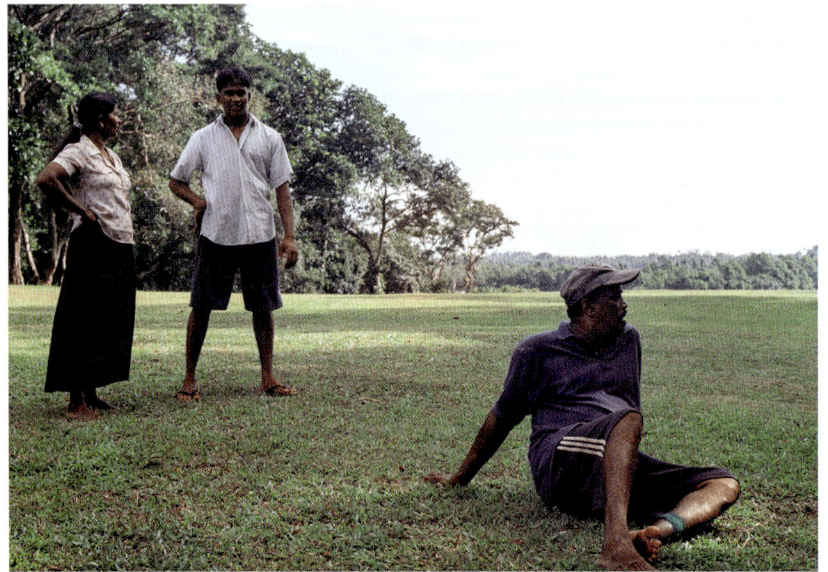

Gardeners on the Lawn

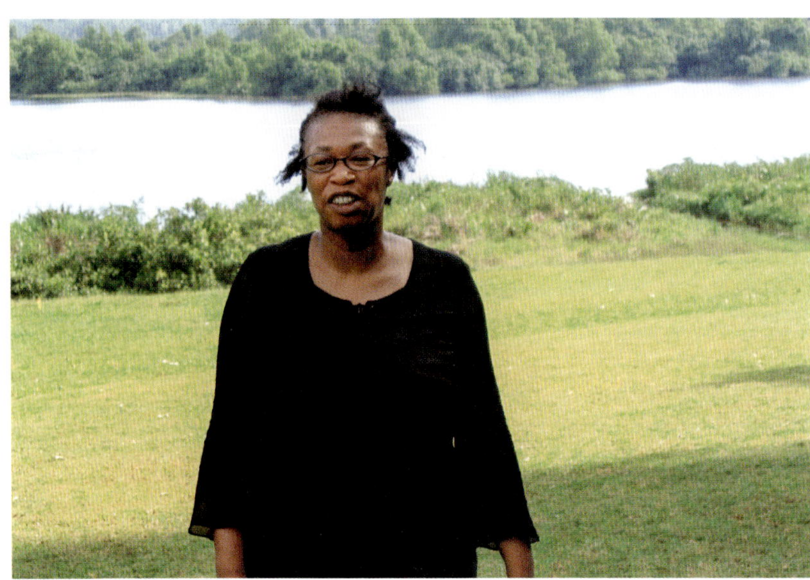

Joy by Krishna

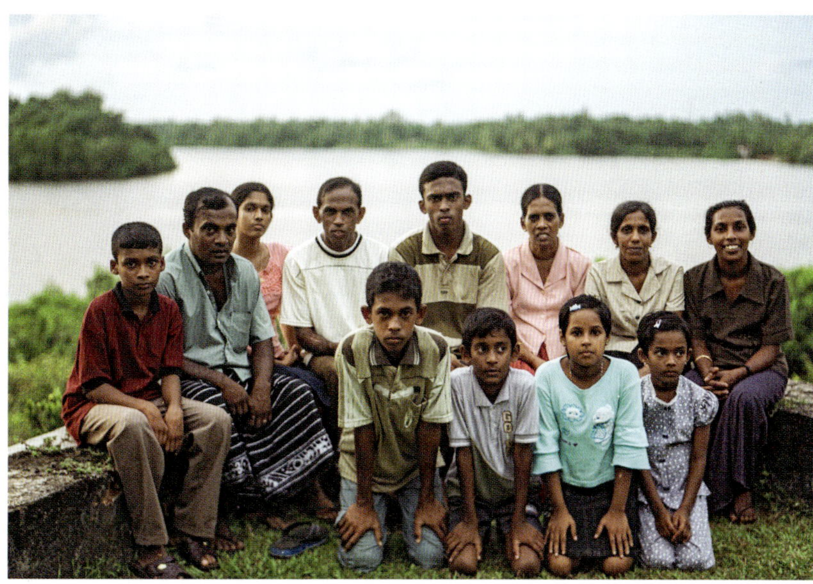

Amarasiri's Family by the Lake

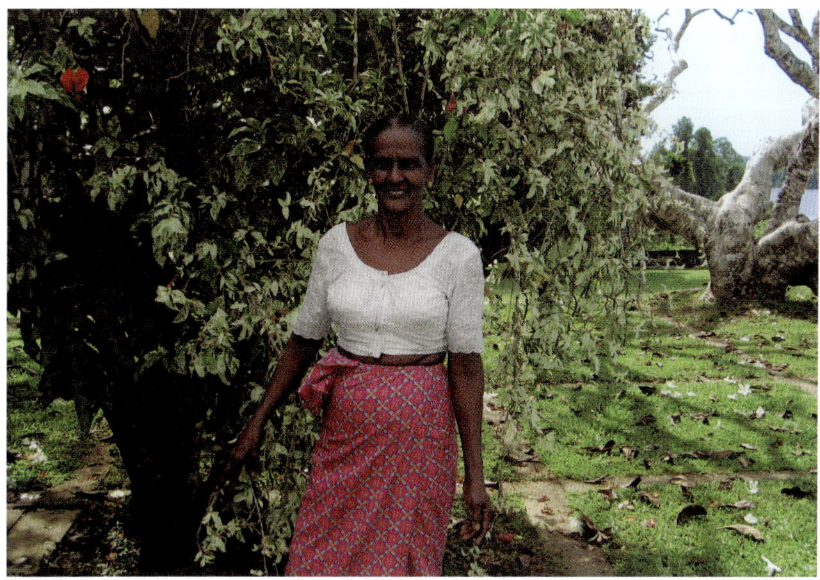

Katherine by Joy

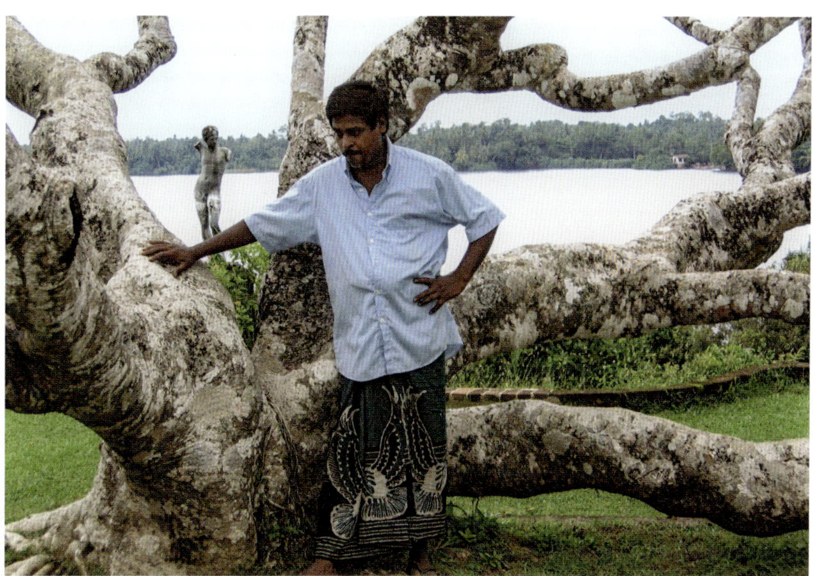

Amarisiri by Joy

Portraits, Lunuganga, Sri Lanka 2004

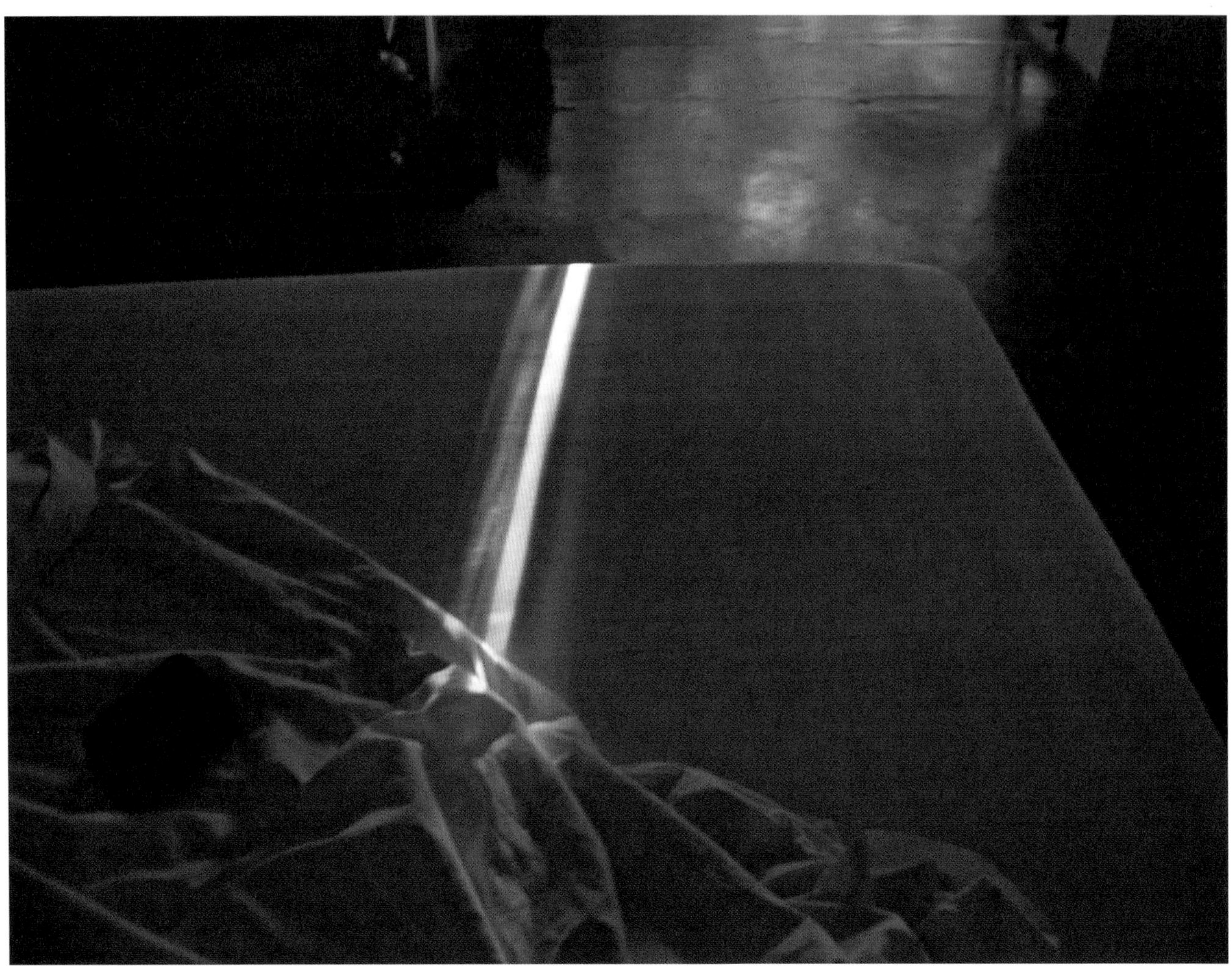

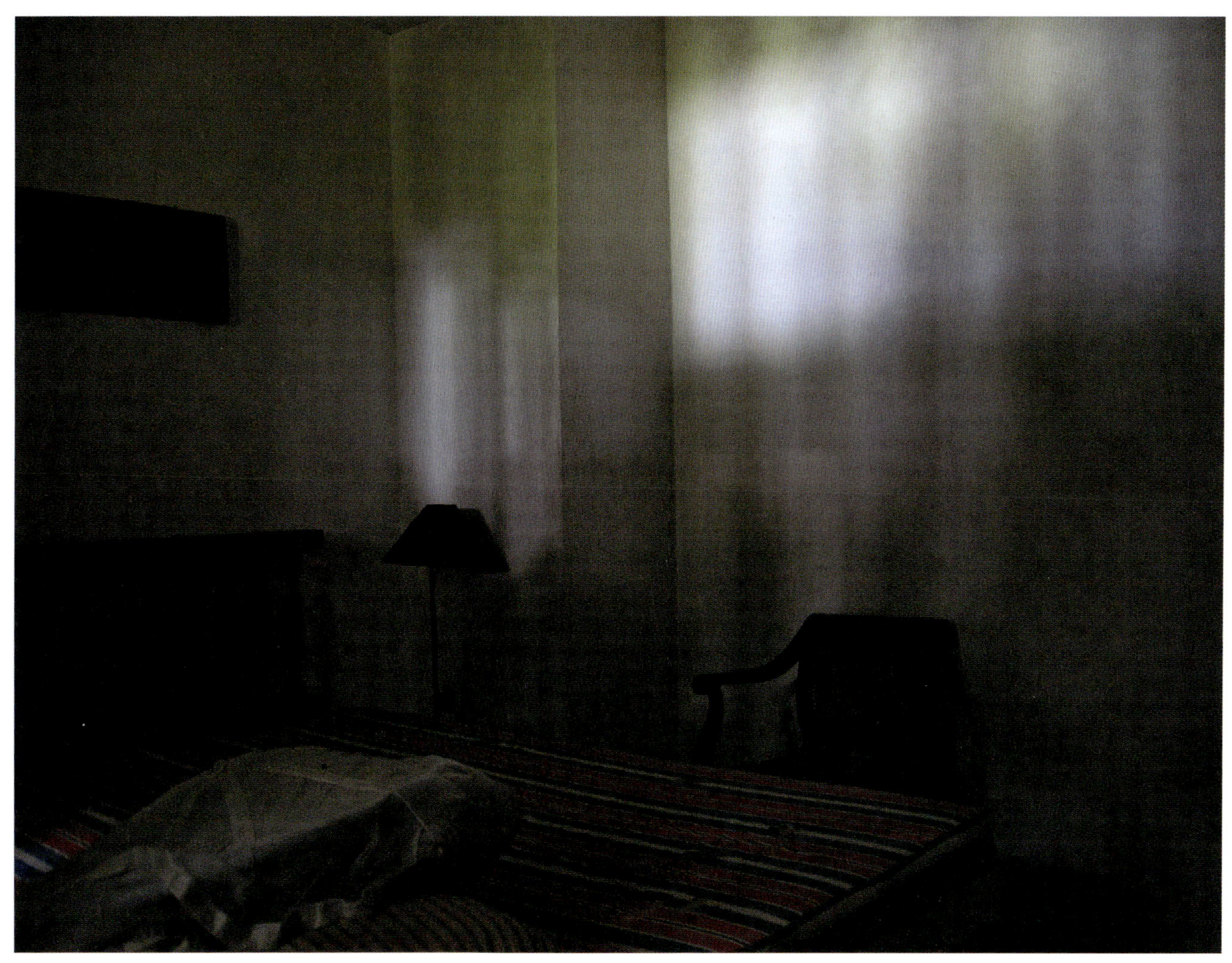

Candy Stripe Bed

Interiors, Lunuganga, Sri Lanka 2004

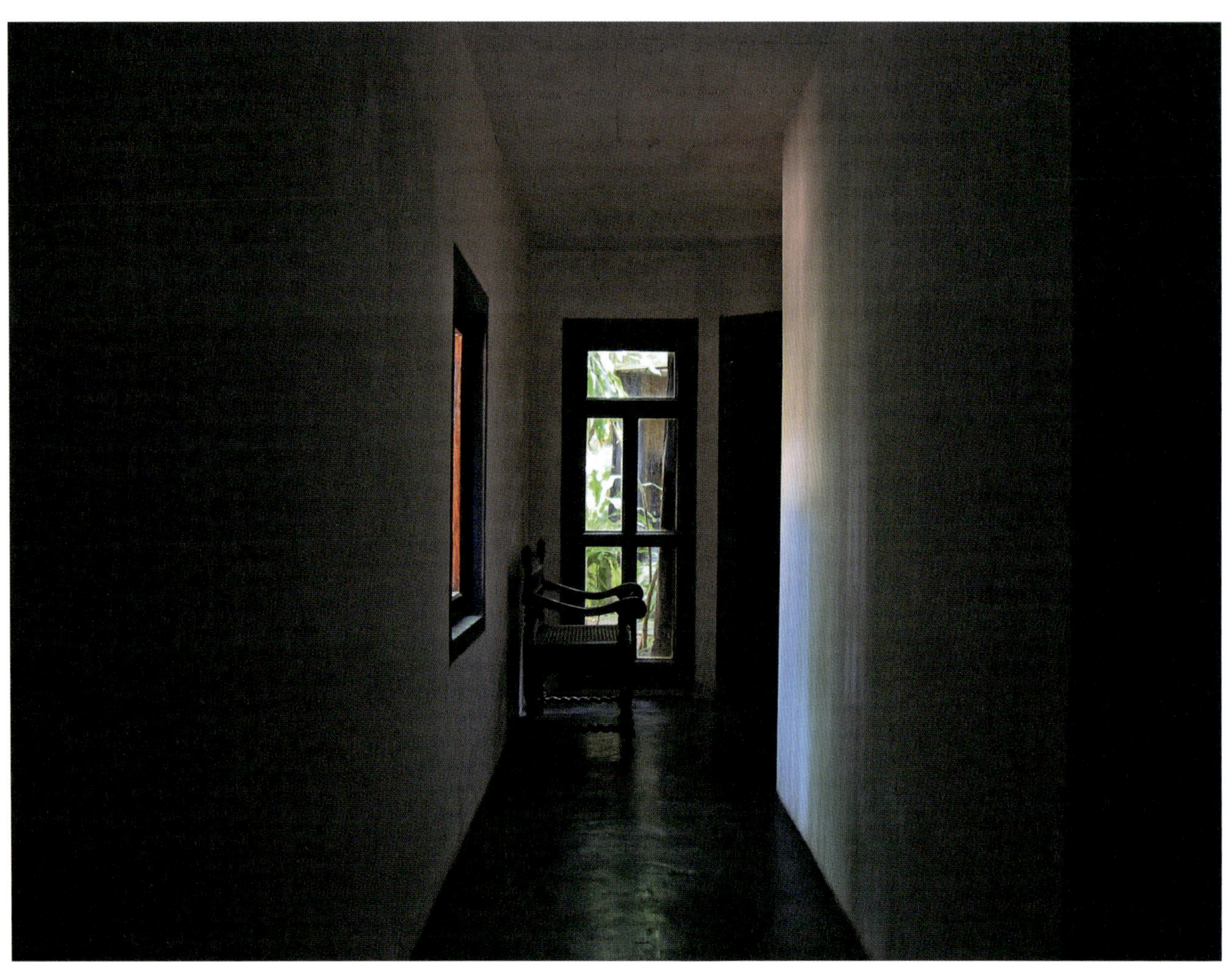

Corridor

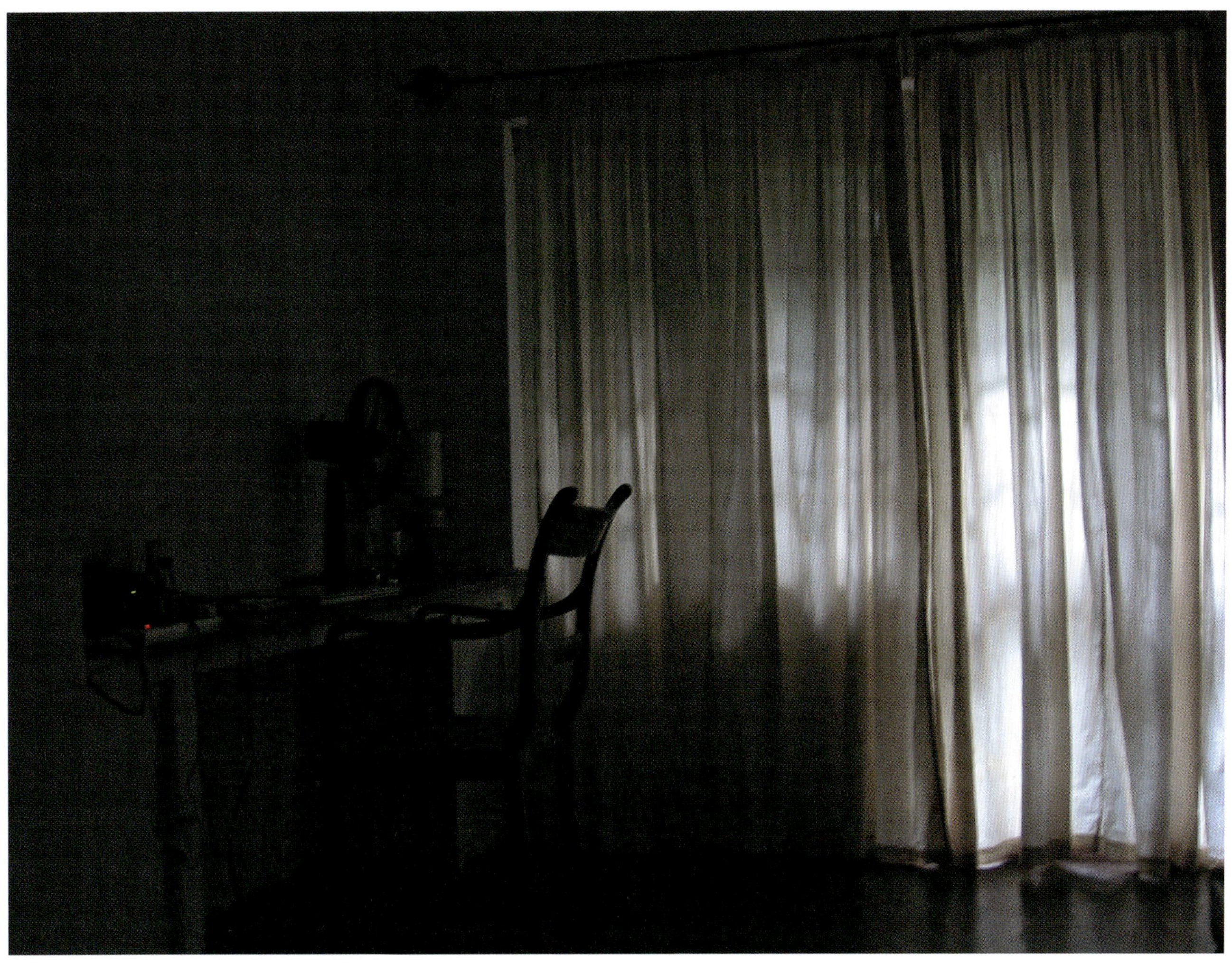

Interiors, Lunuganga, Sri Lanka 2004

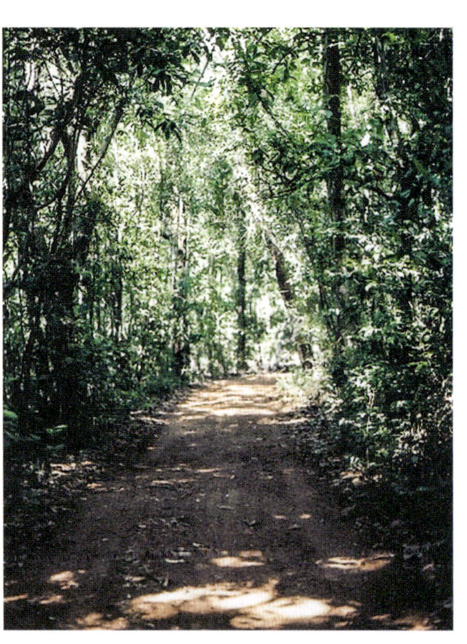

Forest Path

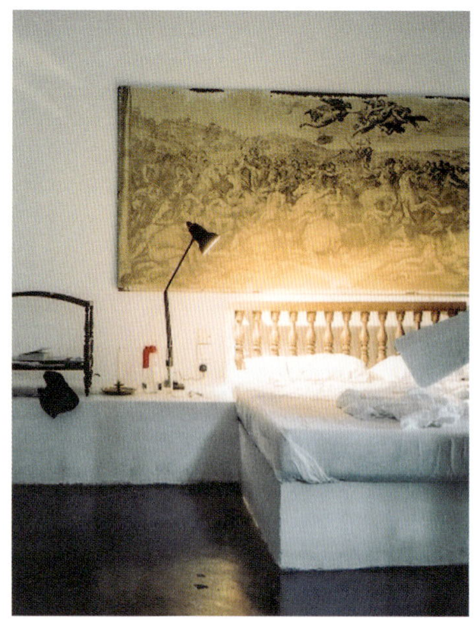

Bedside Lamp

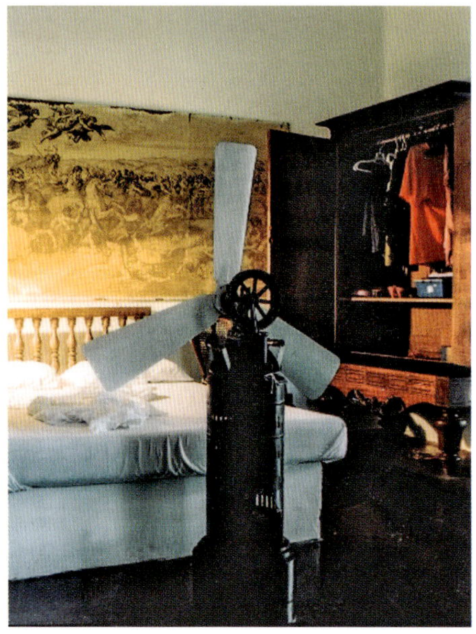

Bedside Fan

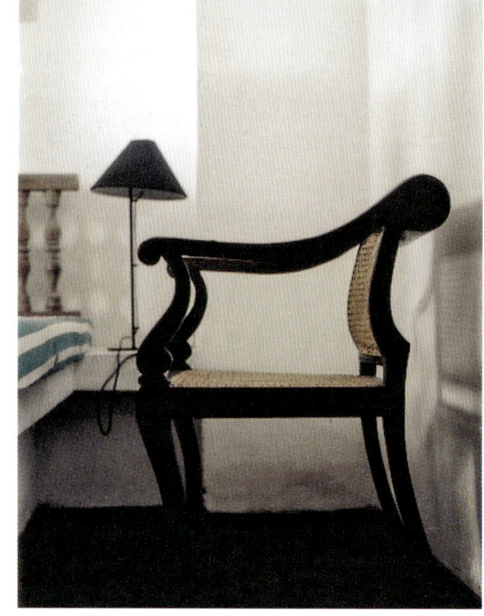

Regency Wratten Chair

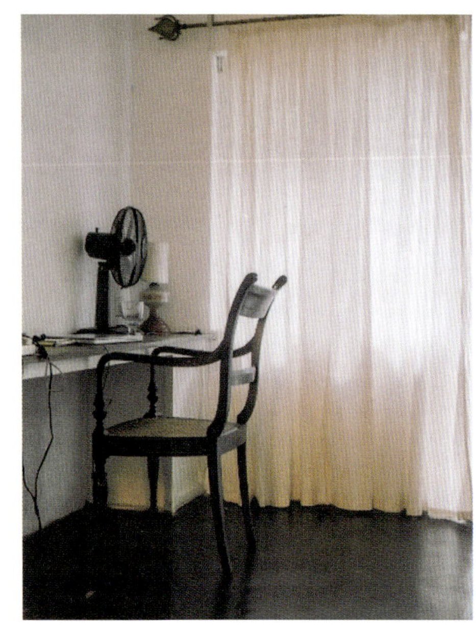

Chair

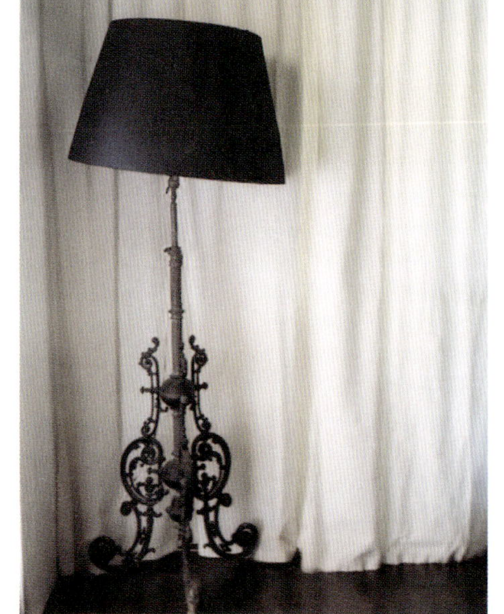

Table Lamp

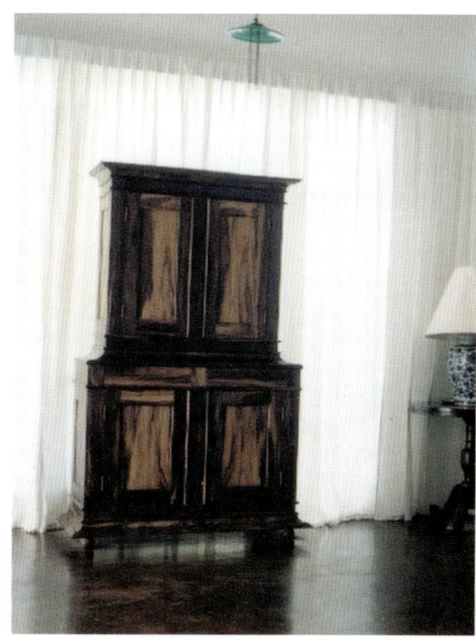

Dresser

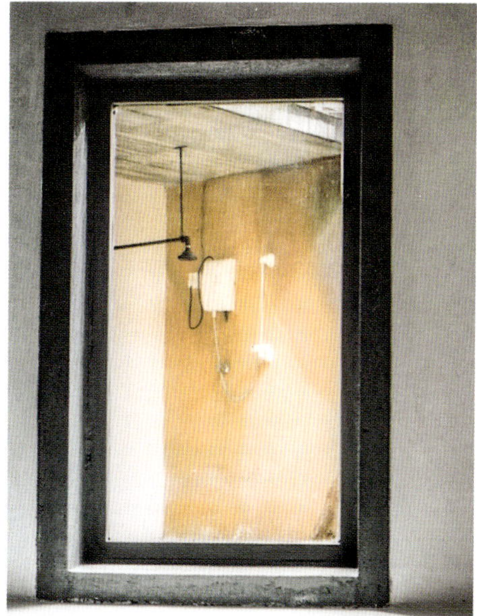

Shower

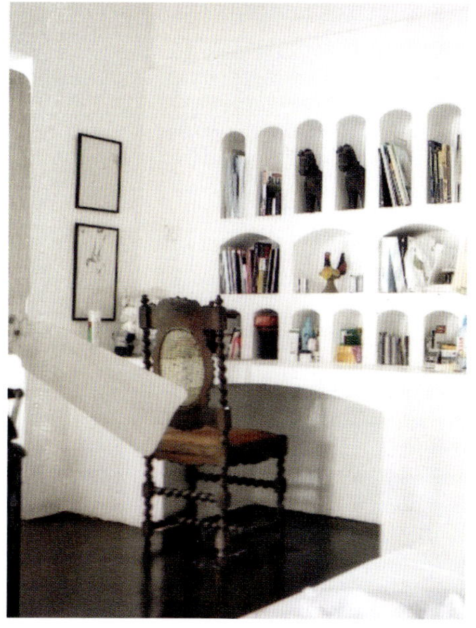

Shelves

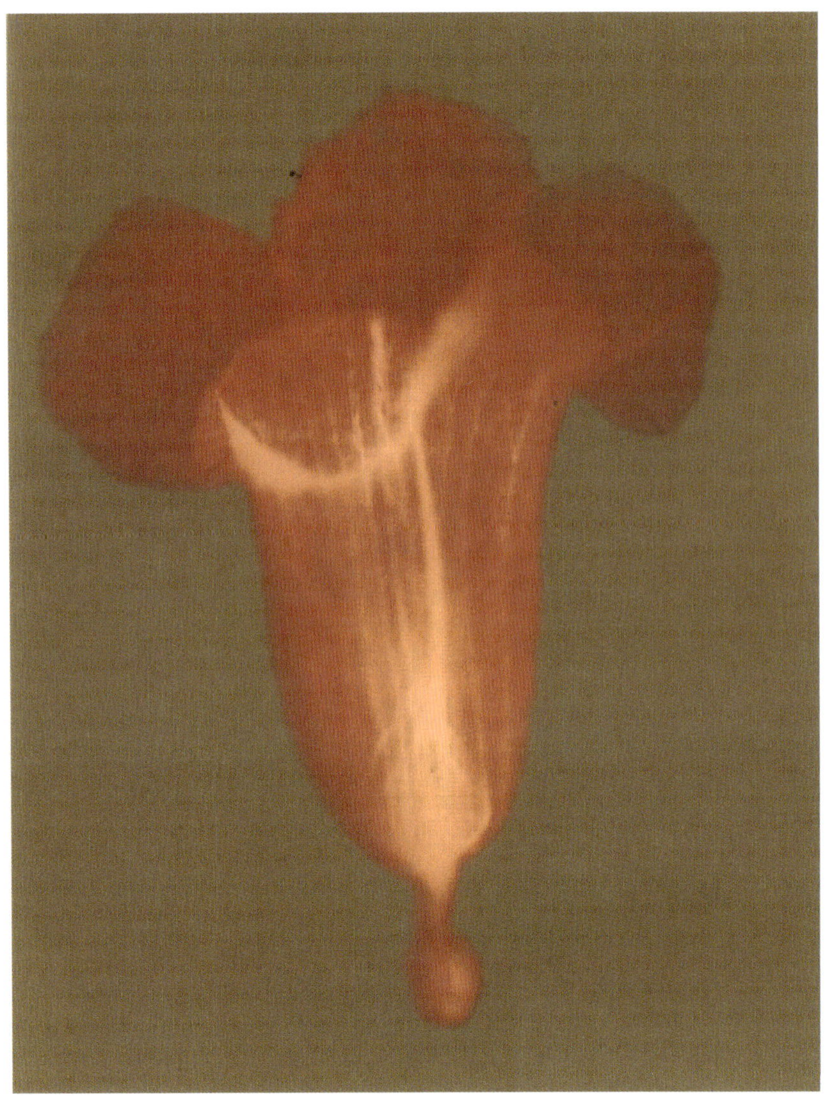

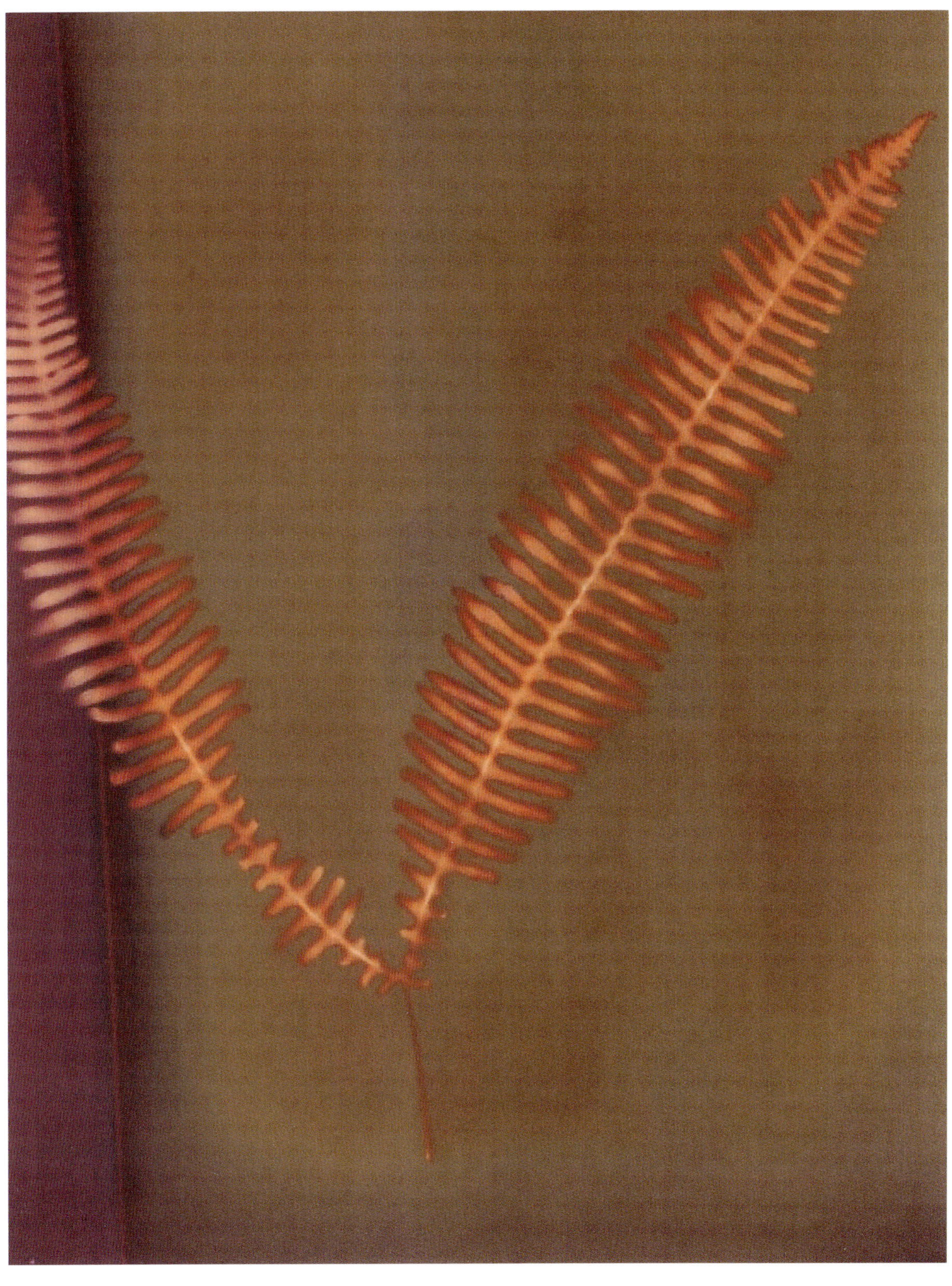

Fern 3

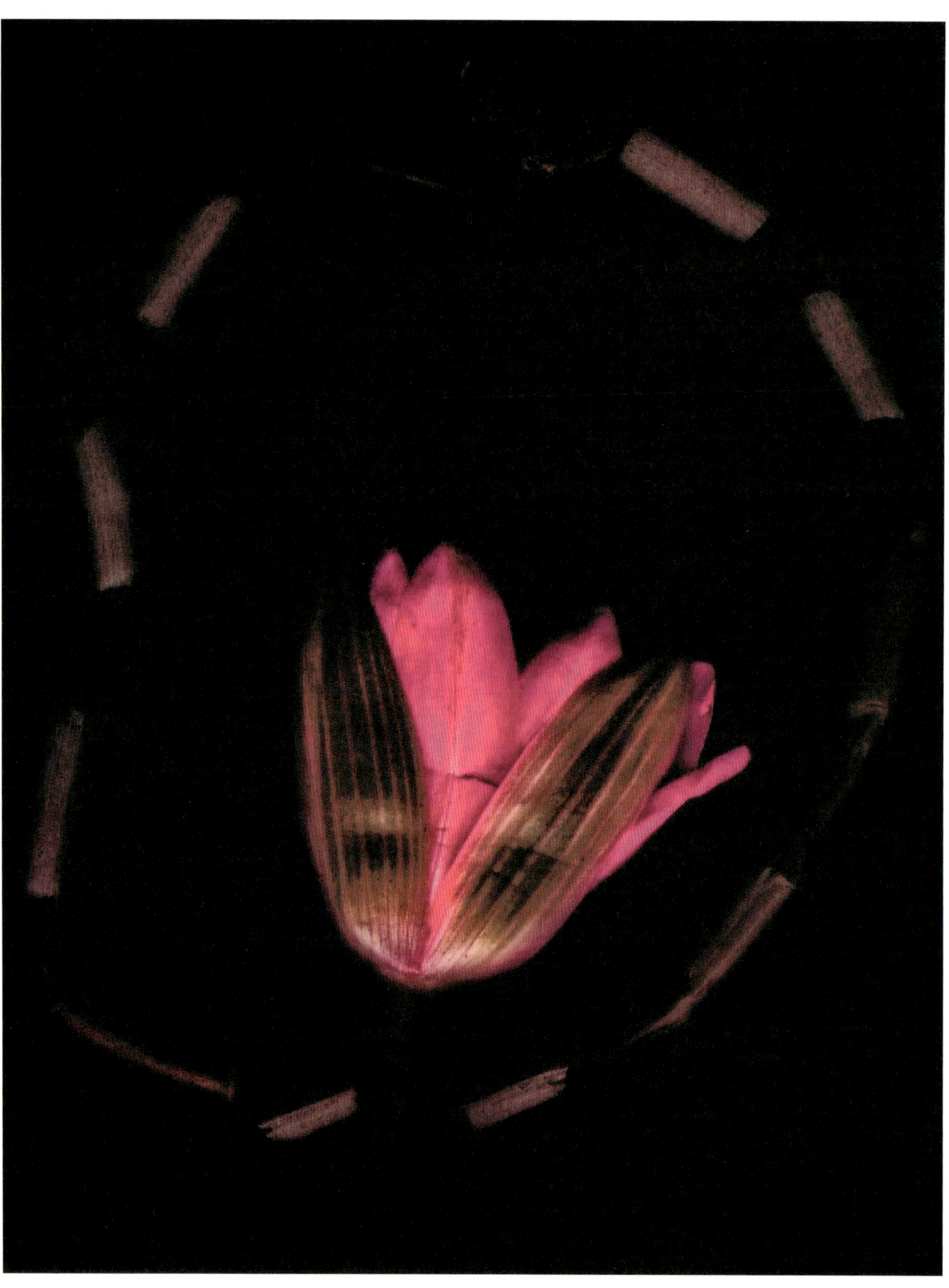

Lotus Flower

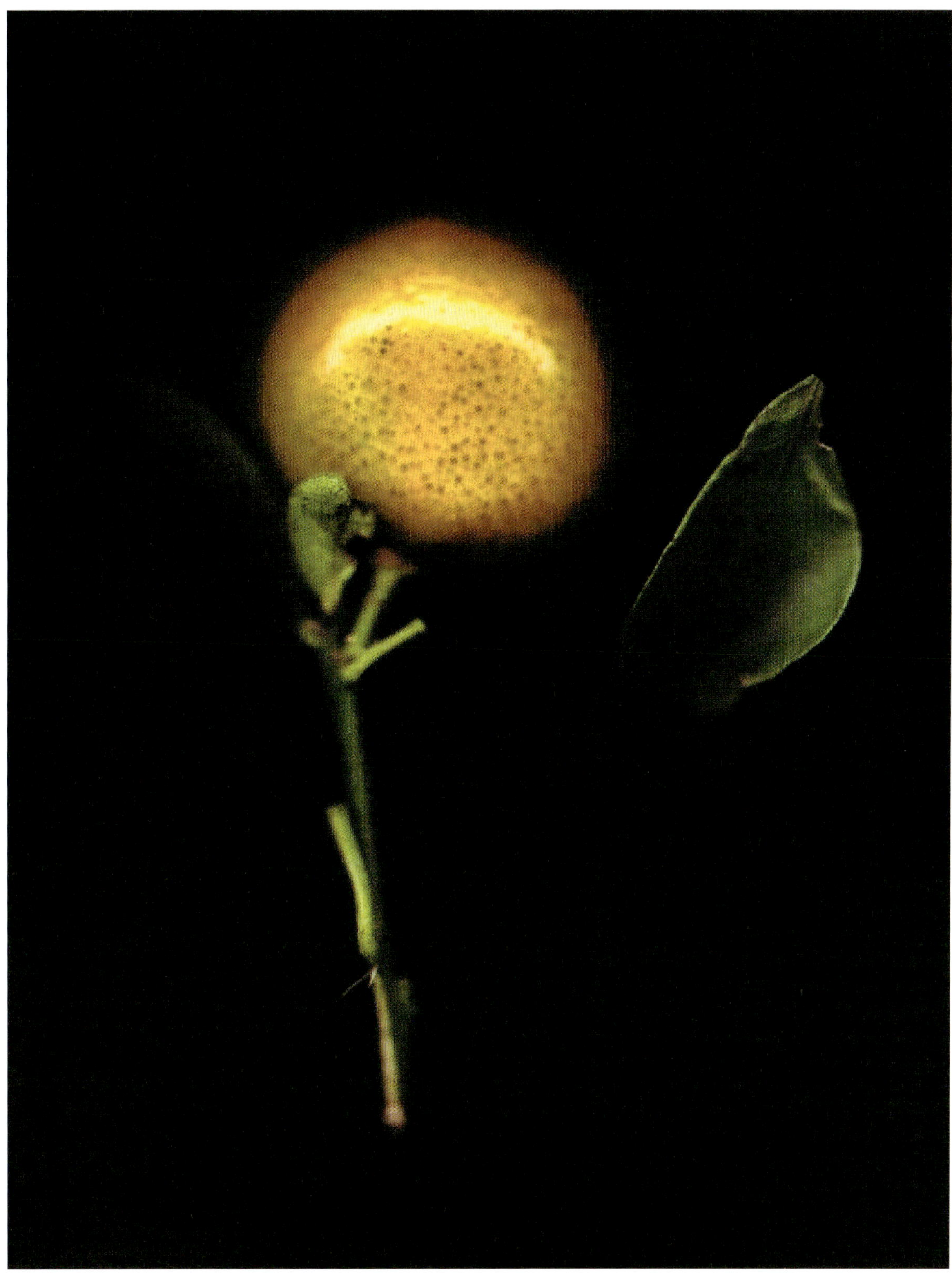

Scanned Plants, Lunuganga, Sri Lanka 2004

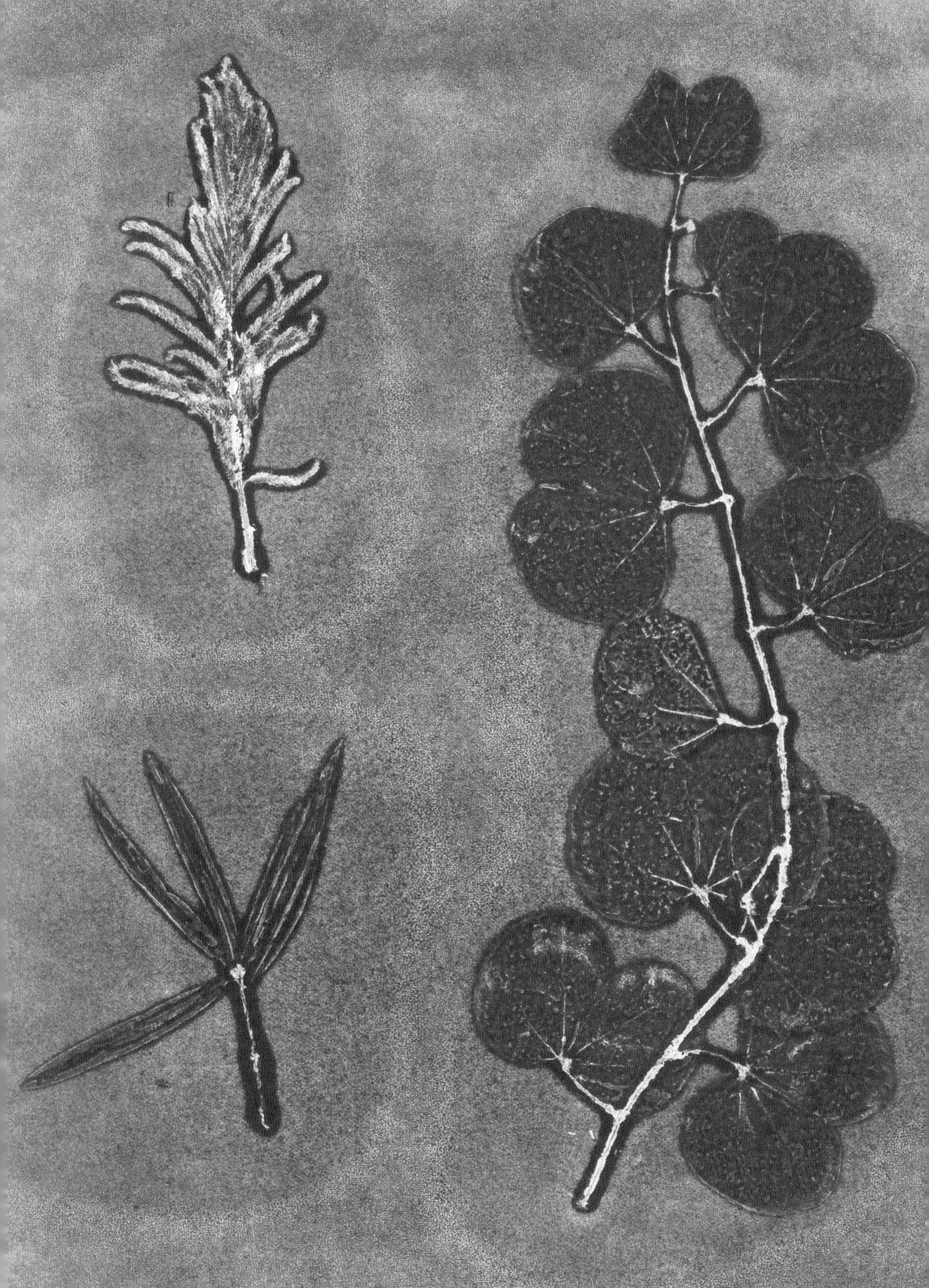

Cheryl Finley

*G*i*ving* T*hem* T*heir* F*lowers*

For forty years, Joy Gregory has developed an artistic practice informed by a passion for humanity, history, place and beauty. Mastering nineteenth-century photographic processes – sun prints, calotypes, photograms, cyanotypes – she captures time and place to enlist her viewers in contemplative visual understanding. Writing thirty-five years ago in the artist's seminal *Autograph ABP* monograph, Sunil Gupta, asserted, 'Gregory is best appreciated in the context of the international'.[1] By then she had exhibited her foundational series *Autoportraits* (1990), the *Language of Flowers* (1993–95) and *Objects of Beauty* (1995) in the UK, Australia, France, Brazil, Chile and South Africa. Artist residencies have played a key role in her drive to deepen and expand her practice as well as her desire to meet new people and experience different places and cultures. In doing so, Gregory has travelled as far and wide as the Kalahari Desert, Sri Lanka, South America and the Caribbean, noticeably, perhaps intentionally, to nodal points of the Global South. For Gregory, travelling to and negotiating new places, whether by invitation or on her own initiative, define her artistic practice broadly, and offer a window into the power of her evolving public art programme and the deep research ethos that informs it.

Accessibility, compassion and the human connection frame her public art works in London: *Love of a Long Vocation* at St Mary's Hospital (2024); *A Little Slice of Paradise* (2023), a London Underground Tube map cover; and *A Taste of Home* (2024), at Heathrow airport, Terminal 4. 'Making something for the public suits my style', Gregory says, 'the idea

1 Sunil Gupta, 'Beauty and the Beast: The Work of Joy Gregory', in *Joy Gregory Monograph* (London: Autograph, 1995), np.

that people don't have to go into a particular space to enjoy art'.[2] Her four decades of journeying around the world, photographing, teaching and meeting people have prepared her for this kind of public-facing, site-specific work.

Migration, memory and botany long have served as thematic anchors of Gregory's oeuvre amplified uniquely by her approach to process and technique. In *Love of a Long Vocation*, the Imperial College Healthcare NHS Trust commissioned her as artist-in-residence to work closely with long serving staff members across five hospitals to create a series of photographic portraits and oral histories that incisively weave collective and institutional memory to reveal a rarely told story of care and community.[3] For this commission, Gregory photographed hospital workers – doctors, nurses and technicians, who are mostly Caribbean, South Asian and African immigrants – and asked them about their greatest desires, their professions, their friendships and their hopes for future generations. Her inviting albumen portraits of them now enliven the hallways of Charing Cross Hospital, providing respite for patients, of course, but for Gregory's purpose, too, the hospital workers, who have limited access to leisure time, let alone the ability to travel abroad freely to visit loved ones due to increasingly restrictive visa and immigration policies.[4] This poignant series has the trademark of Gregory's participatory practice; that is, of her desire to not only picture her subjects, but to involve them in the process, through interviews, observations and often the gift of the photographic image created. Reminiscent of portraiture styles found in her earlier series, such as those of the grounds workers, gardeners, she encountered at the VAFA / Lunuganga Trust residency in Sri Lanka in 2004, she is compelled to exchange ideas as well as give those photographed copies of their own portraits. These serve as keepsakes for sure, indeed testaments to their relationship to place, where they labour, but also, to their humanity. This special gift

2 Joy Gregory quoted in Ravi Ghosh, 'Joy Gregory on Crafting Migrant Solidarity: "Home is where you feel most comfortable"', *British Journal of Photography*, 25 July 2024.

3 *Love of a Long Vocation* was commissioned by the Imperial College Healthcare NHS Trust in 2023 as part of the Art in Hospitals programme. It toured the main hospital sites [St. Mary's, Hammersmith and Charing Cross Hospitals] in 2024 and is now installed permanently at Charing Cross Hospital. Gregory photographed and conducted oral histories with 14 staff members across five hospitals, who had tenures of at least ten years or more.

4 Joy Gregory's critically acclaimed *Cinderella Tours Europe*, 2001, foreshadowed the restrictive immigration and travel policies enacted following the establishment of the European Union in 2002. Her recent public works at St Mary's Hospital and Heathrow Terminal 4 harken back to her critique of immigration policies affecting Caribbean migrants.

of Gregory's, that of translating place, makes her public artworks emphatically personal, memorable and legible. Her portraits of hospital workers exhibit a sense of longing and melancholy that aligns with and mirrors the title of the series, *Love of a Long Vocation*.

From her undergraduate studies at Manchester Polytechnic, Gregory's familiarity with the language of advertising as well as her persuasive power of visual storytelling embolden the messages she conveys in the public arena with both subtlety and intentionality. Undeniably, it is her skilled way with words, images and cadence that welcomes viewers to want to see and learn more. A teacher at heart, Gregory's public commissions also serve an educational function in tune with the day's most pressing issues. In her first commission for the London Underground, *A Little Slice of Paradise*, Gregory met with London Underground workers about the gardens they keep nearby their places of work. She collected their stories as well as their seeds and flowers to create a collage of immense beauty layered with the bounty of the collective harvests. Appealing to the millions of yearly London Underground passengers, people who use the transport for work, school, play and tourism, Gregory's *A Little Slice of Paradise* demonstrated the gardeners' sense of pride as well as the power of their stories and gardens to blossom metaphorically from 'underground'. As a tube map cover, her compelling image was available in handheld format as well as on digital advertising screens, amplifying its communicative power as a public artwork.

Installed on a series of twenty-four billboards in the Piccadilly line ticket hall rotunda of Heathrow Terminal 4 station, *A Taste of Home* greets visitors arriving to or leaving from one of the world's busiest airports. Notably, presciently, Sunil Gupta, asserted of Gregory that hers is 'an art that is engaged with contemporary concerns which draws viewers in by using aesthetic pleasure to trigger a response'.[5] This is clear in her decades-long concern with plant life: flowers, seeds, petals and their dispersal through historic and detrimental colonial practices that gave way to diasporic communities. The works created for Art on the Underground are girded in this concern and its effect on migrant communities, notably refugees and asylum seekers living in abeyance far afield from central London and within close proximity of Heathrow. This series affirms a timely social impact that is subtle, yet direct. Involving the asylum seekers in a series of photographic workshops, Gregory employed the aesthetics of collage to combine essential ingredients and personal experiences of home and migration with fragments from the poetry of Khaled Abdallah and Warsan Shire.[6] For these works, she also selected fragments from recipes that evoke the sensibilities of home through

5 Sunil Gupta, 'Beauty and the Beast: The Work of Joy Gregory', in *Joy Gregory Monograph* (London: Autograph, 1995), np.

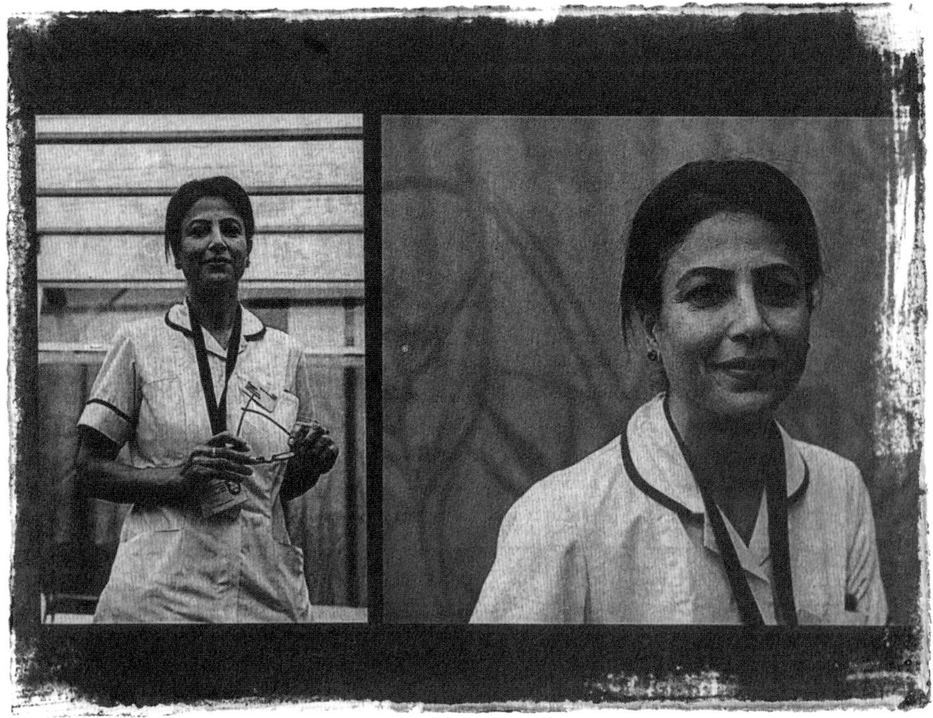

foodways and plant life that recall communal practices of planting, harvesting, cooking, sharing, eating, ceremony and dreaming.

The images Gregory produced for *A Taste of Home* are informed by tactile interaction with objects, flower petals, seeds and plant matter, and the interplay between the lines of poetry and the cyanotype images strikes the kind of delicate balance Gupta refers to in the artist's use of 'aesthetic pleasure to trigger a response'. Together, her images and the poetry invite viewers transiting through Heathrow airport to consider what home means to them in the midst of global migration crises. Through her heartfelt installation, Gregory's seeds of wisdom ultimately cultivate a sense of belonging no matter where home is.

6 Khaled Aballah, *Seeds in Flight* translated by Sarah Vaghefian with the Poetry Translation Workshop, 2021, and Warsan Shire, *Home*, 2023. Born in Gaza, Abdallah is an award-winning Palestinian poet now living in Paris. Shire is a Somali British poet and 2013–14 Young Poet Laureate for London.

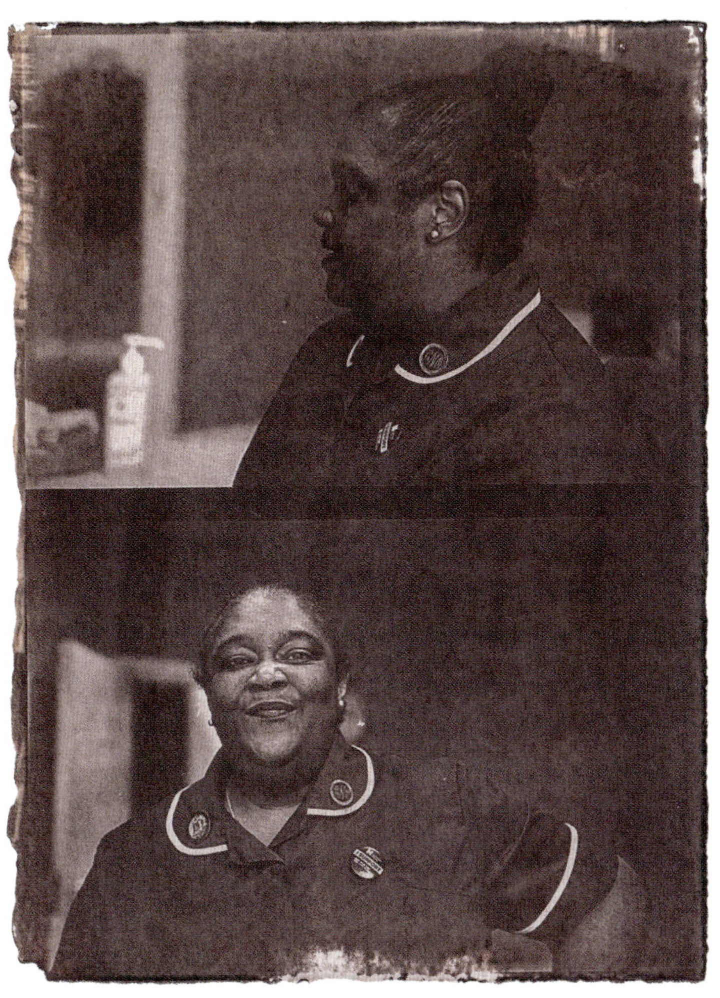

Winny

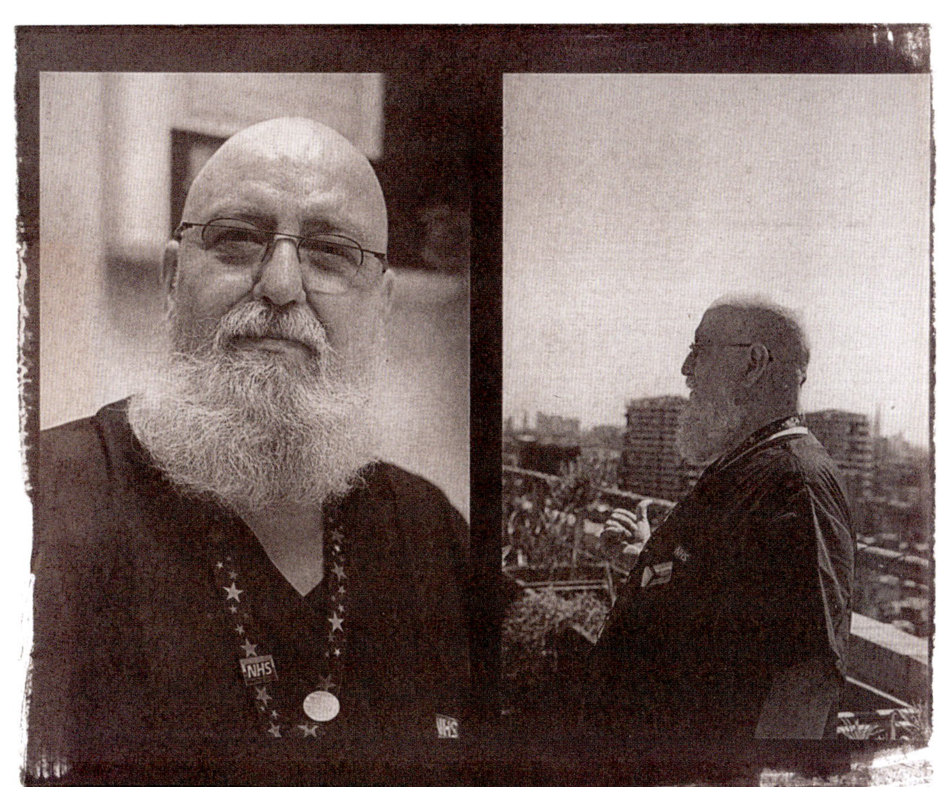

Ricky

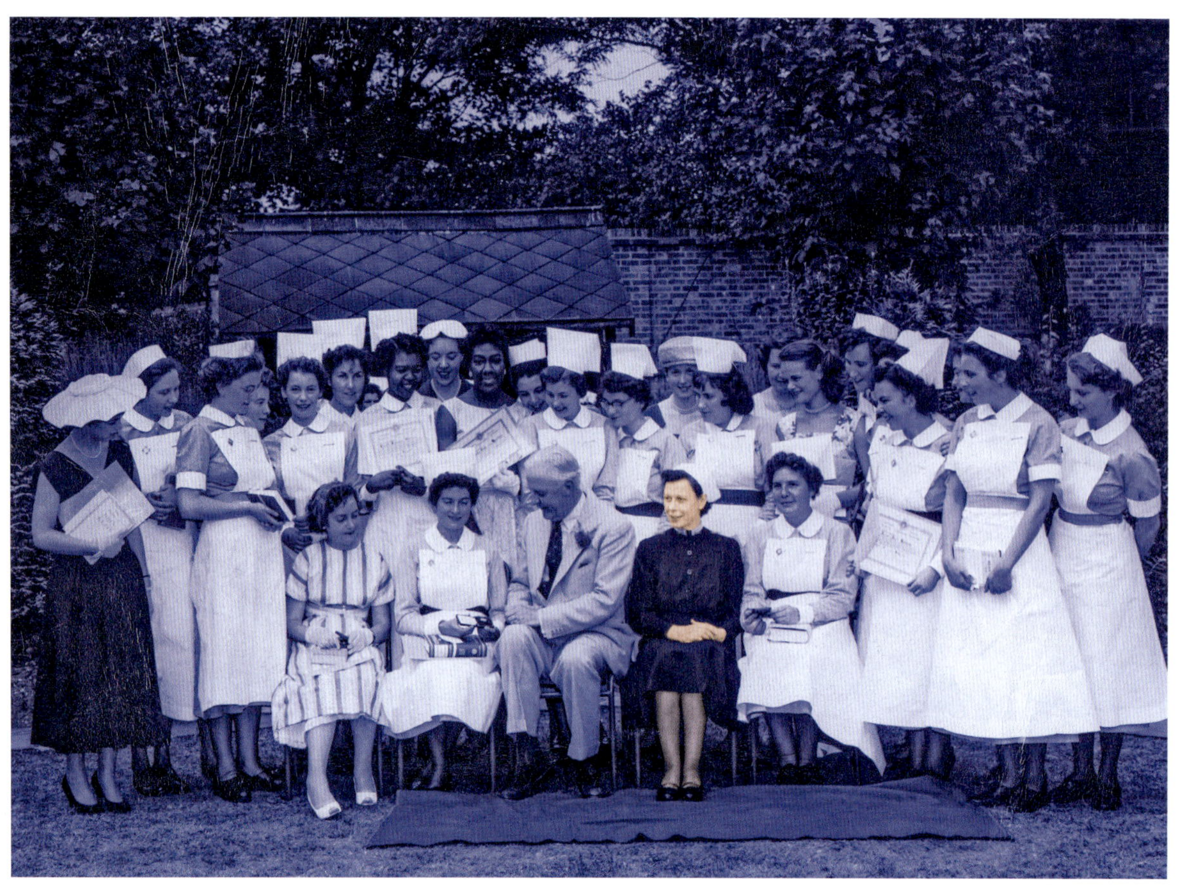

Passing Out

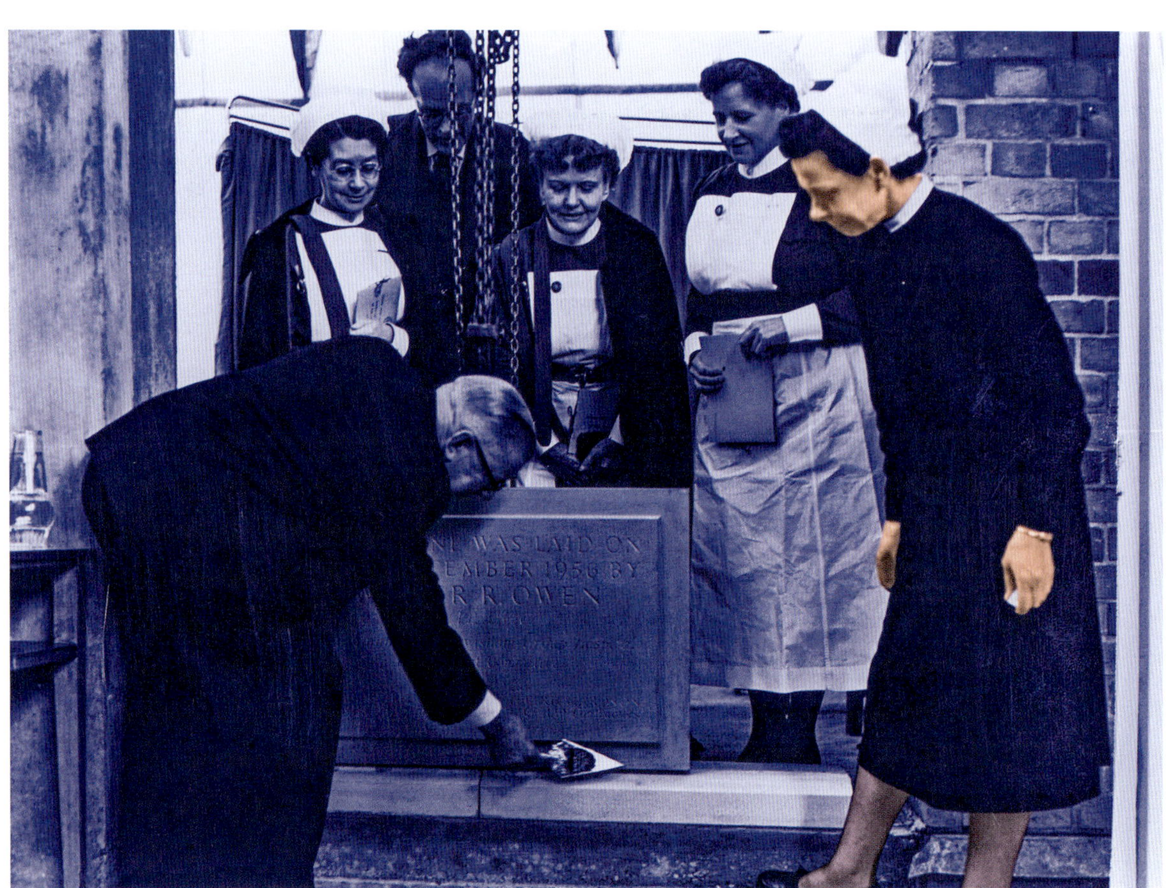

Outpatients Foundation-Stone

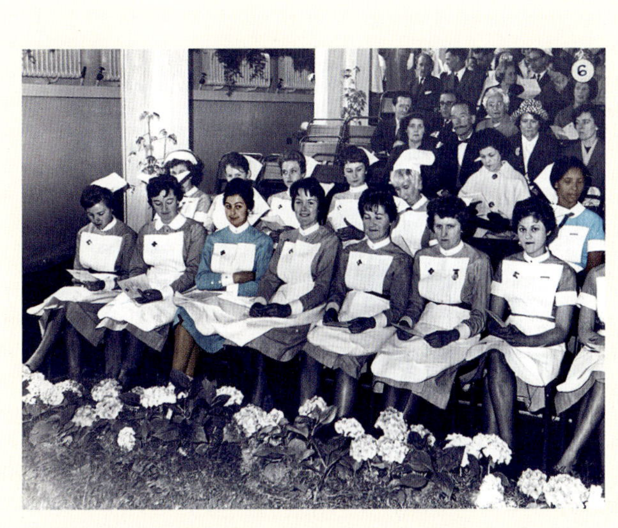

Alongside Matron Bell there…

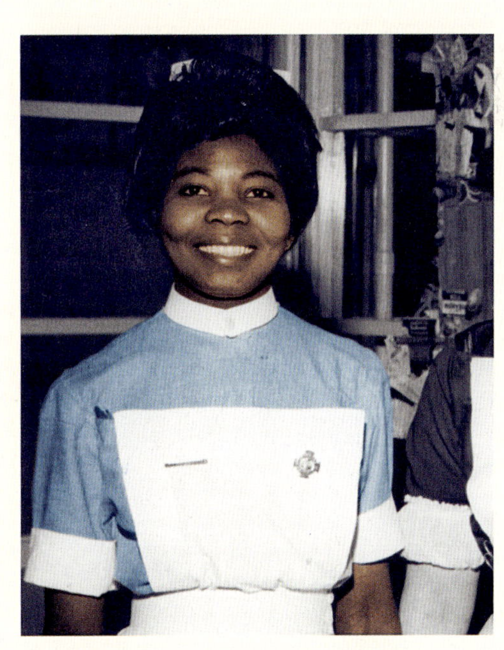

were a wealth of nurses and healthcare workers

Left **Matron Bell** 2008
Right **Alongside Matron Bell** 2020

Charlotte Gardener
Hung at this site for her
part in the Gordon Riots

TOWER HILL

She was part of the
Black resistance movement
which sprang up in London
in the 1760s

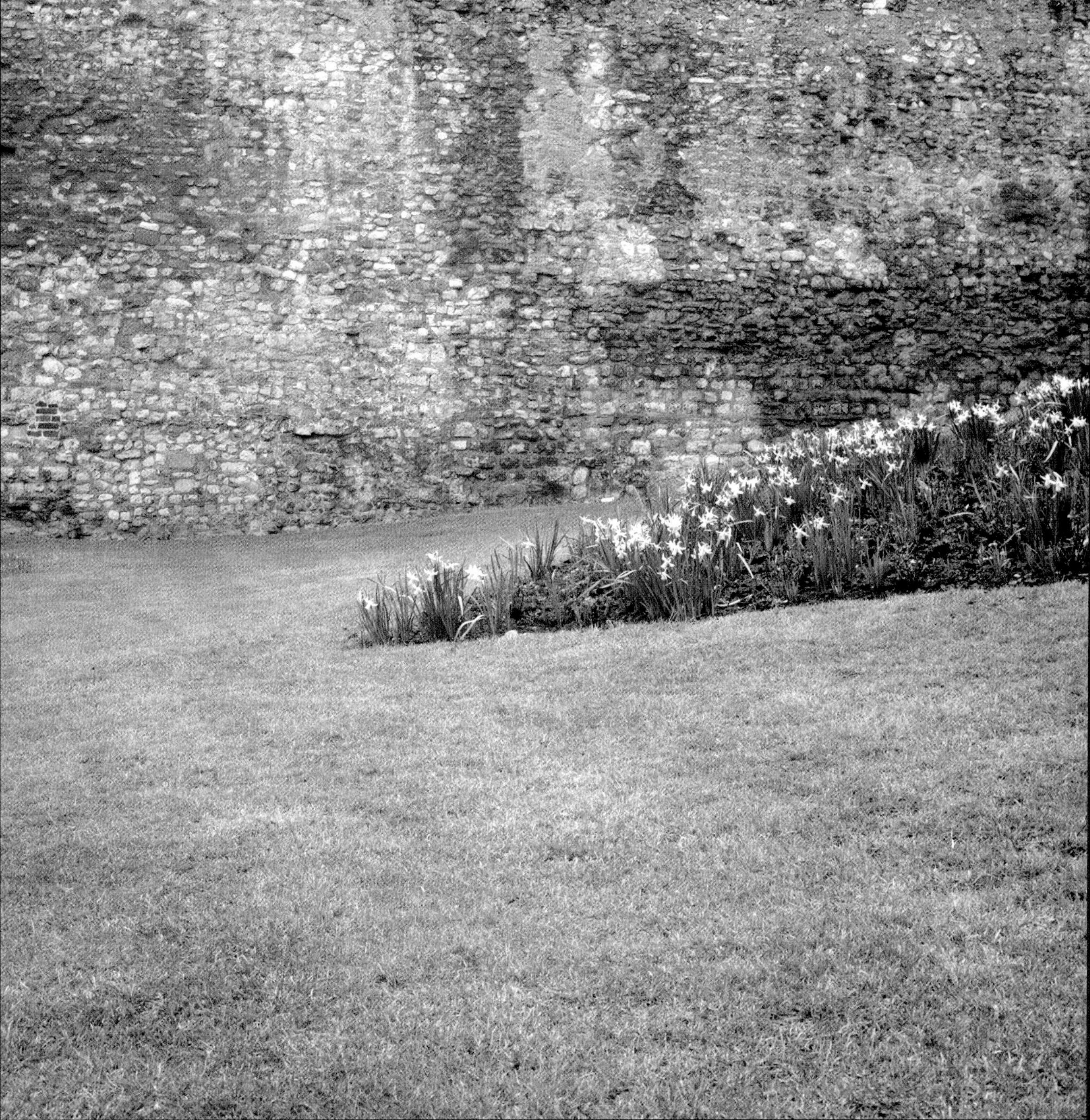

BRICK LANE

1787

Site of a protest meeting
against a law to expel all
Africans from Britain

Street market close to Whitechapel

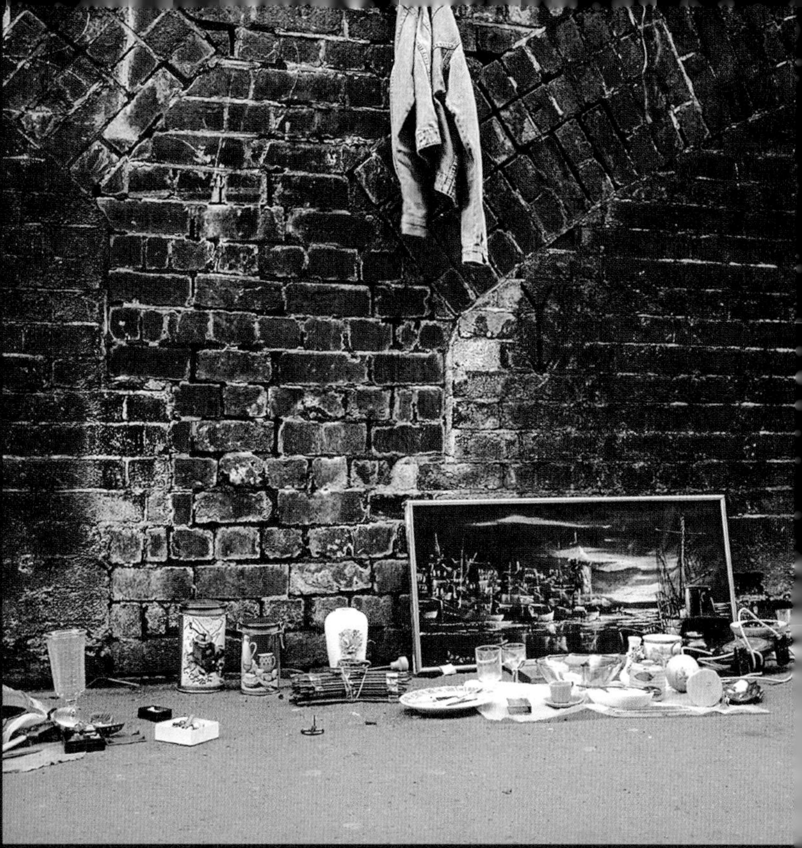

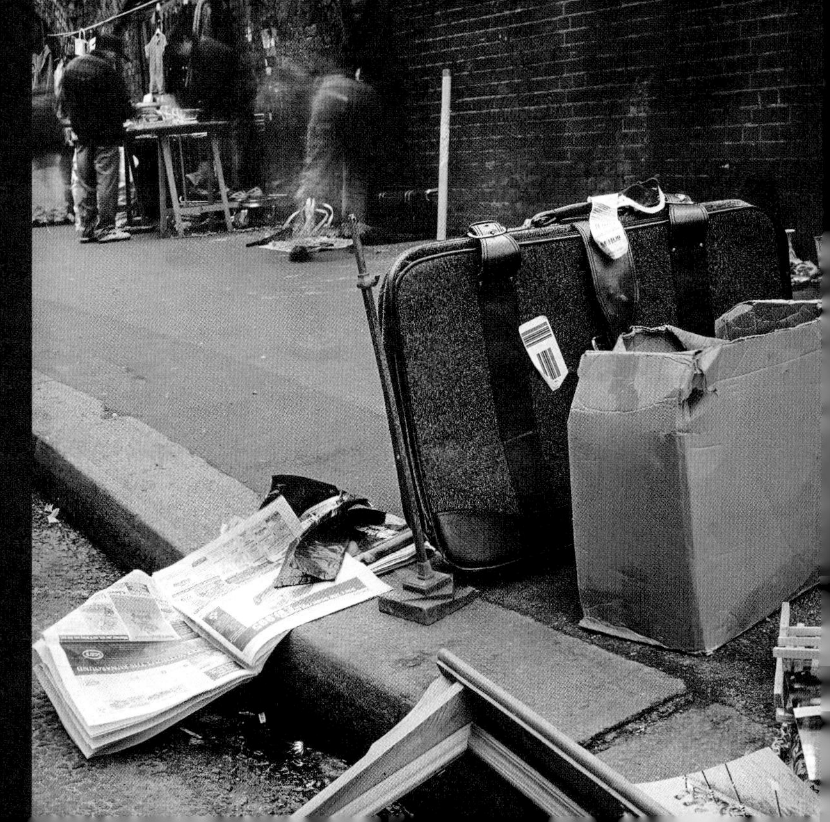

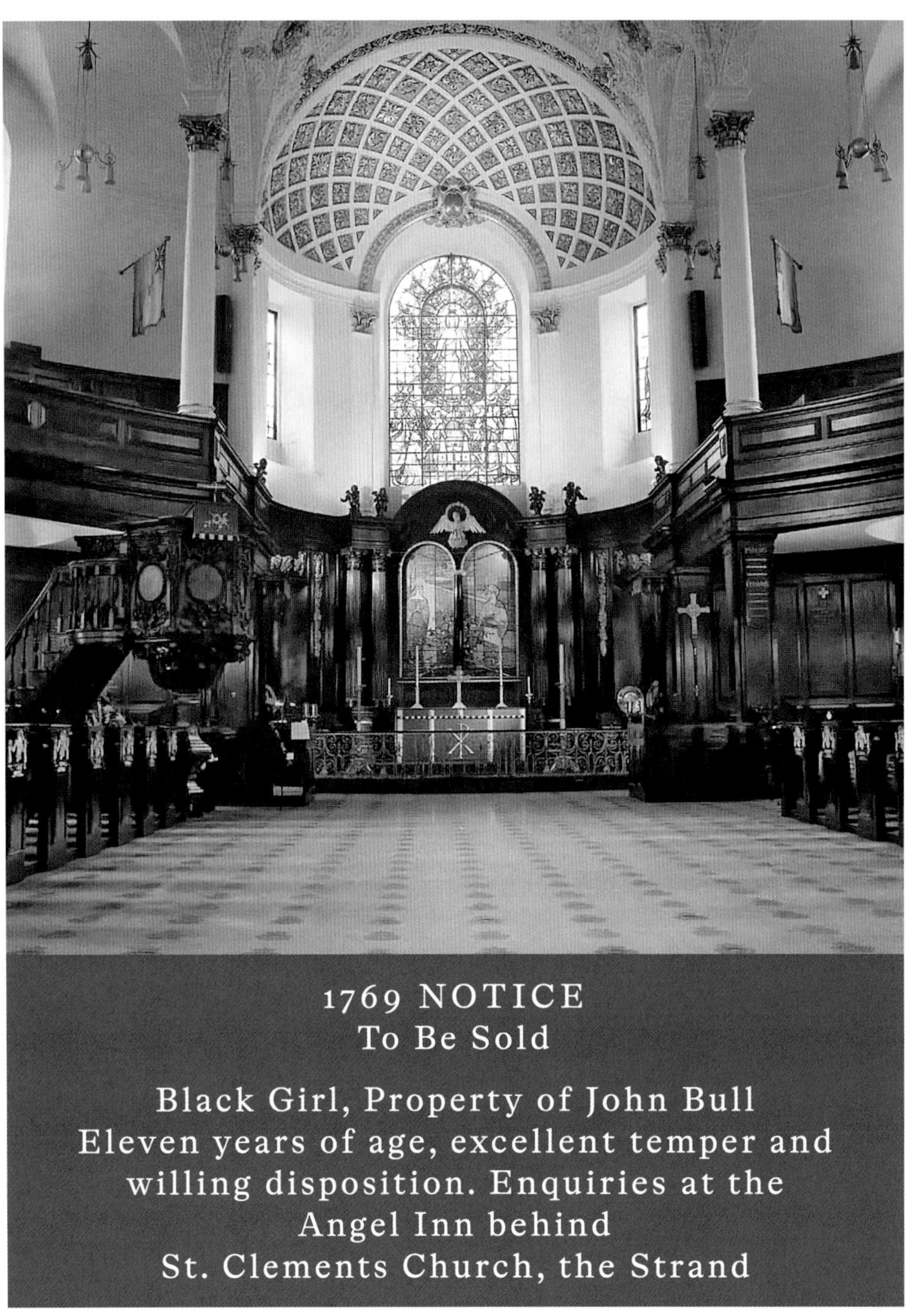
1769 NOTICE
To Be Sold
Black Girl, Property of John Bull
Eleven years of age, excellent temper and
willing disposition. Enquiries at the
Angel Inn behind
St. Clements Church, the Strand

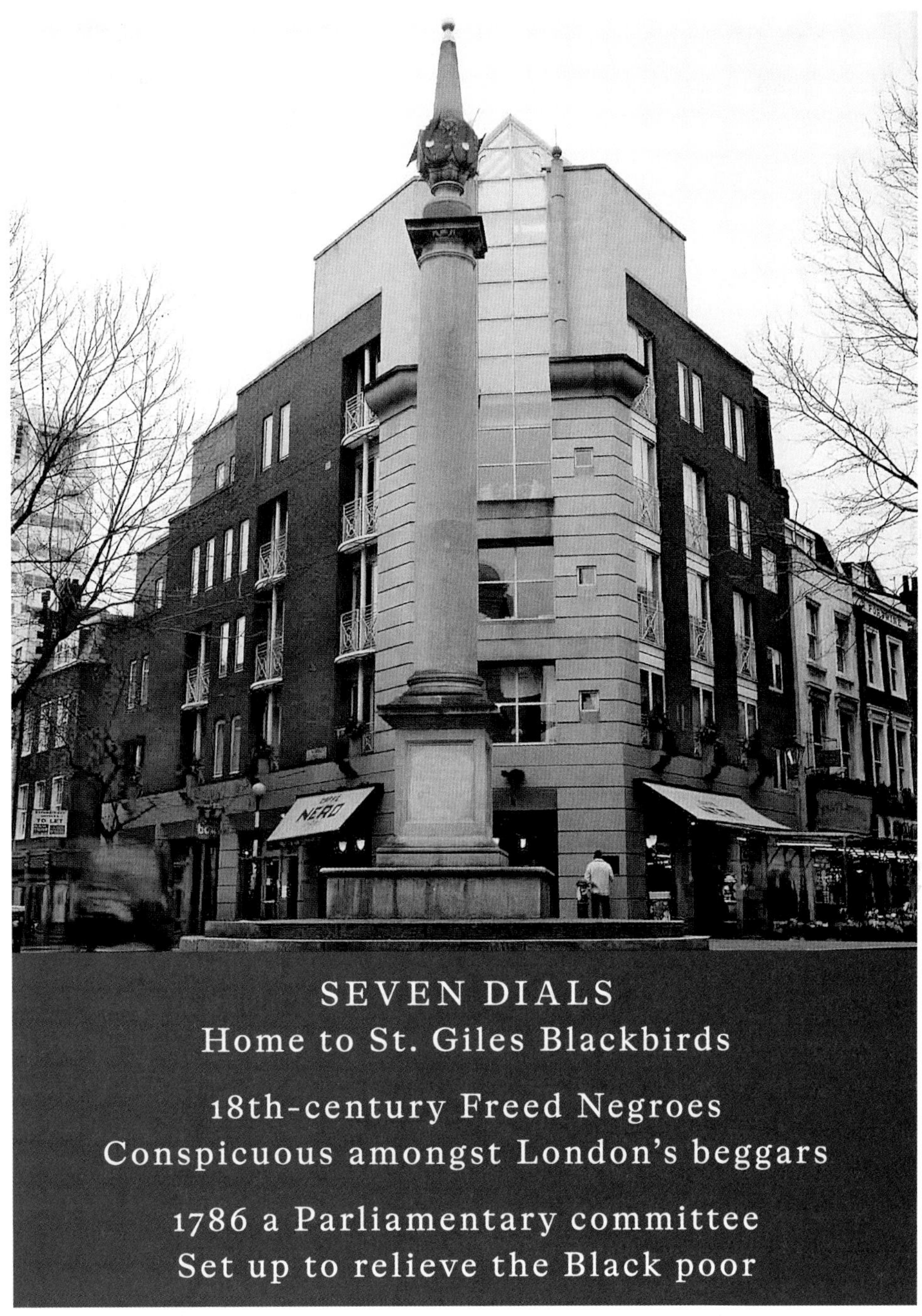
SEVEN DIALS
Home to St. Giles Blackbirds
18th-century Freed Negroes
Conspicuous amongst London's beggars
1786 a Parliamentary committee
Set up to relieve the Black poor

Semiramis

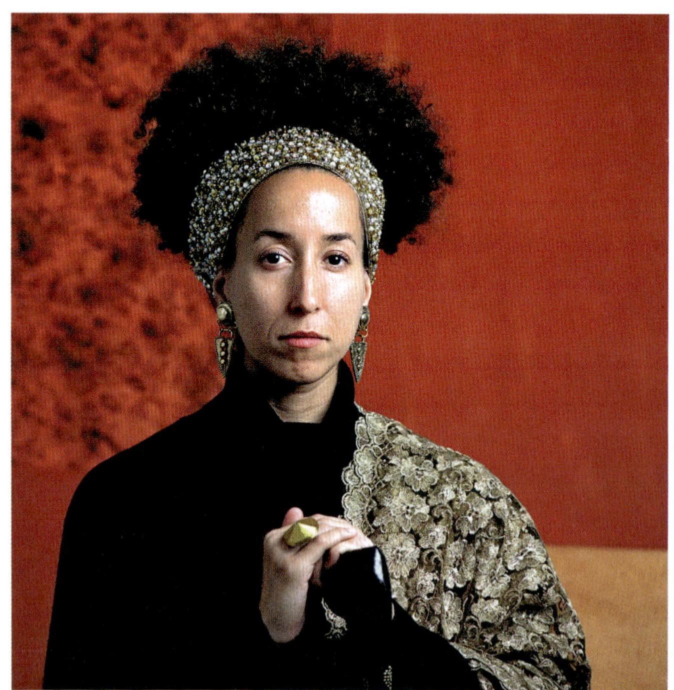

semiramis, assyrian queen of babylon
mighty conqueror of barbary & ethiopia

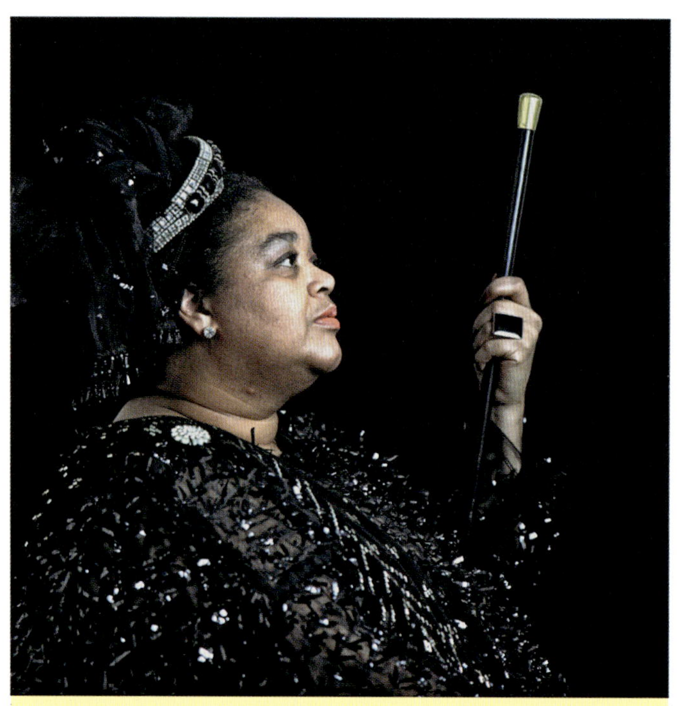

the noble triumph of lady dayfele placed
the great duke of athens in perpetual exile

Lady Dayfele

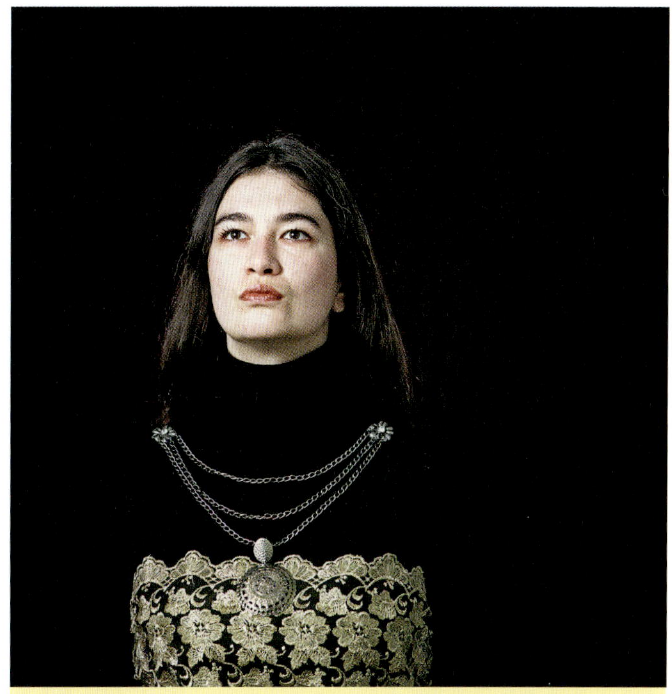

Hippolyta

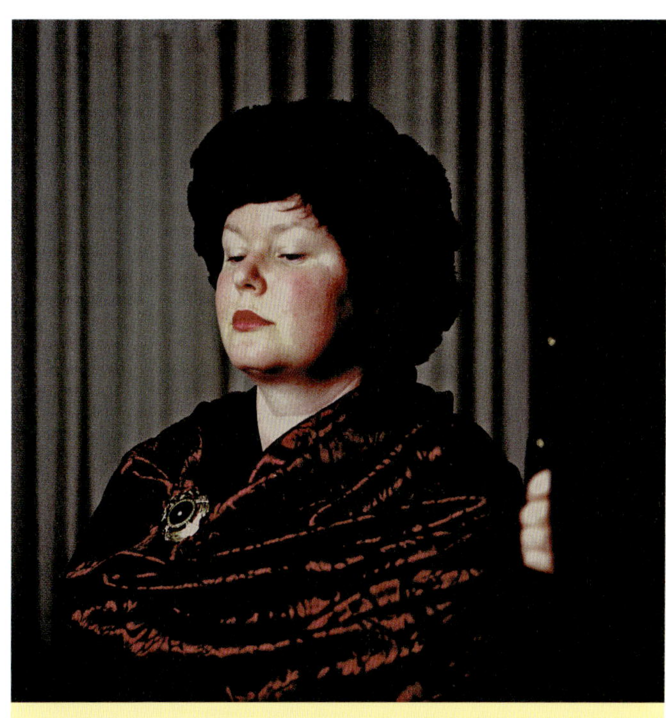

Thomyris

**The Amberley Queens,
Heroines of Antiquity** 1999

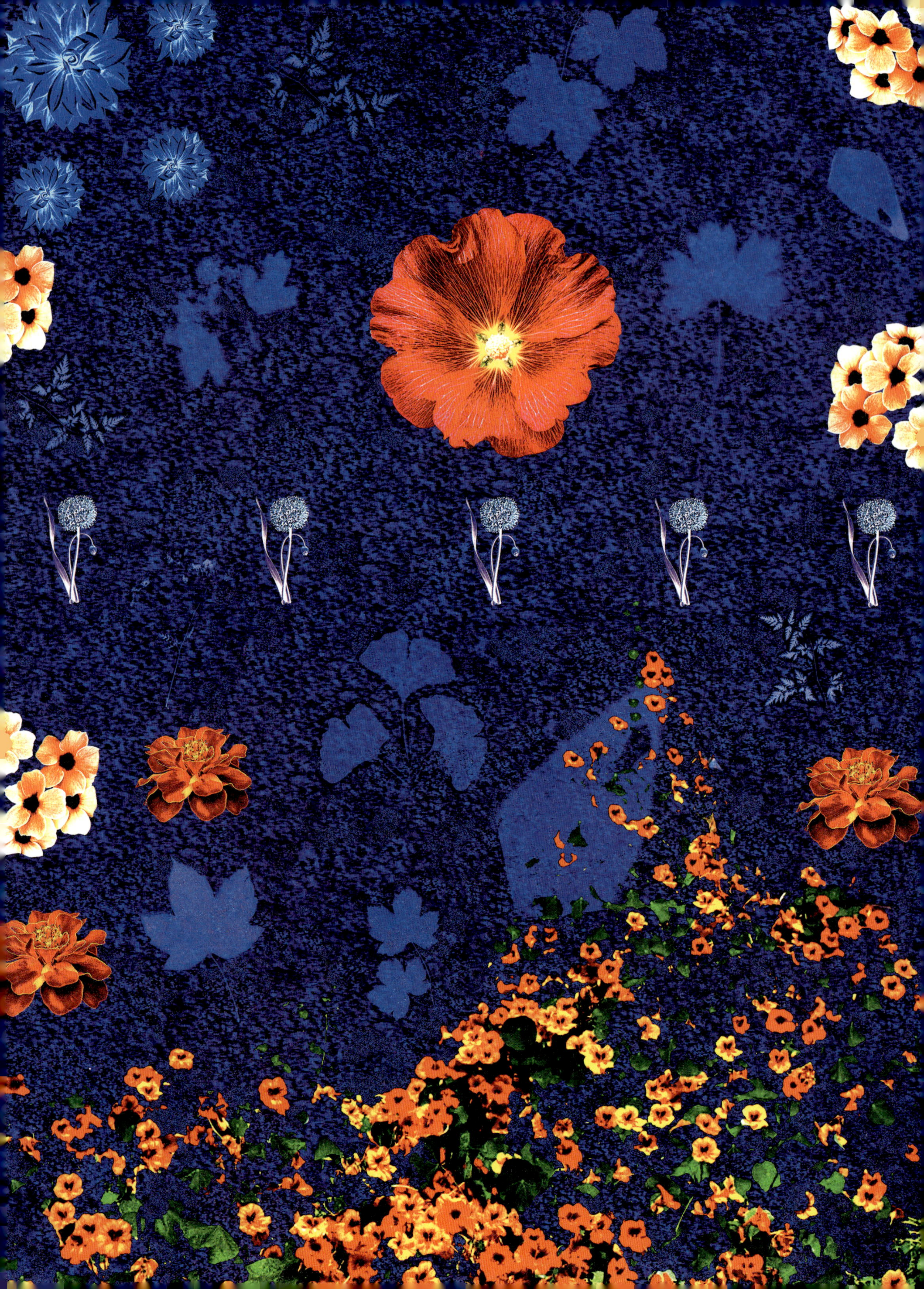

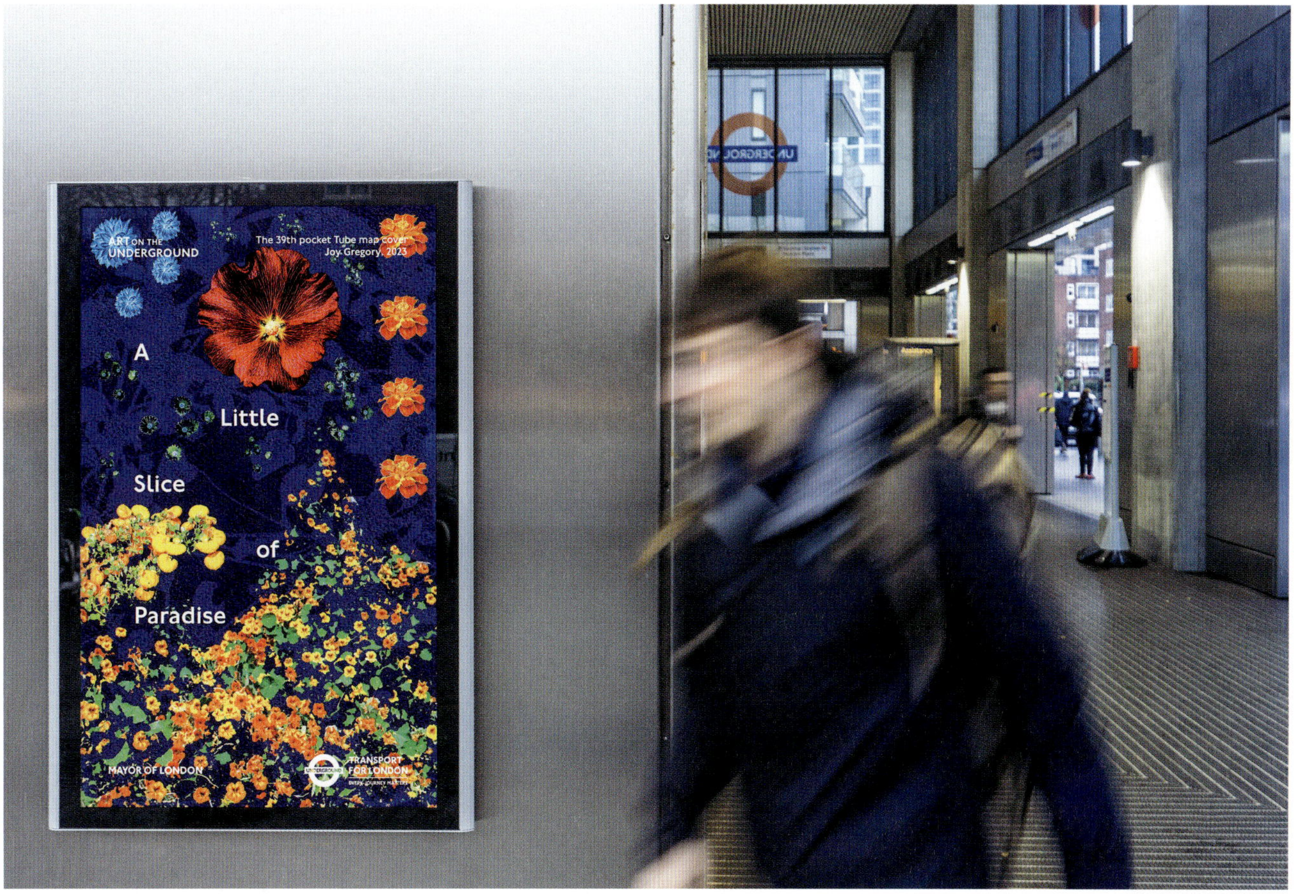

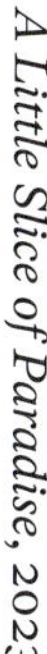

A Little Slice of Paradise, 2023

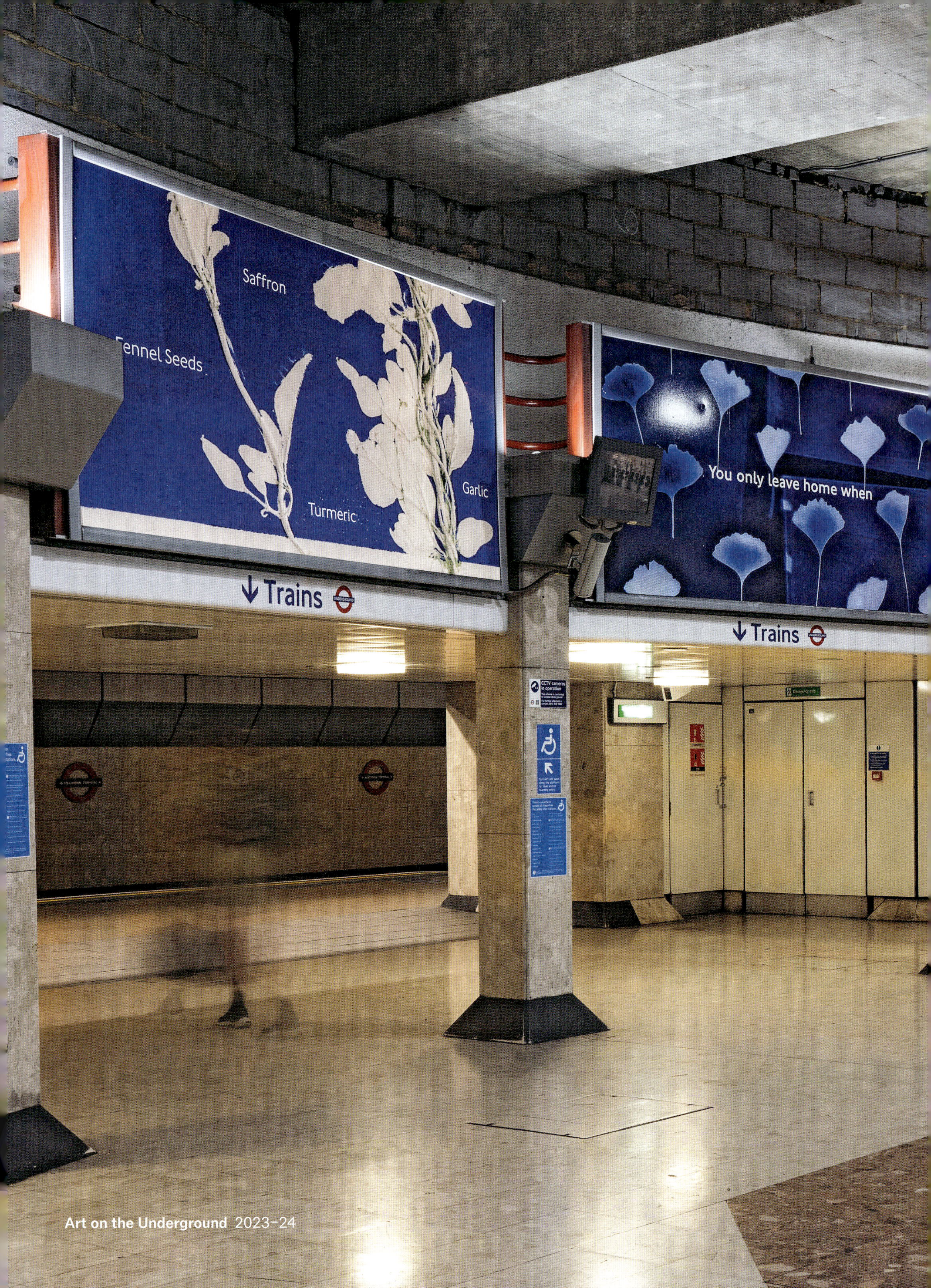
Saffron
Fennel Seeds
Turmeric
Garlic
You only leave home when
↓ Trains
↓ Trains

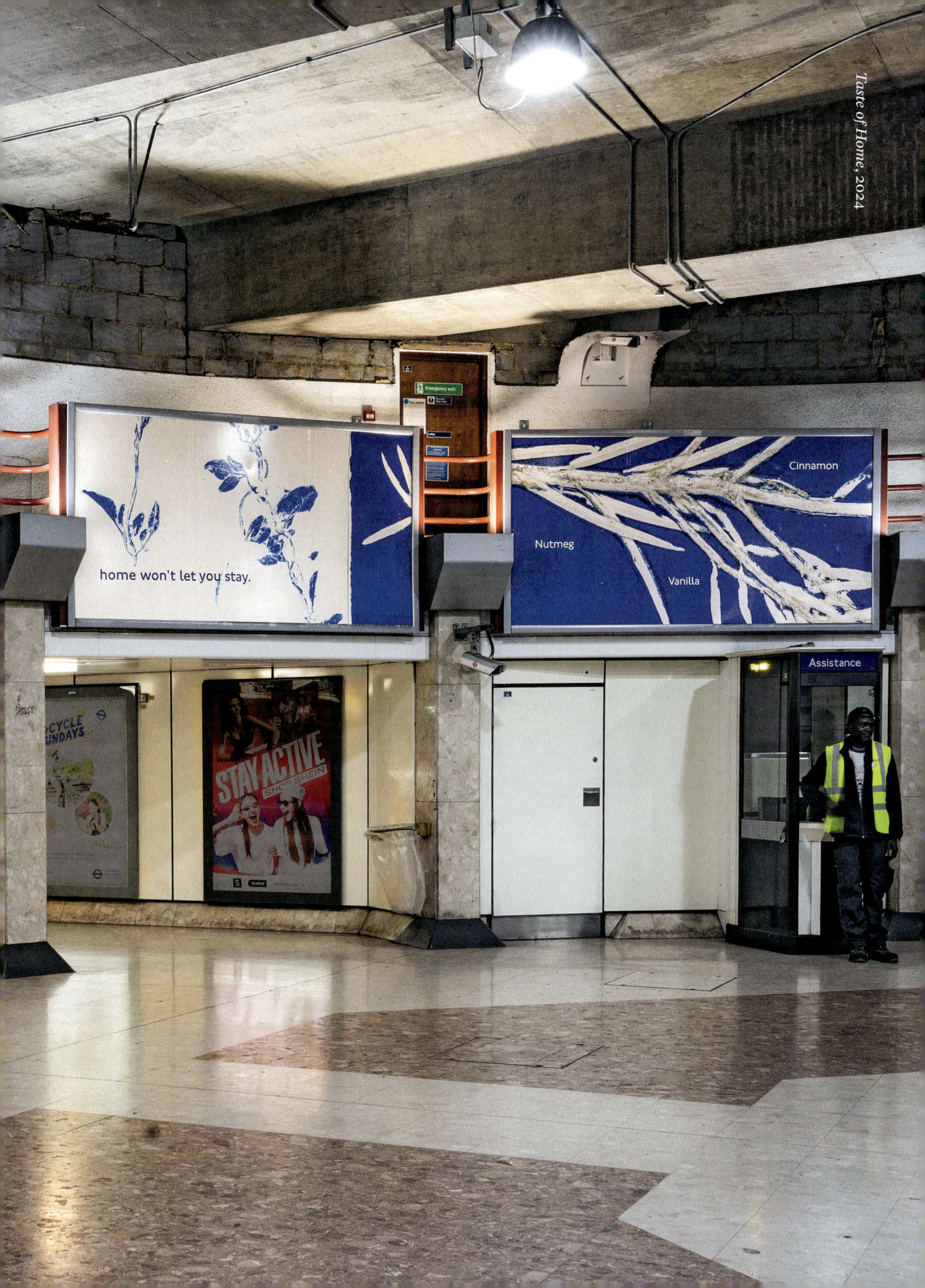

Taste of Home, 2024

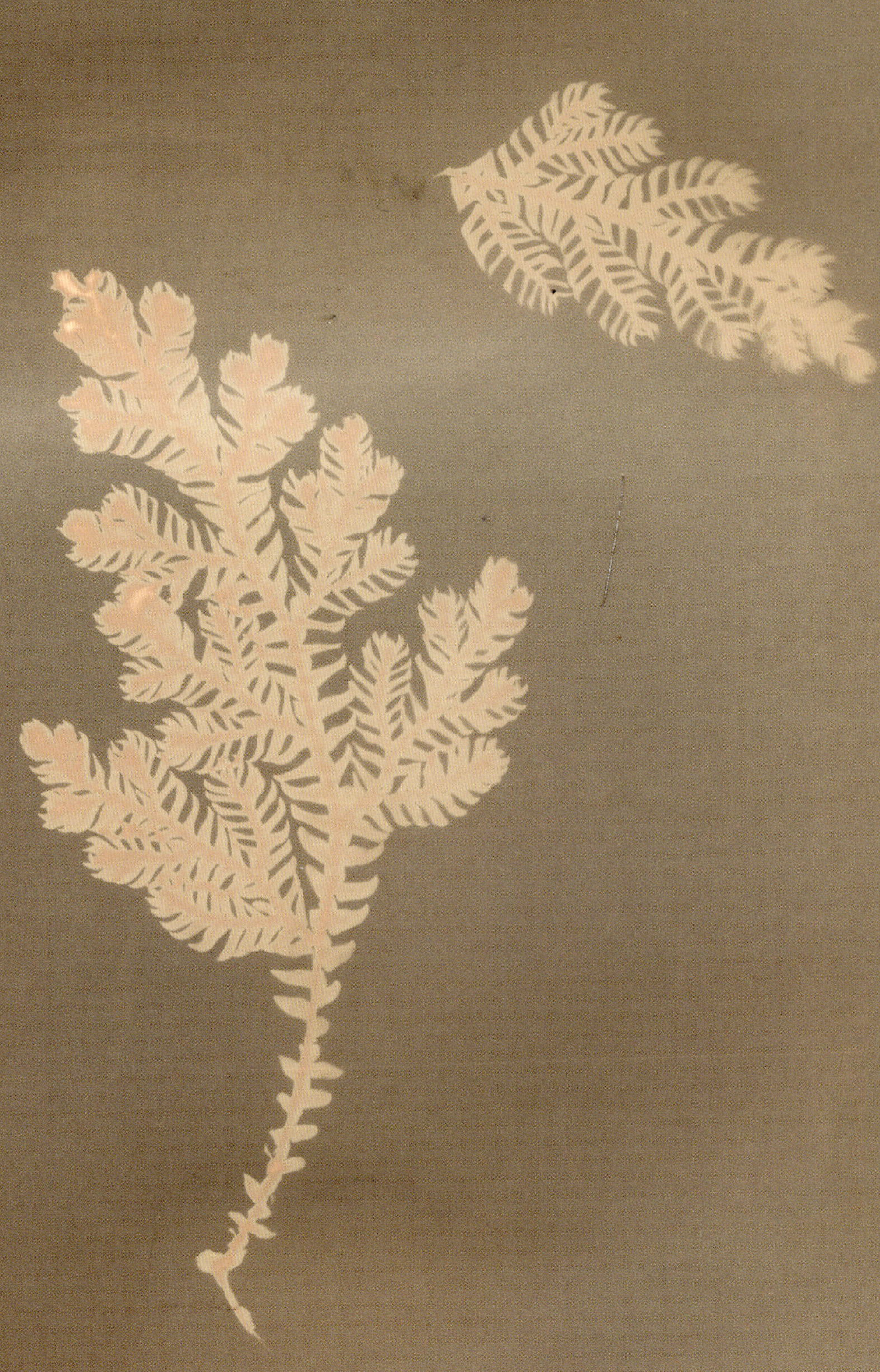

Fixed Plants, Lunuganga, Sri Lanka 2004

List of Works

Autoportrait

Autoportrait, 1989–90,
silver gelatin lith print.
Courtesy the artist and DACS
cover, pp. 7–9

Women and Space

Hotel Normandia #2, Andorra La Vella, 1988, liquid light silver gelatin print on watercolour paper
p. 16

Plaza Sagrada Familia #1, Barcelona, 1988, liquid light silver gelatin print on watercolour paper
Plaza Sagrada Familia #2, Barcelona, 1988, liquid light silver gelatin print on watercolour paper
Hotel Normandia #1, Andorra La Vella, 1988, liquid light silver gelatin print on watercolour paper
Villaroel, Barcelona, 1988, liquid light silver gelatin print on watercolour paper
p. 17

Holland Park, 1989, silver gelatin print
p. 18

Barcelona, 1988, liquid light silver gelatin print on watercolour paper
pp. 11, 21

The Honeymoon Project

The Honeymoon (Staten Island Ferry), 1992, kallitype
p. 19

Silence, 1991–95, kallitype
p. 20

Shame, 1991–95, kallitype
p. 22

Reflection, 1991–95, kallitype
p. 23

Touch, 1991–95, kallitype
p. 24

Uncertainty, 1991–95, kallitype
p. 25

Silence (II), 1991–95, kallitype
p. 35

Self Portraits 1997–2010

Amy in Wood Panelling, 1997–2010, c-type print
Grooming, 1997–2010, c-type print
Alone, 1997–2010, c-type print
p. 26

Sleeping, 1997–2010, c-type print
p. 27

Black Ski Hat

Self Portrait in Wool Hat & Polo Neck [Scratched], 1987–98, silver gelatin film
p. 28

Self Portrait in Wool Hat & Polo Neck, 1987–98, silver gelatin film
p. 29

Self-Portrait in Black Ski Hat, 1988, colour negative contact sheet
pp. 30–1

Old Clothes

Santa Maria (Cowboy & Angels) Top, 2007–present, c-type print
Cream-Gold-Brocade, 2007–present, c-type print
p. 32

Red Sleeveless Top, 2007–present, c-type print
Blue & Gold Twin-set with Gold Lamé Collar, 2007–present, c-type print
p. 33

Constructed Interiors

Grey Room [Janet standing], 1985, colour transparency / cibachrome
Grey Room [Janet sitting], 1985, colour transparency / cibachrome
p. 40

Fairest / The Blonde

Zara, 1997, fuji crystal archive print, still from the film *Fairest*
p. 43

Ingrid (The Blonde), c-type contact sheet, from the series *The Blonde*
Stockwell Siren, 2003, performance / c-type print, from the series *Celebrity Blonde*
p. 45

Language of Flowers

Magnolia – Perseverance, 1986–2004, cyanotype
p. 47

3 Lime Tree Leaves, 1986–2004, cyanotype
Peony, 1986–2004, cyanotype
Catkins, 1986–2004, cyanotype
Mallow, 1986–2004, cyanotype
p. 48

Chickweed, 1986–2004, cyanotype
Carnation, 1986–2004, cyanotype
Dandelion, 1986–2004, cyanotype
Puffball, 1986–2004, cyanotype
p. 49

Objects of Beauty

Knickers, 1992–95, kallitype
Hairpiece, 1992–95, kallitype
p. 14

Shoes, 1992–95, kallitype
p. 50

Stockings, 1992–95, kallitype
Scissors, 1992–95, kallitype
Bustier, 1992–95, kallitype
Bow, 1992–95, kallitype
p. 51

Earrings, 1992–95, kallitype
Hairgrip, 1992–95, kallitype
Comb, 1992–95, kallitype
False Eyelashes, 1992–95, kallitype
p. 52

Gloves, 1992–95, kallitype
p. 53

Girl Thing

Ultramarine Velveteen Bikini, 2002–04, cyanotype
p. 54

Big Haired Barbie, 2002–04, cyanotype
p. 55

White Rose Corset, 2002–04, cyanotype
p. 56

White Lace Dressing Table Doilies, 2002–04, cyanotype
p. 57

Black Satin & Lace Half-Petticoat, 2002–04, cyanotype
p. 58

Wooden Fan, 2002–04, cyanotype
p. 59

The Handbag Project

Claire's Bag, 1998–2008, salt print
p. 36

Black Bead, 1998–2008, salt print
Maggie Thatcher's Handbag, 1998–2008, salt print
p. 39

Big Beauty, 2002–04, salt print
p. 60

Two Metal Evening Bags, 2002–04, salt print.
Tate: Purchased with funds provided by the Photography Acquisitions Committee 2022
p. 61

Seeds of Empire

Little or No Breeze, 2021, archival digital print on fine art paper
p. 62

Observations: A Little Breeze, Joy Gregory and Philip Miller, 2021, HD video with sound, duration: 4 minutes 14 seconds, exhibited at Danielle Arnaud Gallery. Installation photography by Oskar Proctor
p. 65

Observations: Rose, Joy Gregory and Philip Miller, 2021, HD video with sound, duration: 14 minutes 50 seconds
p. 66

The Staircase (Little or no breeze), 2021, archival digital print on fine art paper
p. 68

The Drawing Room (Little or no breeze), 2021, archival digital print on fine art paper
p. 69

Joy Gregory and Philip Miller, *A Little or No Breeze*, 2021, vinyl record sleeve
p. 70

Still Breeze, 2021, archival digital print on fine art paper
p. 71

Cotton Tree, Hope Botanical Gardens, Saint Andrews, Jamaica, 2021, archival digital print on fine art paper
p. 93

Memory and Skin

Girl in Red Dress, 1998, digital print
p. 72

Canefield, Spanish Town, 1998, digital print
p. 73

Junie Sweeping, Kingston, 1998, raster print
p. 74

Native Beach, Jacmel, Haiti, 1998, raster print
p. 75

Sheila Ketwaru, Paramaribo, Suriname, 1998, c-type print
Man on a bicycle, Kingston, Jamaica, 1998, c-type print
p. 76

Manuel Pina, 1998, c-type print
p. 77

Indra and Christine, 1998, c-type print
p. 78

Rocio and Romina, 1998, toned black-and-white print
p. 79

Typing Pool, Port au Prince, 1998, raster print
p. 80

Carlos, 1998, toned black-and-white print
p. 81

Skin, 1998, miscellaneous objects and vinyl text, part of the exhibition 'Memory and Skin'
Women, 1998, miscellaneous objects and vinyl text, part of the exhibition 'Memory and Skin'
p. 82

Sugar and Tobacco, 1998, miscellaneous objects and vinyl text, part of the exhibition 'Memory and Skin'
p. 83

Proella, 1998, wax and copper, part of the exhibition 'Memory and Skin'
pp. 84–5

Watching Windows, Nantes, 1998, c-type print
p. 130

Cooking Class, 1998, c-type print
p. 132

Cinderella Tours Europe

Patio, Alhambra, 1998–2001, fuji crystal archive prints
p. 86

Palace of Westminster, London, 1998–2001, fuji crystal archive prints. Courtesy Government Art Collection, UK
UN, Geneva, 1998–2001, fuji crystal archive prints. Courtesy Government Art Collection, UK
Rialto Bridge, Venice, 1998–2001, fuji crystal archive prints
Zaanse Schans, 1998–2001, fuji crystal archive prints. Courtesy Government Art Collection, UK
Eiffel Tower, Paris, 1998–2001, fuji crystal archive prints
Cadiz, 1998–2001, fuji crystal archive prints
p. 87

St. Mark's Square, Venice, 1998–2001, fuji crystal archive prints
Cristo Rei, Lisbon, 1998–2001, fuji crystal archive prints
Plaza de Espana, Seville, 1998–2001, fuji crystal archive prints
Versailles, 1998–2001, fuji crystal archive prints. Courtesy Government Art Collection, UK
Mosteiro dos Jeronimos, 1998–2001, fuji crystal archive prints
Reichstag, Berlin, 1998–2001, fuji crystal archive prints
p. 88

Bridge of Miracles, Venice, 1998–2001, fuji crystal archive prints. Courtesy Government Art Collection, UK
p. 89

The Sweetest Thing

The Sweetest Thing, 2022, cyanotype and chintz cotton with rayon, polyester and metal threads. 290 × 180 cm. Commissioned by the Royal Albert Memorial Museum & Art Gallery, Exeter, 2023
pp. 90, 94, 97–101

Lost Histories

Viewed & Viewing, 1997, kallitype
Memory Flickers, 1997, kallitype
Breathing Out, 1997, kallitype
To survey from a distance, 1997, kallitype
p. 102

Families II, 1997, kallitype
p. 103

Kalahari

Rosedale, Upington, 2005, c-type print
p. 105

Salt Pan 2, 2005, c-type print
p. 106

Sign, 2006, c-type print
p. 107

Sarah with Hoodia, 2006, c-type print
Red Dunes, 2016, c-type print
p. 108

Ouma |una and Piet, 2006, c-type print
Visiting Ouma Kheis's Grave, 2006, c-type print
p. 109

Sara and Ouma |una in the Park, 2006, c-type print
p. 110

Magdalena in the Park, 2006, c-type print
p. 111

Orange River, Upington, 2005, c-type print
p. 112

Nigel, Magdalena and Magdeaena's House, 2005–16, contact strip
p. 113

Horizon 2, 2006, c-type print
p. 114

The Last Speakers

Invisible Life Force of Plants

I'm Home

Portraits, Lunuganga, Sri Lanka

Interiors, Lunuganga, Sri Lanka

Fixed Plants, Lunuganga, Sri Lanka

Leaf 2, 2004, silver gelatin
p. 144

Stripped Gypsophila and garden leaves, 2004, silver gelatin
p. 145

Jacaranda, 2004, silver gelatin
p. 160

Fern 3, 2004, silver gelatin
p. 161

Floating Ferns, 2004, silver gelatin
p. 184

Garden Fern with Double Hue, 2004, silver gelatin
endpaper

Scanned Plants, Lunuganga, Sri Lanka

Lotus Flower, 2004, digital print
p. 162

Strange Fruit, 2004, digital print
p. 163

Love of a Long Vocation

Cagan, 2024, albumen print
p. 168

Winny, 2024, albumen print
Ricky, 2024, albumen print
p. 169

Matron Bell / Alongside Matron Bell

Passing Out, 2008, duratran lightbox, from the series *Matron Bell*
Outpatients Foundation-Stone, 2008, duratran lightbox, from the series *Matron Bell*
p. 170

Presentation Day, 2020, duratran lightbox, from the series *Alongside Matron Bell*
Passing Out with Matron Bell, 2020, duratran lightbox, from the series *Alongside Matron Bell*
p. 171

Sites of Africa

Tower Hill, 2001, billboard design
pp. 172–3

Brick Lane, 2001, billboard design
pp. 174–5

To Be Sold, 2001, billboard design
p. 176

Seven Dials, 2001, billboard design
p. 177

The Amberley Queens, Heroines of Antiquity

Semiramis, 1999, c-type print
Lady Dayfele, 1999, c-type print
p. 178

Hippolyta, 1999, c-type print
Thomyris, 1999, c-type print
p. 179

A Little Slice of Paradise

A Little Slice of Paradise, 2023, poster design. © Art on the Underground, photography by Benedict Johnson
pp. 180–1

A Taste of Home

Souls in Flight, 2024, monoprint, study for *A Taste of Home* (2024)
p. 164

A Taste of Home, 2024, billboards. © Art on the Underground, photography by Thierry Bal
pp. 182–3

Acknowledgements

It has taken me a long time to attempt a list of formal acknowledgments; there are simply too many people to thank. Across time and place, every encounter has played a meaningful role in shaping who I am and the work I create.

First and foremost, I thank my family for their unwavering support, and I pay tribute to my exceptionally talented brother, Douglas, who passed away earlier this year.

I am deeply grateful to Zelda Cheatle, Amanda King, Anne McNeill, Mark Sealy, Gary Stewart and Sunil Gupta, as well as to the brilliant essay contributors whose inspiration, encouragement and belief in my work have sustained me over the past forty years.

I am especially thankful to everyone in the studio who meticulously assembled the archive, making both the exhibition and publication possible. I also extend my sincere gratitude to Gilane Tawadros and the team at Whitechapel Gallery, whose continued support and vision brought this project to life.

To all of you – named and unnamed – thank you. I carry your contributions with me every step of the way.

Joy Gregory

Joy Gregory: Catching Flies with Honey has been generously supported by:
Freelands Foundation through the Freelands Award 2023
Cockayne – Grants for the Arts: a donor advised fund held at The London Community Foundation
Joy Gregory Exhibition Circle and Patrons: Maria Sukkar, WooP, Lord Peter Palumbo, Grace Wales Bonner and those who wish to remain anonymous
Research for the exhibition, and the production of this publication, have been supported by the Paul Mellon Centre for Studies in British Art

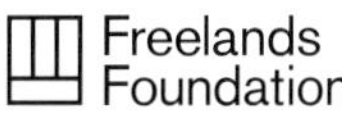

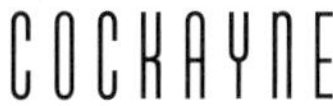

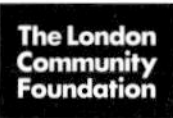

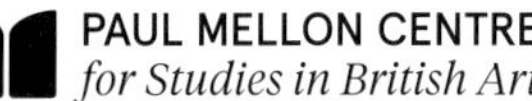

With additional support for the artist from The Elephant Trust.

Whitechapel Gallery would like to thank its supporters, whose generosity enables the Gallery to realise its pioneering programmes:

Major Donors and Supporters
Arts Council England Catalyst Endowment Fund
Sir Frank Bowling
Bloomberg Philanthropies
City Bridge Foundation
D. Daskalopoulos Collection
Ford Foundation
Foyle Foundation
Freelands Foundation
Garfield Weston Foundation
Paul Mellon Centre for Studies in British Art
The Rose Foundation
Terra Foundation for American Art
Michael and Nina Zilkha
and those that wish to remain anonymous

Exhibitions Programme
Aldgate Connect BID
The Ampersand Foundation
John Booth
Cockayne – Grants for the Arts
Henry Moore Foundation
Hiscox (Artworks Insurance Partner)
Iwona Blazwick Artistic Ambition Fund
Amrita Jhaveri
Marcelle Joseph
Sir Isaac Julien
Kevin Kane
Frank Krikhaar
Paul Mellon Centre for Studies in British Art
Pilgrim Trust
Russell Tovey
Pat Wang Maugüé
Whitechapel Gallery Commissioning Council
Whitechapel Gallery Patrons
and those who wish to remain anonymous

Participation & Public Programmes
The 29th May 1961 Charitable Trust
Aldgate Connect BID
Capital Group
The Centre for Public Engagement at Queen Mary University of London
Kurt Forrest Foundation
Tower Hamlets Arts & Music Education Service (THAMES)
The London Borough of Tower Hamlets
Glenn Sujo
Stanley Picker Trust
Whitechapel Gallery Education Council

Whitechapel Gallery Corporate Patrons and Members
Alma
Bloomberg Philanthropies
Gazelli Art House
Lisson Gallery
Phillips

Whitechapel Gallery Corporate Supporters
Aldgate Connect BID
Bloomberg Philanthropies
Champagne Pommery
Crozier Fine Arts
Frame London (Editions Framing Partner)
Fedrigoni
Hiscox (Artworks Insurance Partner)
Little Greene (Paint Partner)
Max Mara
Collezione Maramotti
Omni Colour (Signage Partner)
Phillips

Whitechapel Gallery Commissioning Council
Dorota Audemars
Erin Bell
Émilie De Pauw

Whitechapel Gallery Education Council
Julie and Debashis Dey
Alex Sainsbury

Whitechapel Gallery Global Circle
Faisal Tamer and Sara Alireza
and those who wish to remain anonymous

Whitechapel Gallery Director's Circle
Erin Bell and Michael Cohen
Pilar Corrias
Julie and Debashis Dey
Bimpe Nkontchou
Anthea Peers
and those who wish to remain anonymous

Whitechapel Gallery Curator's Circle
Annette Anthony
Bella Kesoyan
Oba Nsugbe
Audrey Wallrock
and those who wish to remain anonymous

Whitechapel Gallery Patrons
Cedric Bardawil
Sadie Coles HQ
Francesca Consigli
Sarah Elson
Joanna and Alan Gemes
Mark Harris
Pippy Houldsworth
Frank Krikhaar
Kate MacGarry
Mary E McNicholas
Heike Moras
Maureen Paley
Darryl de Prez and Victoria Thomas
Maria-Cruz Rashidian
Alex Sainsbury and Elinor Jansz
Cherrill and Ian Scheer
Elisabeth von Schwarzkopf
Bina and Philippe von Stauffenberg
Christoph and Marion Trestler
and those who wish to remain anonymous

We remain grateful for the ongoing support of Whitechapel Gallery Members.

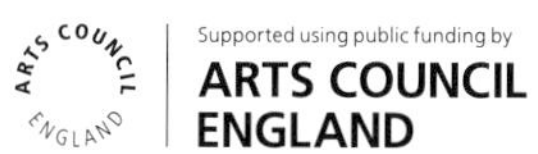

Whitechapel Gallery is proud to be a National Portfolio Organisation of Arts Council England.

Published on the Occasion of the Exhibition

Joy Gregory: Catching Flies with Honey

Whitechapel Gallery, London
8 October 2025 – 1 March 2026

Arnolfini, Bristol
17 October 2026 – 7 February 2027

Curated by Gilane Tawadros
and Katrina Schwarz

Whitechapel Gallery
Director Gilane Tawadros
Head of Exhibitions Leila Hasham
Curator, Special Projects Katrina Schwarz
Assistant Curator Hannah Woods
Gallery Technical Manager Luke Edwards
Exhibitions Technician Chris Elliott
Technical Production Manager Sam Williams

Arnolfini
Director Suzanne Rolt
Head of Exhibitions Gemma Brace
Exhibitions Producer Kiara Corales
Technical and Sustainability Producer Jack Friswell
Head of Engagement Keiko Higashi
Engagement Producer Eleanor Sanghara Güstard

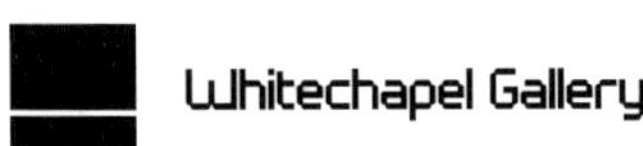

ARNOLFINI
EST. 1961

Publication
Editors Gilane Tawadros and Leila Hasham
Publications Manager Joel Cosson
Editorial Coordinator Rochelle Roberts
Copy Editing Hannah Young
Production Management Corinna Pickart

Design Wolfe Hall
Separations Reproline mediateam, Unterföhring, Germany
Printing and binding Livonia Print SIA, Riga
Paper Magno Volume

A member of Penguin Random House
Verlagsgruppe GmbH
Neumarkter Strasse 28 · 81673 Munich
produktsicherheit@penguinrandomhouse.de

First printed 2025

Library of Congress Control Number
is available; a CIP catalogue record for this
book is available from the British Library.

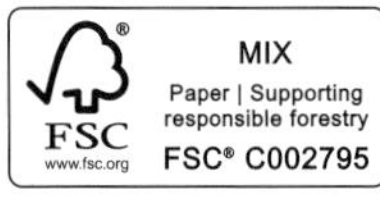

Penguin Random House Verlagsgruppe
FSC® N001967

Printed in Latvia
ISBN 978-3-7913-7661-5

www.prestel.com

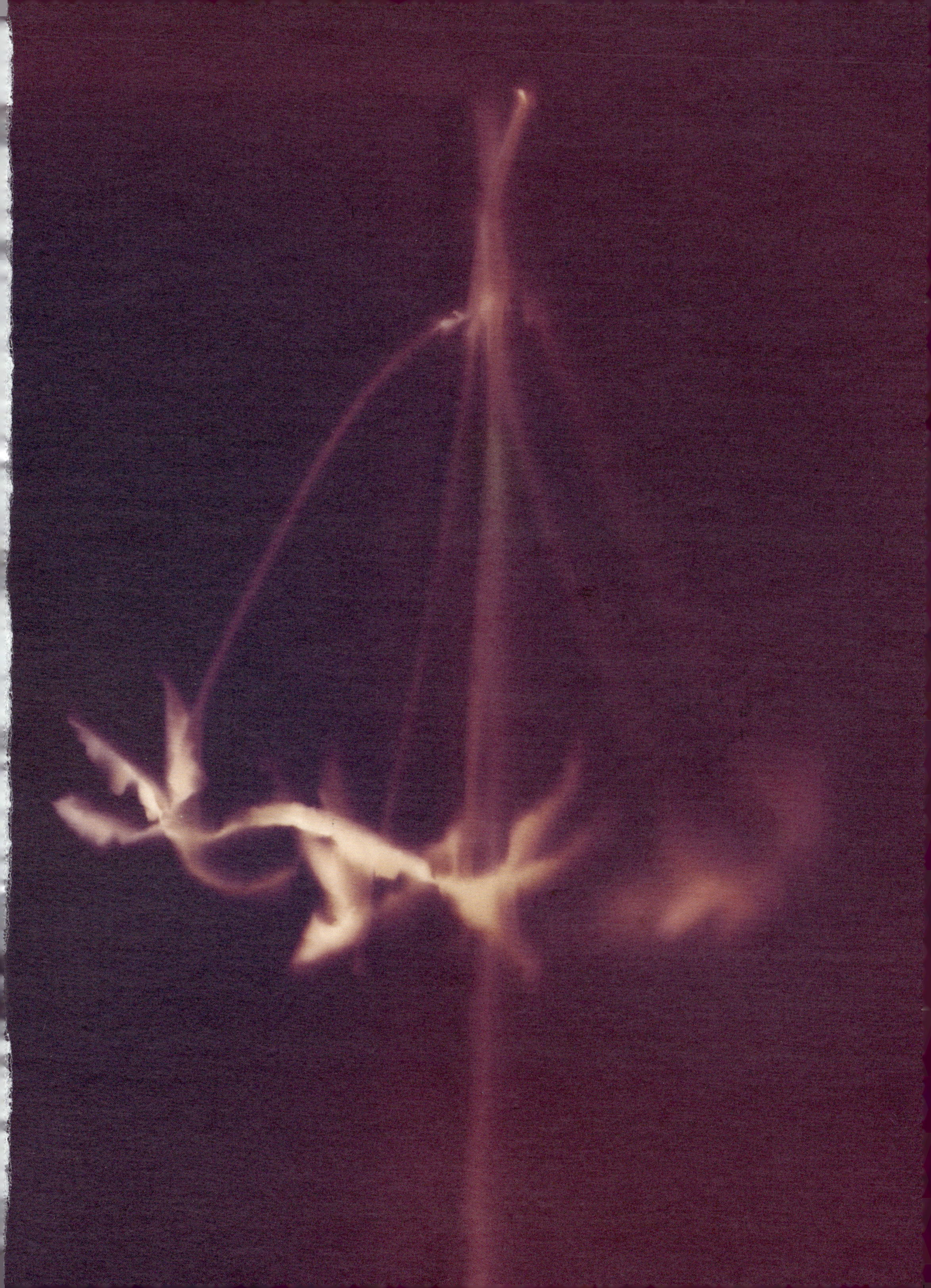

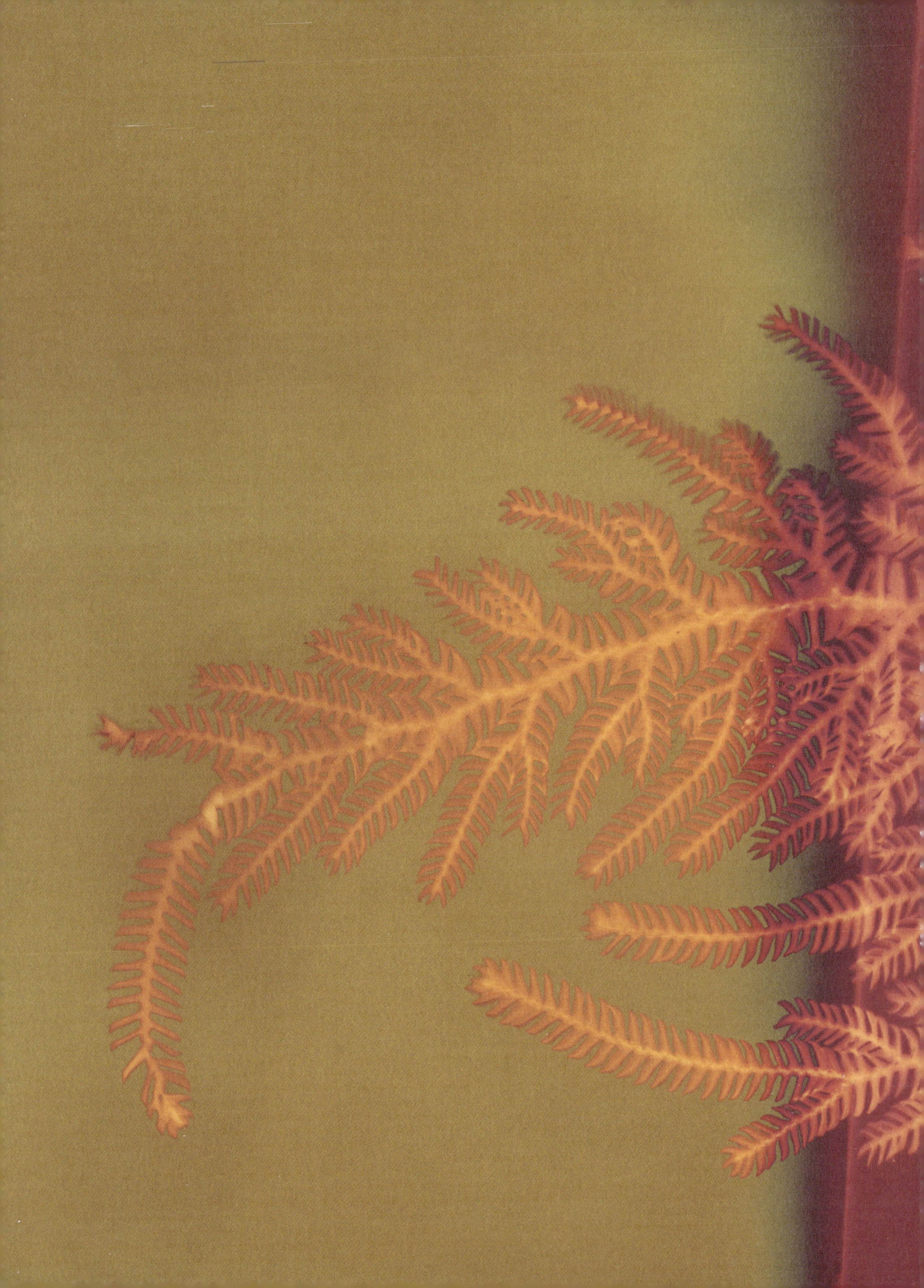